Adorno's *Minima Moralia* in the 21st Century

photography: Stefan Moses | © Stefan Moses Archiv

Adorno's *Minima Moralia* in the 21st Century

Fascism, Work, and Ecology

Edited by Caren Irr

BLOOMSBURY ACADEMIC
LONDON • NEW YORK • OXFORD • NEW DELHI • SYDNEY

BLOOMSBURY ACADEMIC
Bloomsbury Publishing Plc
50 Bedford Square, London, WC1B 3DP, UK
1385 Broadway, New York, NY 10018, USA
29 Earlsfort Terrace, Dublin 2, Ireland

BLOOMSBURY, BLOOMSBURY ACADEMIC and the Diana logo are trademarks
of Bloomsbury Publishing Plc

First published in Great Britain 2022
This paperback edition published 2023

Copyright © Caren Irr and Contributors, 2022

Ryan McInerney has asserted his right under the Copyright, Designs and Patents Act,
1988, to be identified as Author of this work.

For legal purposes the Acknowledgments on p. xvi constitute an extension of this copyright page.

Cover image Stefan Moses | © Stefan Moses Archiv

All rights reserved. No part of this publication may be reproduced or transmitted in any form or by
any means, electronic or mechanical, including photocopying, recording, or any information storage
or retrieval system, without prior permission in writing from the publishers.

Bloomsbury Publishing Plc does not have any control over, or responsibility for, any third-party
websites referred to or in this book. All internet addresses given in this book were correct at the
time of going to press. The author and publisher regret any inconvenience caused if addresses
have changed or sites have ceased to exist, but can accept no responsibility for any such changes.

A catalogue record for this book is available from the British Library.

Library of Congress Cataloging-in-Publication Data
Names: Irr, Caren, editor.
Title: Adorno's 'Minima Moralia' in the 21st century: fascism, work, and
ecology / edited by Caren Irr.
Description: London; New York, NY: Bloomsbury Academic, 2021. | Includes bibliographical
references and index.
Identifiers: LCCN 2021025992 (print) | LCCN 2021025993 (ebook) | ISBN 9781350198838
(hardback) | ISBN 9781350198845 (ebook) | ISBN 9781350198852 (epub)
Subjects: LCSH: Adorno, Theodor W., 1903-1969. Minima Moralia. | Critical theory. |
Utopias. | Fascism.
Classification: LCC B3199.A33 M5324 2021 (print) | LCC B3199.A33 (ebook) |
DDC 170–dc23
LC record available at https://lccn.loc.gov/2021025992
LC ebook record available at https://lccn.loc.gov/2021025993

ISBN: HB: 978-1-3501-9883-8
PB: 978-1-3501-9893-7
ePDF: 978-1-3501-9884-5
eBook: 978-1-3501-9885-2

Typeset by Deanta Global Publishing Services, Chennai, India

To find out more about our authors and books visit www.bloomsbury.com and sign up
for our newsletters.

Contents

List of Contributors	vi
Foreword: Rehearsals for the Right Life *Peter E. Gordon*	viii
Acknowledgments	xvi
An Adorno for the 21st Century: Introduction	
Diana Filar and Caren Irr	1

Part I Thought after Fascism

1	*Minima Moralia* and the Contradictions of Postwar Pedagogy *Jakob Norberg*	13
2	"Breathtaking Leaps" or from Doorknobs to Fascism *Oshrat C. Silberbusch*	28

Part II The Effects of the Aphorism

3	Adorno's Senses of Critique: Gesture, Suffering, Utopia *S. D. Chrostowska*	45
4	Negative Dialectics, Negative Events: The Aphorism and Melancholy Historicism *Wyatt Sarafin*	61

Part III A Labor Theory of the Present

5	"The Whole of Life Must Look Like a Job": *Minima Moralia* and the Capitalocene *Clinton Williamson*	77
6	Life Still Doesn't Live: Adorno's Guide to the Realm of the Dead *Caleb Shaoning Fridell*	90

Part IV Adorno's Ecology

7	Adorno and Animality after Auschwitz *Andrea Dara Cooper*	113
8	Adorno's Anthropocene *Caren Irr*	129

Notes	143
Index	175

Contributors

S. D. Chrostowska is Professor of twentieth-century intellectual history in the Department of Humanities and the Graduate Program in Social and Political Thought at York University, Canada. Among her books are *Matches* (2015, 2nd ed. 2019, with a foreword by Alexander Kluge) and *Utopia in the Age of Survival: Between Myth and Politics* (2021). She has contributed articles to *Common Knowledge*, *New German Critique*, *Public Culture*, *New Literary History*, *Telos*, *Constellations*, *Boundary 2*, and elsewhere.

Andrea Dara Cooper is Assistant Professor in the Department of Religious Studies and Leonard and Tobee Kaplan Fellow in Modern Jewish Thought and Culture at the University of North Carolina at Chapel Hill. She works at the intersection of Jewish thought, cultural theory, and continental philosophy, emphasizing connections between religious studies and critical theory. Her book *Beyond Brotherhood: Gendering Modern Jewish Thought* is forthcoming with Indiana University Press in the series New Jewish Philosophy and Thought. Her next research project examines post-Shoah ethics, animality, and narratives of sacrifice.

Diana Filar is a PhD candidate in English at Brandeis University. Her expertise lies in contemporary immigrant literature and critical race theory.

Caleb Shaoning Fridell is a PhD student at the Graduate Center, CUNY, studying modernism and critical theory. His article "The Extractive Logic of Fossil Capital in H. G. Wells' Scientific Prophecy" appears in *Modern Fiction Studies*, in the March 2020 special issue "Literature and Extraction." He teaches at Queens College.

Caren Irr is Professor of English at Brandeis University. She is the author of *Toward the Geopolitical Novel: US Fiction in the 21st Century* (Columbia 2013), *Pink Pirates: Contemporary American Women Writers and Copyright* (Iowa 2010), and *The Suburb of Dissent: Cultural Politics in the US and Canada during the 1930s* (Duke 1998). She has also co-edited two collections of essays on critical theory, both published by SUNY.

Jakob Norberg is Associate Professor of German at Duke University. He is the author of *Sociability and Its Enemies: German Political Thought After 1945* (Northwestern UP, 2014) and over twenty articles on political theory and modern literature in journals such as *Cultural Critique, New German Critique, PMLA, Telos,* and *Textual Practice.*

Wyatt Sarafin is a PhD candidate in English at Harvard University. He studies contemporary literature, media, and art in the Americas. His essay, on Chris Ware's "diagrammatic epistemology," was published in *ASAP/Journal.*

Oshrat C. Silberbusch holds a PhD in philosophy from Tel Aviv University and an MA in German studies from the Université de la Sorbonne Nouvelle Paris 3. She is the author of *Adorno's Philosophy of the Nonidentical: Thinking as Resistance* (Palgrave Macmillan, 2018), and has published articles on Theodor W. Adorno, Jean Améry, Günther Anders, George Orwell, post-Shoah thought and German Jewish history. She lives in Brooklyn with her husband and three children.

Clinton Williamson is a PhD candidate in English at the University of Pennsylvania, specializing in nineteenth- and twentieth-century American literature. His dissertation, "Nebulous Figures: A Cultural History of an American Riotocracy, 1848-1929," looks to the ways in which a so-called *lumpenproletariat* crafted refusals to work as strategies for restaging value and assembling improvisatory commons in the latter half of the long nineteenth century. Assembling a heterodox cultural archive, this project proposes that representations of and from those living on the margins of wage labor expose new ways of modeling potential worlds rooted in labor's absence.

Foreword

Rehearsals for the Right Life

Peter E. Gordon

Minima Moralia is a work of exile. Published seventy years ago in 1951, the greater share of it was written during the war, when its German-born author Theodor Wiesengrund Adorno was living in Los Angeles county, not far from his colleague Max Horkheimer and other artists and intellectuals who had the good fortune to escape the Third Reich. "The violence that expelled me," he explains, left him with an enduring sense of guilt at the very fact of his survival. The book's subtitle, "Reflections from Damaged Life," is a record of this unhealed wound, a bitter confession that even to write about individual experience already suggests the undeserved privilege of survival, or even something like complicity with "unspeakable collective events." But Adorno did not shirk from the challenge. Instead he worked at the trauma and made of it an irritant for thinking, sand for the pearls of insight that would fill each page. Taking as its thematic point of departure "the narrowest private sphere, that of the intellectual in emigration," it is beyond all doubt the most personal book he ever wrote, and even at the highest peaks of philosophical abstraction, it does not efface its origins in autobiography. Like Montaigne's *Essais*, Adorno's book is not only a series of philosophical experiments but also an exercise in self-portraiture. *Car c'est moi que je peint*, wrote the humanist Montaigne. "Subjective experience," wrote Adorno, must serve as an ineliminable element for all criticism if it does not wish to contribute to the further destruction of humanity.[1]

How can we classify an intellectual who abhorred classification? Critical of all group loyalty and always keen to take his distance from his social surroundings, Adorno was nonetheless a recognizable type, known to sociologists as a *Kulturträger*, an itinerant intellectual who carries his erudition on his back as the only possession that matters. In the first aphorism of the book, Adorno offers a homage to Marcel Proust as an embodiment of European spirit who draws back in horror from the noise and ruin that now passes for culture. He is especially ill-suited to the conventions of the modern university. "The son of well-to-do parents who, whether from talent or weakness, engages in the so-called intellectual profession, as an artist or a scholar, will have a particularly difficult time with those bearing the distasteful title of colleagues." In the "competitive hierarchy" of official culture he is seen as a "dilettante, no matter how well he knows his subject," not least because he objects to the "departmentalization of spirit." If he dares to think of himself as an "independent intellectual," he is nonetheless exposed to the "practical" demands of the institutions he has left behind. If he refuses to comply with the customary division of labor that governs this profession, its rules will nonetheless have their revenge. "[S]ome have to play the game because they cannot otherwise live, and those who could live otherwise are kept out because they do not want to play the game."[2]

Adorno admired Proust but he was also describing himself. His father Oscar Wiesengrund was an assimilated Jew, a wine merchant in Frankfurt, and the young boy known as "Teddie" often played with friends among the wine-bottles that were stored in the cellar. Years later, after his father's business had been destroyed, Adorno came to feel that his philosophy was like a *Flaschenpost*, "messages in a bottle," thrown out to sea onto the "rising tide of barbarism."[3] *Minima Moralia* itself is a work that flouts the official categories, a *Wunderkammer* or cabinet of curiosities comprising insights and aphorisms that are arranged in no particular order and honor no disciplinary rules. "Cultural criticism" is one name we might attach to this anti-genre of free-ranging commentary that can encompass both bitter reflections on fascism and loving memories of the author's own childhood. No published work by Adorno better conveys his inimitable persona, his special gift for intermingling the sociological and the autobiographical, the nostalgic and the austere. The genius of his writing is that he never permitted himself to rest completely in either domain. Even at the highest pitch of philosophical abstraction he never unbinds himself from the social world, and even when writing in admiration about the aesthetic realm he interlaces formal analysis with grim reminders of the suffering that art cannot transcend.

Minima Moralia, to be sure, is scored with nostalgia. It is the transcript of an embattled spirit, of the innocent cast overboard into a society that no longer offers the comforts he once knew. Perhaps his fondest recollections from childhood were of evenings with his mother, Maria (*née* Calvelli-Adorno), and her sister Agathe, a pianist, when Teddie would sit beside his aunt to play pieces transcribed for four hands. "Four hand playing," he would later recall, "was the gift the geniuses of the bourgeois nineteenth century placed at my cradle at the beginning of the twentieth." It was "music with which one could still interact and live, before musical compulsion itself commanded solitariness and secretive craft."[4] One of the later entries in *Minima Moralia* has the title "Regressions," in which Adorno writes of his early memories of the "Cradle Song" by Brahms, that he then associates with the curtain around his childhood bed that shielded him from light so that he could sleep "in an unending peace without fear."[5]

Still, it is altogether typical of Adorno that he cannot permit himself the consolations of Proustian nostalgia but always remains alert to the hidden links between innocence and brutality. No island of perfection escapes his critical eye. Dreams of immediacy or the "authentic" that may have once enraptured Kierkegaard are now condemned as harbingers of barbarism.[6] In aphorism 123, Adorno writes, without embarrassment, that "I ought to be able to deduce Fascism from the memories of my childhood." He recalls schoolyard bullies who teased him as a boy, who beat him and took delight when he, the *primus* or top of his class, made an occasional error. He sees in them the harbingers of those who later tortured prisoners and Jewish detainees. The bull-headed kids who interrupted the teacher and "crash[ed] their fists on the table" have now become a *Männerbund*, whose members now preach "worship for their masters." In such passages Adorno leaps across the decades. Untroubled by the scruples of historicism, he sees the catastrophe that was prepared long ago. The wounds of the sensitive child have not yet healed when the adult takes up his pen to condemn the mindless collective, whose brutality has now metastasized into the modern state. "In Fascism," he concludes, "the nightmare of childhood has come true."[7]

All of these memories speak of displacement. During his period of exile, first the few, lonely years in Oxford where he was dismissed as an eccentric, then in the States where he kept close to the émigré community and looked upon most of American life with a mixture of alienation and disdain, Adorno never felt at home. Aphorism 18 is entitled "Asylum for the Homeless." But it is an argument *against* the ideal of a permanent home. "Dwelling in the authentic sense," he writes, "is no longer possible." Little in Adorno's work better expresses his mistrust of "dwelling" and "authenticity," those cherished themes of Heideggerian existentialism.[8] It is true that the sunny climate in California reminded him of Tuscany. Still, is there anything more incongruous than the image of Adorno in Los Angeles? In the brave new world of America he witnessed Huxley's dystopian novel as reality. The music irritated his ears, the products of Hollywood offended his eyes, and even the door handles were unfamiliar. With his astonishing gift for overstatement the experience of trying to open or close them became, in the astonishing aphorism 19, yet another occasion for meditating on the rise of fascism. "What does it mean, for the subject," he asks, "that there are no more casement windows to open, but only sliding frames to shove, no gentle latches but turnable handles, no forecourt, no doorstep before the street, no wall around the garden?" His questions already anticipate the answer. "The movements machines demand of their uses already have the violent, hard-hitting, unresting jerkiness of Fascist maltreatment."[9] For those who already dislike Adorno this passage ranks among the more notorious in the entire book. For those who admire him it is a sign of his refusal to exempt anything from criticism. When seen up close by means of what he called the "micrological" glance, the smallest fragments of everyday life lose their innocence and become signs of surrounding catastrophe.

Displacement, then, was more than a personal experience. It was the intellectual premise, the precondition for critical practice. Only in the book's final aphorism is the method that animates the entire book condensed into a single formula: "Perspectives must be fashioned that displace and estrange the world, reveal it to be, with its rifts and crevices, as indigent and distorted as it will appear one day in the messianic light."[10] This statement should not be misunderstood as a declaration of pessimism or a surrender to thoroughgoing negativity. In Goethe's *Faust*, Mephistopheles declares that "Ich bin der Geist der stets verneint, und das mit Recht, denn alles was entsteht, ist Werth, daß es zu Grunde geht." Adorno, too, has a reputation as a spirit who always negates. But he was no Mephistopheles, nor did he believe that "all that comes to be deserves to go under." Criticism remains dialectical only if it resists the allure of such totalizing verdicts. "The Whole is the False," he writes, in a dark rejoinder to Hegel's triumphant statement, "The True is the Whole." But it does not follow that Adorno was prepared to condemn present society as wholly false. It meant that every image of a coherent society had to be resisted as ideological so long as even one individual remains in despair. Among the many *obiter dicta* from *Minima Moralia* that have earned Adorno his reputation for total negativity is the seemingly decisive statement: "There is no right living in the false." But even this dictum should not be inflated into a Gnostic condemnation of the entire world. It was meant as a warning against false-transcendence, against the consoling thought that one could live a life of private happiness and moral rectitude in the midst of generalized suffering. Properly construed, it is a warning against the very sins of elitism and aesthetic quietism that his uncomprehending critics have so often accused him of. Adorno is often portrayed as a scowling contrarian who looks down upon a debased reality from the privileged remove of a "Grand Hotel Abyss." But this is mere caricature. It does a disservice to his dialectical method, his penchant for identifying partial moments of redemption even in the midst of an unredeemed world.

In form, *Minima Moralia* is a book in aphorisms, a genre that Adorno learned from exemplars such as Nietzsche and Kraus. Like Nietzsche, it conveys its claims in lightning strikes of paradox and wit; and, like Nietzsche, it trades rather too often in blusterous certitudes. We may find it ironic that Adorno, the critic of all fetishism, is widely celebrated for the overstatements that lend themselves to fetishistic quotation. "In psycho-analysis," he writes, "nothing is true except the exaggerations"[11] (aphorism 29). A philosopher less enchanted with hammer-blows might respond that in Adorno's thinking whatever is true must be salvaged *from* his own exaggerations.[12] The burden is often shifted to the reader, who must complete Adorno's thoughts for him but can assent only to what survives rational elucidation. "Thinking that renounces argument," Adorno once said, "switches into pure irrationalism."[13]

This is one reason why Adorno's book needs its expositors and why the interpretation of his work remains an ongoing task. Where arguments are not advanced, even the most compelling dictum can harden into a cliché. Perhaps this is always a risk in the aphoristic form of which Adorno was a recognized master. At its best, his writing is furrowed and self-referential; it often shifts direction mid-course, or even midsentence, leaving the reader in a state of vertigo where it is no longer clear which thoughts may have survived the process of negation. This was the formal principle that Adorno would later call "negative dialectics," a practice that borrows from Hegel the gesture of negation but resists the allure of a final reconciliation.[14] For Adorno the arrogant claim to "absolute knowing" that concludes Hegel's *Phenomenology of Spirit* was no longer tenable: to insist on the "identity of identity and non-identity" was little more than an ideological demand that the last margins for criticism be shut. Once achieved, the final identity that concluded the dialectic was just a lapse into thoughtless affirmation. More than anything, Adorno feared that all claims to a triumphant identity could only abet the mind's surrender to what positivists call "the given." Any philosophical practice that pretends to closure is in reality little more than regression to the unreflective immediacy that it wished to leave behind. "Reflection that takes sides with naivety condemns itself" (aphorism 46).

When confronted with a book that places such enormous emphasis on the negative it is altogether natural to pose the question of whether it furnishes any guidance whatsoever in the moral domain. Its title alludes to the treatise known as the *Magna Moralia*, or "Great Ethics," a work once attributed to Aristotle but now considered a compendium of Aristotelian ethical principles by a later writer. It is therefore tempting to read *Minima Moralia* as an ironic rejoinder to the tradition, a chastened commentary on the minimal hopes that remain for us in the modern world now that the chasm has opened beneath us. It is true that the book describes a darkening landscape—how could it not given the years when it was written? The grim epigraph to Part I is taken from the nineteenth-century Viennese writer Ferdinand Kürnberger: "Life does not live." But it sounds like something that Adorno could easily have written himself. It is the sort of sentence, self-referential and enigmatic, that seems to have delighted him. *Minima Moralia* bears the subtitle "Reflections from Damaged Life," and the entire book could be read as a set of variations on this theme. More than once, it laments the "withering of experience" (19, 33) and the rise of "administered beneficence" that no longer leaves room for "human impulses." The human being who loses "live contact with the warmth of things" is at risk of making himself into "thing" and thereby "freezes" (21).

In such a glacial landscape what remains as a moral vision? In the opening dedication to Horkheimer, we read that the book is meant as a contribution to what was once considered philosophy's highest mission: "the teaching of the good life." But is such instruction still possible? Adorno knows that with the professionalization of philosophical inquiry this mission has suffered neglect. To ask how we should live our lives only conceals the bitter truth that little in human life still retains its substance or depth. We cannot pretend that people "still have the capacity to act as subjects" when in fact they are "no more than component parts of machinery." And yet Adorno does not fully capitulate to what he calls "the administered society," nor does he surrender his devotion to the good. At the margins of capitalist society where the imperatives of production and exchange have still not wholly colonized consciousness we are still dimly aware of the fact that the world has gone hopelessly wrong. Only if we sustain our opposition to the current order and its imperatives can we "bring about another [order] more worthy of human beings." Adorno has grown suspicious of grand theories. Although he sustains a seldom-stated bond with the Marxist critique of capital he is not primarily interested in political economy, nor could we say that he has any real talent for institutional or economic analysis. Instead he is drawn to what Matthias Benzer has called "microsociology," the inspection of lived experience in all of its exquisite detail. The starting point for such an inquiry must be the embattled subject whose individual experience even in its decay might still contribute to knowledge.

It is on this level of individual experience that Adorno seeks the requisite sources of moral insight. Despite the nearly overwhelming tones of hopelessness that pervade his book Adorno remains attuned to the fleeting moments of individual happiness even in the midst of despair. These moments are signs of the "nonidentical," traces in everyday life of the subject-in-exile who has not succumbed to the false social whole. We should not be surprised to learn that Adorno told his publisher that Part III of *Minima Moralia* was his favorite. It is there that we find one of the book's most affecting passages, "Toy shop" (146), in which Adorno gives free rein to his interpretative skills. Not incidentally, it is also the entry that more than any other bears a resemblance to the dialectics-in-miniature that were the special bequest of his friend Walter Benjamin, who had died a mere six years earlier and whose memory hangs over Adorno's writing like a melancholy muse. (The bond is readily apparent: *Minima Moralia* draws much of its inspiration from two of Benjamin's most original works, the episodic memoir, *Berlin Childhood around Nineteen Hundred*, and the kaleidoscopic study of urban experience, *One-Way Street*.) Benjamin harbored a special fascination for children's books and toys. Here Adorno reflects on the purposeless wonder that enwreaths a child's world, and the disenchantment that sets in once capitalism imposes its demands.[15] When the imperative of "earning a living" colonizes our experience, all of the aimless activities of childhood must be abandoned and the very specificity of things is lost. This is the logic of the "equivalent form" as Marx has theorized in *Capital*, that invades even the sensorium, and drains everyday objects of their uniqueness and color. Hence the significance of child's play. "In his purposeless activity the child, by a subterfuge, sides with use-value against exchange value," resists the demand that things should be valued only in exchange. The child still knows what the adult has forgotten, that the things have value beyond their value as commodities, and when the child tends to this value "he seeks to rescue in them what is benign towards men." Under the sober gaze of the adult children's games may seem superficial but it is capitalism that has robbed human life of its depth. "The unreality of games gives notice that reality is not yet real. Unconsciously they rehearse the right life." Because children are not yet fully tethered to the mechanisms of production and commodification that have disfigured our nature, they also retain an instinctive love for animals whose very existence seems to beckon as an undisguised utopia. "In existing without any purpose recognizable to men, animals hold out, as if for expression, their own names, utterly impossible to exchange."

To accuse Adorno of sentimentalism would be mistaken. The micrological task of *Minima Moralia* is to assist us in seeing the redemptive surplus that lies unrealized at the interstices of everyday experience. This is what Rahel Jaeggi means when she describes the book as a "critique of forms of life."[16] It does not draw back in horror from the totality of the world and condemn it all as false;

it burrows deeply into the crevices of life to alight upon its small moments of enduring truth. In his more formal philosophical argumentation, and especially in *Dialectic of Enlightenment,* the work he had coauthored with Horkheimer just a few years before he set about writing *Minima Moralia,* Adorno identified such experiences as remnants of mimesis, the fragile relationship that still obtains between human nature and the nature that exceeds the subject's will to domination. The "live contact with the warmth of things" (aphorism 21) that he cherished most of all was the *point d'appui* for all his criticism, not only in everyday life but also in his sociology and even in his aesthetics. To lie on the water and look peacefully at the sky, "Rien faire comme une bête," became in *Minima Moralia* the poetic image for this utopia. All the same, since, Adorno refused to isolate artistic or individual experience as a privileged domain beyond social conditioning. Nor was he so naïve as to imagine that such moments, in art or in everyday life, could suffice as a respite for social suffering. In a distorted world such experiences, too, are distorted. They offer not only a refuge for mimesis; they are also seismographs of the despair that pervades modern civilization. What they promise could only be fulfilled in a society that would at last become worthy of human beings. Until that day they too must remain in exile, promises of a life that will one day live.

The same may be said of *Minima Moralia* itself. If Adorno's book still retains its relevance today, this is not because it equips the reader with a settled doctrine that can be applied as a changeless schema to any and all problems that happen to arise. Books (or the best of them anyways) are not closed in their meanings, nor are they confined to only one time or place. The historicist conceit that a thinker belonged to their *own* time and therefore not to ours is a bad inference from a good premise. It is also a symptom of provincialism. Although it is true that Adorno had only a specific range of problems in view and could hardly have anticipated all of the questions that may trouble us today, this truism can hardly warrant the dismissive verdict that he should now be cast aside as obsolete. Instead it is a provocation: in reading his book our efforts are transformative; they make of it something it was not before. Commentary, after all, is not external to a book; it is an essential part of its continued life. This is how we demonstrate its ongoing grip on things unforeseen, or what in German is called its *Aktualität*. Seen in its proper light, *Minima Moralia* proffers not finished theories but exercises in criticism. The chapters in this volume are a reminder that, even when we disagree with him, Adorno can still furnish us with critical models that may challenge us to think in ways we may not have imagined.

Acknowledgments

The symposium for which the chapters were originally developed took place at Brandeis University in Fall 2019, during a world of in-person conversation that, from the point of view of a pandemic, feels like an artifact of the distant past. Generously supported with funding from the Mandel Center for the Humanities, the English department, and the Office of the Dean of Arts and Sciences, the symposium brought together an interdisciplinary group of scholars for a full day of lively discussion and new connections. The symposium would not have been possible without the dedicated and creative research of Diana Filar, Emiliano Gutierrez-Popoca, Ryan Hitchcock, and Lynn Kaye. I extend to these co-organizers my sincerest thanks as well as to my colleagues Stephen Dowden and Eugene Sheppard. In the year leading up to the symposium, Daniela Gati, Diana Filar, Lynn Kaye, Matthew Schratz, Grace Wilsey, and I studied *Minima Moralia* together, reading closely and slowly. Our shared learning shapes this volume, and I dedicate this work to all such efforts at collaborative thinking.

Caren Irr, January 2021

An Adorno for the 21st Century

Introduction

Diana Filar and Caren Irr

The austere portrait of Theodor Adorno alone in an office that appears on the cover of this volume poses a question. Observing Adorno in the mirror, the viewer sits in his position. His reflection appears as if it were our own. The question, then, is how Adornian are we now and in this place? Studying this portrait, perhaps we attempt to catch the philosopher's shadowed and bespectacled eyes and study the slight awkwardness of his in-turned and oddly illuminated right foot. And, in so doing, we are prompted to ask how our twenty-first-century insights may have been shaped by an Adornian posture. Or, more pointedly, we might reverse the gaze and ask how Adorno's eye perceives our fallen world. What vantage point on the present does Adorno's complex, sober, and slyly witty perspective provide? In which ways do his writings anticipate contemporary concerns, and where are corrective lenses required?

While exploring these questions, we should remind ourselves that this photo is a self-portrait staged by the celebrated German photographer Stefan Moses. As Gerhard Richter recounts, "Moses traveled all over Germany with a kitschy chrome mirror on wheels, borrowed from the dressing room of a department store, to visit his subjects in their 'own' environments and to encourage them to photograph themselves in front of the department store mirror with his camera. In the process, he too made a series of photographs of these sessions." Captured in the act of observing himself through a commercial reflection that intrudes into his own quiet space, the Adorno that Moses observed shrinks into his suit—almost disappearing into its featureless anonymity. He collaborates with Moses to stage his own evaporation into a pattern of dark and light vertical stripes. He peers out through the implicit bars of a cage whose contours his gaze reveals.

In other words, as we examine this selfie from the age of film and analog machines, we witness the pre-history of conditions that have only accelerated since the photo was taken. Adorno's gaze illuminates our own situation by carefully studying the modes of capture and damage of its own moment. Precisely because Adorno's thinking is so firmly planted within the horrors of fascism, synthetic and commercial environments, never-ending workplace routines, and tiny gestures, it offers twenty-first-century readers of his image and his words a strikingly contemporary perspective.

Nowhere in Adorno's corpus are these themes developed in a more accessible manner than in *Minima Moralia: Reflections from Damaged Life*. Carefully ordered in flows that rise from apparently autobiographical, even confessional, passages toward more properly philosophical statements, Adorno's aphorisms and vignettes—his fractured bits of stories—offer *Reflexionen*. In German, as in English, reflections associate the movement of thought with the multidirectional bouncing of light. Rebounding from layers and shards placed in complex arrays, Adorno's reflected thought in *Minima Moralia* travels toward its twenty-first-century readers from oblique angles.

Set in counterpoint to Aristotle's *Maxima Moralia* (or Greater Ethics), Adorno's investigations expose the small moments, little spaces, and subtle gestures that allow us to perceive the damage that permeates his world and our own. His thinking offers an ethical way of living—and a way of thinking—within conditions of control. He also bounces the rubber ball of his ideas off the apparent solidity of "damaged life" so that we understand this concept in new ways. Damaged life, as Adorno teaches us to read it, consists not only of the horrors of the war and the concentration camps he observed from an exile's safe distance in Los Angeles but also of the very conditions of safety and banality that coexist with that barbaric depravity. To be able to live at all in a condition of barbarism is necessarily a form of damage for Adorno.

These, then, are motifs of considerable relevance to a contemporaneity colored not only by a revival of explicitly fascist symbolism and virulent racisms but also by a perhaps irreparably damaged natural environment and a psychic and social life that offers few prospects for thinking beyond the present. This volume begins from the premise that Adorno speaks to twenty-first-century conditions in *Minima Moralia* precisely because he offers his own openly partial perspective from the late 1940s.

Of course, it comes as no surprise that historical markers of the mid-twentieth century saturate *Minima Moralia*. Adorno's aphorisms start, for example, from a conventionally gendered idea of marriage as a "community of interest" (#10) that degrades both parties, but especially the woman. This is a conception of marriage that predates and seems not to anticipate gay marriage and the sexual revolution of the 1960s and 1970s. Adorno also finds the question of race in fewer places than we are learning to do today. Further, the as-yet incomplete domination of popular culture by mass media in his moment prompted some of the more infamous (although often mischaracterized) pronouncements on film and music. "Every visit to the cinema," he memorably complained, "leaves me dumber and worse than before" (#5). In the age of social media and its relentless synchronization of what remains of free time, this is probably not a formulation that makes sense in the same terms anymore. We must acknowledge that although Adorno's thought creatively elaborates upon and ultimately overturns many views advanced by his contemporaries, these do nonetheless remain his starting points and serve in some degree as limits for his thinking.

Consequently, when we engage in twenty-first-century readings that borrow from Adorno to think through the questions that occupy this volume—fascism, work, ecology, and the aphoristic form of thinking itself—it is essential that we not initiate a project of transference. We cannot simply pick up shiny pebbles from the path that Adorno has strewn through the forest and put them to our own purposes any more than we might "cancel" this work because its concerns do not reproduce our own. Avoiding both pitfalls, we find that the worthwhile labor of historical translation is required if we are to approach *Minima Moralia* from a contemporary perspective.

Historical translation here does not refer to a process of contextualizing and explaining away the damaging effects of period prejudices in hopes of creating a purified and ahistorical perfect form. Such a project would be entirely antithetical to Adorno's thought. After all, in "Famished" (#65) he cautions his reader against idealizing "the speech of the subjugated" since "the poor chew words, in order to feel full." Romanticizing the effects of hunger and subjugation is no solution to the injustices that created them, and the same surely holds true for our relation to the damage inflicted by history. Rather than acclimating oneself to an abusive environment (be it hunger or war), in the same aphorism Adorno instead recommends "speech which sublates writing into itself"—that is, a "strict linguistic objectivity" that transforms and moves past its damaged condition.

Turning this thought back toward its thinker entails consideration of ways in which Adorno's own writing shares features with the writing of the famished. Produced in a condition of loss—of friends, family, culture, nation, politics, and tradition—Adorno's writing knows itself to be scarred and damaged. As his subtitle reminds us, this is writing that emerges from a specific life situation. The damage that Adorno reflects upon is also internal to his thought, ravaging its workings, and it cannot simply be burned off like garden waste. Even where Adorno's thinking apparently leaps ahead of its historical moment (as, for instance, in his pointed criticism of a purportedly race-blind language of "tolerance" of difference in aphorism #66), the task of the translator remains.

Much scholarship on *Minima Moralia* undertakes this task of historical translation, firmly situating Adorno's most popular book within its moment and culture. This work, too, continues Adorno's own advocacy of a critical interdisciplinarity that "addresses the challenges and the prospects of society as a whole."[1] Reexamining normative interpretations of his work in light of later crises, scholars engage in historically nuanced forms of critique. As Gerhard Schweppenhäuser notes, "critique is crystallized in situations of crisis, as negation of the existing condition. However, the objective purpose of the negation is a better condition."[2] Those following this line of thinking uncover Adorno's "positive dialectic," or the "utopian dimension"[3] of his work, and they often revisit Adorno's understanding of key philosophical concepts as well as his relationships with other philosophers—peers, influences, and adversaries alike.

In this spirit, a growing body of scholarship explores concepts either long thought to be outside Adorno's philosophical scope or upheld as evidence of a particular kind of interpretation, including autonomy,[4] human action,[5] theology,[6] nature,[7] and democracy.[8] For Christopher Craig Brittain, an investment in the "enduring and determined search for a better world" grounds Adorno's "relentless criticism," suggesting he should be read for an "inverse theology . . . motivated by a deep and sustained commitment to confront the realities of human suffering."[9] In the same vein, Deborah Cook focuses on "Adorno's idea of natural history [which] reveals the dynamic, and potentially catastrophic, interaction between nature and history."[10] Cook contends that Adorno's work has much to offer contemporary environmental movements, a perspective inimical to those who position Adorno as inherently apolitical. Shannon Mariotti, too, insists on Adorno's politics, recuperating his English writings as a "nascent form of negative dialectics direct[ed] to an American audience to inform them of the problems and possibilities of their own political culture."[11]

Taking Adorno seriously as a philosopher, other scholars explore his "contestatory dialogue" with important figures in the Western philosophical canon.[12] Peter Gordon's *Adorno and Existence*, for instance, claims that throughout his career, Adorno "remained caught in a troubled yet productive bond" with philosophies of "bourgeois interiority,"[13] specifically theories of existence and existentialism as outlined by Kierkegaard, Heidegger, and Husserl.[14] Fabian Freyenhagen further reveals how Kant influenced Adorno's conception of "the gap between human beings as they are now—damaged, reduced to appendages of the machine, lacking real autonomy—and their potential—their humanity yet to be realised—[which] provides the normative resources for a radical critique of our social world."[15] Similarly, Adorno shared a defense of plurality and reflective judgment with his contemporary Hannah Arendt, an approach that cleared a path for "critical theorizing of political modernity and democracy."[16] And although Adorno cannot be said to believe inherently in the idea of art as revolution, nor lauded as someone for whom literature and the literary object in particular would be sufficient to redress social ills, *Minima Moralia* suggests the potential for a different life, one uncovered through a negative dialectics at the level of what might be called a literary form at the crux of philosophy and art.

When it comes to linguistic rather than historical translations of Adorno's writing, we also enjoy an abundance of riches. Since its publication in German in 1951, *Minima Moralia* has been recast in other languages many times. Influential early translations include Renato Solmi's Italian version (1954),[17] Maurits Mok's translation into Dutch (1971),[18] Norberto Silvetti Paz's Spanish edition (1975),[19] and E. F. N. (Edmund) Jephcott's translation into English in 1974.[20] With the aid of Solmi's interpretation, a particularly vibrant critical conversation surrounding *Minima Moralia* has developed in Italian, accompanying the substantial body of scholarship in German. For scholars like those included in this volume, who are based in North America and write primarily in English, however, Jephcott's translation has been enormously influential. A comparatist who wrote a dissertation on Proust and Rilke at the University of Cambridge, Jephcott went on to become a leading translator of many of Adorno's works (including a 2002 edition of *Dialectic of Enlightenment,* one that follows the widely read 1972 version by John Cumming), as well as editions of key works by Walter Benjamin and many books by the German Jewish refugee sociologist Norbert Elias. Jephcott also worked on editions of Gustav Mahler and Richard Strauss's letters, as well as books on European art, fashion, and music. It is no doubt thanks to Jephcott's careful annotations that the many allusions to German literature and philosophy that pepper *Minima Moralia* are comprehensible to Anglophone readers.

That said, every translator has preferences, and a brief comparison between Jephcott's careful and enjoyable translation of *Minima Moralia* and Dennis Redmond's 2005 version suggests one or two ways in which the concerns of the intellectual world of the 1970s permeate Jephcott's treatment. "The melancholy science from which I make this offering to my friend," Jephcott's translation of the opening sentence of the "Dedication" reads, "relates to a region that from time immemorial was regarded as the true field of philosophy, but which, since the latter's conversion into method, has lapsed into intellectual neglect, sententious whimsy and finally oblivion: the teaching of the good life."[21] Where Jephcott selects "region," "true," "conversion," "neglect," "whimsy," and "oblivion," Redmond opts for "realm," "authentic," "transformation," "disrespect," "caprice," and "forgetfulness."[22] Somewhat less poetic and slightly more technical in its use of philosophical terms, Redmond's decisions remind us that the occasionally plaintive and mournful voice of *Minima Moralia* is one that has been emphasized and, to some extent, invented in the Jephcott version. That is, Jephcott's linguistic translation is also a historical one, responsive to the psychoanalytic preoccupations of the 1970s and the rising interest in memory. The mist of a more humanistic sensibility rises through these pinholes, and in light of these considerations several chapters in this volume ask how or whether moments of translation might be considered afresh as well as how the psychic life of the twenty-first century returns us to different moments in Adorno's prose.

While a close analysis of the many factors influencing translations into languages other than English exceeds the mandate of this introduction, the timing of the various waves of translation is interesting to observe. During the late twentieth century, editions of *Minima Moralia* appeared in Greek (1984),[23] French (1980),[24] and Portuguese (1993).[25] Then, in the 2000s, more than fifty years after its first publication, *Minima Moralia* came to the attention of East Asian translators, and editions in Korean (2005)[26] and Japanese (2009)[27] appeared. New editions in Dutch,[28] Spanish,[29] and Portuguese[30] were also published in the early years of the new millennium, and translations into Scandinavian and Slavic languages proliferated as well. During the first decade of the twenty-first century, *Minima Moralia* appeared for the first time in Norwegian (2006),[31] and early Croatian (1987)[32] and Swedish (1986)[33] versions were joined by publications in Polish (1999),[34] Romanian (1999),[35] Slovenian (2007),[36] and Czech (2009).[37] Adorno's signature work also became available in Turkish in 1998[38] and Azerbaijani in 2018.[39] These later translations suggest not only that Western European scholars are revisiting *Minima Moralia* in light of current developments but also that the increasingly global reach of neoliberalism has brought scholars and readers in so-called new capitalist economies of Eastern Europe and Eastern and Western Asia to this text as well. An assessment of the value of Adorno's writing for this expanded readership and the resonances his ideas might have in parts of the world where consumerism, mass society, and the authoritarian state are emergent contemporary questions are topics very much on our minds as we prepare this volume.

Most of the scholars represented in this volume hail from literature departments, and their analyses draw upon and complement the many studies of Adorno's work that begin from the standpoint of literary and cultural studies. *Minima Moralia* has attracted the attention of literary scholars both because of its engagement with everyday life and its generic commitment to the form of the aphorism. The work as a whole offers a masterclass in significant relations between form and content. The text's form embodies the "ability of the work of art to break through, at least momentarily, the mythic veil that capitalism has cast over society."[40] If—as Peter Hohendahl intimates—critique is at the center of aesthetic theory and the truth of art,[41] then Adorno's position on the precipice of damaged life commits him to a form capable of articulating a critique of "what exists in the name of what does not yet exist."[42] The splintered form of collected but individual aphorisms, a whole composed of fragments, is the damaged form necessary to reflect damaged life.

Literary scholars also turn to Adorno for insight into writing as a mode of thinking. They attend to the ways that the advice on the writing process offered in "Memento" (#51), for example, opens up a consideration of exile's homelessness. "Properly written texts are like spiders' webs: tight, concentric, transparent, well-spun and firm," Adorno proposes. Fittingly, then, "the movement of [Adorno's] thought through language is at the same time an inward, condensing movement of language within itself, a movement toward what is . . . a fusion of dialectics and *style* at the level of such language's smallest moving part: the sentence or short, aphoristic sequence of sentences."[43] In such analyses, the writer's private subjectivity anchors philosophical insight.

Adorno's experiments with and theses on the diminishing value of subjective experience have also been important themes for humanists. Andreas Huyssen, among others, refutes impressions of Adorno that conjure a culture-hating curmudgeon who acts "as the theoretical gravedigger of bourgeois subjectivity."[44] Instead, scholars in literary and cultural studies have identified in *Minima Moralia* a philosophy that "crash[es] against its erected facades."[45] They reveal how *Minima Moralia* discloses objective conditions from the perspective of subjective experience and, in so doing, disavows us of the notion that private experience is separate from the more "objective" social conditions we are more prepared to acknowledge as the wrong life. As noted by Roger Foster, "Coming to grips with how we are all marked by participating in wrong life, is crucial for learning to diffuse [this] dynamic."[46] Drawing on Adorno's profound critique of a "context-transcending" version of the good life,[47] humanistic scholars build on *Minima Moralia*'s model of philosophically informed subjective critique.

For literary scholars, Adorno's negative dialectic is valuable because his writing offers "rupturing, dissonant, critically valuable qualities of experience" that resist a "tendency toward 'identity thinking' that subsumes, homogenizes, and categories all that is other, different, or unique."[48] In addition to "outlin[ing] a theory of modern alienation,"[49] *Minima Moralia* offers a glimmer of utopian potential. The dictum "life does not live," a characteristically chiasmic sentence that at once reflects on (and critiques) damaged life as we know it, "also implies that life and living do have richer possibilities . . . that life differently organized, might in fact more truly live."[50] While indicating the "impossibility of direct access to the good life,"[51] *Minima Moralia* describes a damaged world that nonetheless gestures toward possibility. Adorno's negativism exposes the "unattainability of the right life,"[52] even as it offers a contextually, historically, and formally situated account that "believes in the ability of critical reason to identify"[53] the wrong life. The conditions of its production and its formal innovations "provide an index"[54] for what S. D. Chrostowska calls his "circuitous path to utopia."[55] It follows then that the end of each section and the book's conclusion are meant as non-endings, a *form of literature* that refracts the phenomenology of everyday life out of which emerges a "critique of capitalism as a *form of life*."[56] Whether they describe *Minima Moralia* as a book of aphorisms, a miniature,[57] a collection of "thought-images,"[58] a self-help manual,[59] a book of advice,[60] (somewhat confoundingly) a guide for project management,[61] or a contribution to literary criticism,[62] literary scholars have lauded Adorno's integration of aesthetic experience with the fundamental question of the good life.

To this wide-ranging body of existing scholarship, this collection of original chapters introduces a new generation of scholars. Touching on questions relevant to studies of history, critical theory, literature, the environment, Marxism, and religion, this volume's contributors demonstrate the reach of Adorno's well-loved reflections. Together, these chapters reveal a modest, exploratory, and resilient Adorno quite different from the dated curmudgeon too often caricatured by those less engaged with his work.

The first two chapters situate Adorno's writings in relation to fascism in his moment and our own. Jakob Norberg provides a historical account of *Minima Moralia* as a piece of the anti-fascist pedagogical work Adorno took up as a public intellectual after his return to postwar Germany. Just as *Minima Moralia* promotes "lucid encounters with unfreedom," so too did Adorno's radio appearances, publication record, and teaching speak to the confrontation between an Enlightenment version of individual freedom and a bureaucratic over-management preventative of personal autonomy. Similarly attendant to the relationship between praxis and theory, Chapter 2 zeroes in on *Minima Moralia*'s "breathtaking leaps" (per Rahel Jaeggi)—the limited space between Adorno's fascination with the minute details of daily existence and a proposed universal ethics. Situating the aphorisms in the context of exile, Oshrat Silberbusch suggests that for Adorno's philosophy of exaggeration, the most recognizably mundane objects become foreign; doorknobs and windows can, via historical circumstance, indicate the same damaged life evidenced by the Holocaust.

The authors of the next section, S. D. Chrostowska and Wyatt Sarafin, speak to the formal possibilities of the aphorism, asking how the style of Adorno's prose influences his arguments. In Chapter 3, Chrostowska closely examines the gestural mode of the fragment—a brevity that "resists closure" of critical thought. Fragments simultaneously acknowledge the impossibility of encapsulating the entirety of damaged life even as they resist the idea of suffering as a precondition of our contemporaneity. The philosophical gesture that emerges out of the fragment is not inconsequential or "empty" in the sense of being meaningless. Indeed, Chrostowska argues, the fragmentary gesture leaves space for utopian possibilities. Taking a transnational approach, Sarafin's Chapter 4 notes that the mobility of the aphorism—across national literary traditions and genres—relates to the form's "compression of information." Sarafin contests accusations that the aphorism as Adorno employs it is a Eurocentric form, exploring the vibrant contemporaneous treatment of the form in Caribbean aesthetics.

In Chapters 5 and 6, Clinton Williamson and Caleb Shaoning Fridell move us from considerations of the aphorism's formal capacity and into theories of late modern labor. In Chapter 5, Williamson dissects Adorno's dictum that "the whole of life must look like a job"; he asks, what can be done to cease the ruthless march of work as part and parcel of the "wrong life" as experienced in the 24/7 Capitolecene? One answer, Williamson suggests, lies in the glimpses of idleness described in *Minima Moralia*, moments where Adorno invites us to imagine a life without the exhaustive extraction of work. Fridell's chapter moves between the catastrophe of fascism, the "death of the worker's movement," and the role of nature in the subsumption of human life, to reassert Adorno's place as a capitalist critic for our time. More than an "abstract scheme for a blueprint utopia," Fridell sees Adorno's more tangible decree—to attend to the "coarsest demand: that no one shall go hungry anymore" (#100)—as the path toward the preservation of human life.

The final pair of essays investigates the ecological vision underlying *Minima Moralia*. In Chapter 7, Andrea Dara Cooper posits animality as an epistemological tool for exposing the harmful constructions of difference evident in both interspecies and interhuman relations. The inhumanity of humans toward one another runs parallel to our domination over animals, a hierarchical program of control that propels us toward injustice. "Recognizing animality," then, illuminates the real-life consequences faced by the most vulnerable populations, with further implications for how we approach anti-Semitism, anti-Black racism, and settler colonialism. Adorno's negative dialectics are made apparent in *Minima Moralia* through its methodology of entanglement—intertwining the concrete and abstract, the minor and the major, and in the final chapter, Caren Irr focuses on Adorno's entanglement of nature and history. Through a reading of "Paysage" (# 28)—where Adorno reflects on the simultaneity of beauty and horror in a hypercapitalist American landscape, a space in which we can see both our "obdurate stupidity" and the possibility for adaptation to widespread change—Irr concludes that what we call the Anthropocene, Adorno called damaged life.

Taken together, the chapters in the book demonstrate the value of ongoing attention to Adorno's aphorisms. A work that probes a vanishing literary and philosophical culture for inspiration and defines the terms for the survival of thinking itself, *Minima Moralia* resonates with twenty-first-century conditions. Continuing to think not only about but also with Adorno's methods lays bare the struggle to find a form adequate to the damage we continue to experience.

Part I

Thought after Fascism

1

Minima Moralia and the Contradictions of Postwar Pedagogy

Jakob Norberg

Written in the United States during the mid-to-late 1940s, *Minima Moralia* was published in West Germany in 1951, about two years after Adorno had returned to Frankfurt am Main in the Federal Republic, where he would spend the final two decades of his life—his late forties, fifties, and early sixties. The collection of extended aphorisms or dense essays was the first of Adorno's full-length books to be released in postwar Germany; *Minima Moralia* was a kind of postwar debut. While its form was absolutely singular even within Adorno's varied output, the collection nonetheless encapsulated the paradoxes and tensions of the many public and often political interventions that would follow until his passing in 1969. In this chapter, I sketch out Adorno's self-appointed and urgently felt anti-fascist mission in West Germany, the complex character and purpose of his statements, and then, returning to *Minima Moralia*, indicate how this work embodied and prefigured the intellectual and pedagogical work that he would continue to carry out in the decades after its release.

This contribution thus seeks to situate *Minima Moralia* in Adorno's broader project to repurpose pedagogical practices after the era of Nazi rule, world war, and genocide. As an increasingly prominent voice in postwar debates from 1949 to 1969, Adorno often stated his belief that postwar democracies, among them the Federal Republic, could only function authentically if its citizens achieved genuine autonomy, understood as the ability to make independent and informed decisions and judgments. As an intellectual with a public profile, Adorno professed his commitment to an ideal of civic personhood, and even emerged as a dedicated defender of the Enlightenment program as formulated by Immanuel Kant; he took pains to outline practical reforms required to educate and support independent subjects and responsible citizens. But in his philosophically informed sociological analyses of postwar Germany, Adorno noted how this society constituted a form of organized heteronomy, in which a gigantic complex of interlocking corporations, organizations, and state bureaucracies kept individuals in a state of dependency and fungibility. People were, Adorno believed, continually over-socialized, managed, coerced, and reminded of their own superfluity, and therefore also remained attracted to quasi-fascist promises of invulnerability and invincibility. In this way, Adorno's pedagogical program seems flatly at odds with his sociological analysis; Adorno demanded the cultivation of autonomy, the possibility of which he denied in his critical sociology.

Published in the beginning of his postwar rise to prominence, *Minima Moralia* held these two apparently contradictory strands together, combining an insistence on personal autonomy with an admission of organized heteronomy; it explored the "richness, differentiation, and vigour" of the individual without ever denying that this figure was "enfeebled and undermined" by relentless forces of socialization and control.[1] This tension also structured the text at the level of its form. Adorno himself suggested that his collection was affiliated with the historical tradition of advice or the "teaching of the good life."[2] Yet the very spirit of such wise counsel, defined as suggestions delivered to readers construed as agents ready to consider and implement programs of self-betterment, was hollowed out by the bleak depictions of totalizing sociocultural management exercised over modern individuals; the presuppositions of the genre were contradicted by the content of the aphorisms. By mimicking gestures of advice while repeatedly reminding the reader of the impossibility of efficacious individual action, *Minima Moralia* did not quite set out to facilitate autonomy but rather sought to provoke lucid encounters with unfreedom. In this way, *Minima Moralia* rendered the contradictions of late capitalism transparent by enacting them in the medium of genre and form, setting the stage for Adorno's entire postwar pedagogy and nearly two decades of subsequent interventions.

Professor, Expert, Critic, Counselor: Adorno's Public Roles

Over the first two decades of West Germany's existence, Adorno would emerge as one of the country's most prominent intellectuals, perhaps its most prominent. This is partly a simple claim about his media presence. He published articles in a number of culturally ambitious postwar journals and occasionally contributed to widely circulating newspapers; he published books with West Germany's most prestigious high-brow publisher, the Frankfurt-based Suhrkamp; he appeared in televised roundtables and discussions; and, above all, he was a frequent guest on the radio, commenting on music, literature, and sociopolitical matters over a hundred times, especially on the regional Hessian station.

In all this, Adorno coupled media savvy with an impressive thematic range; he could discuss the high arts and especially music but also pronounce on popular culture; he was a contemporary bearer of the German philosophical tradition as well as an exponent of the modern discipline of sociology. In the 1950s, a decade not known for a frank discussion of the Nazi past, Adorno appeared as a practitioner of modern research methods with US experience, and once the silence about the past gave way to debate about Nazi Germany and the dangers of fascist recidivism in the early 1960s, he emerged as its most persistent and scrupulous voice, an expert on the psychological mechanisms behind authoritarianism and anti-Semitism—again, his interventions were guided by a deeply felt mission of cultural and emotional disarmament aimed to prevent a fascist resurgence. As the most prolific and public representative of the Frankfurt School, Adorno offered young progressives in the early Federal Republic an attractive politico-ethical habitus: radicalism without dogmatic Soviet communism, critique without militancy, moral seriousness without religion.[3] He invented a manner of living somewhat peacefully with the Federal Republic of Germany, namely in the mode of constant, vigilant negativity, and even became a sort of father figure for aspiring intellectuals, but only by projecting an entirely un-fatherlike appearance;[4] Adorno's public demeanor, including his precise but non-commanding diction, displayed none of the authoritarian, patriarchal traits that had traditionally been associated with the paternal role in the German cultural context.

Adorno emerged as West Germany's exemplary public intellectual and yet the phrase "public intellectual" does not quite capture the various roles he played or audiences he targeted and also leaves out many of his reflections on his own engagement with society. Adorno was, to begin with, a professor. Professorships were an explicit goal of Horkheimer and Adorno, for the status and stability it granted its occupants; scholars can lead precarious lives, especially if they belong to an historically marginalized minority, and both friends strove for "security."[5] For Adorno, the road to a full professorship was long—he was granted a tenured chair a decade after his arrival—but toward the end of his career, he would lecture in front of hundreds of students, direct the Frankfurt Institute of Social Research, and preside over the German Association of Sociologists. In other words, Adorno spoke from a well-established institutional position that he himself equated with a certain degree of power.[6] Ironically, it was precisely as a professor, an embodiment of theoretical learning and academic hierarchy, that he became a target for the happening-like disruptions of a politicized phalanx of the largest student generation in the history of Germany, a generation he had at first inspired.[7]

As a professor, Adorno mostly taught philosophy, but he chose to identify himself with the rapidly rising discipline of sociology. In 1960, there were 13 chairs in sociology; 10 years later, the number was 200.[8] The demand for Adorno was related to the demand for a new kind of expertise, largely rejected by the racially oriented Nazis but embraced in West Germany, where empirically based analysis and careful reform of the social system was part of the republic's self-image. Adorno continuously contributed to the redefinition of Germany as a society of interacting individuals and institutions rather than a community of blood and race. And yet he also acknowledged sociology's history of entanglement with a vision of a centralized and bureaucratic total administration, which became a significant target of his critical theorizing.

Adorno would probably not have achieved his ubiquity on the basis of a disciplinary specialization alone but also appeared as a polymathic and aesthetically sensitive critic of cultural artifacts and trends. His first books to appear in West Germany, apart from *Minima Moralia*, were collections of essays on culture and music such as *Prismen* (1955) and *Dissonanzen* (1956). This role, too, was a kind of retrospective resistance to fascist ideology—Adorno himself pointed to the Nazi hatred of supposedly corrosive criticism and helped re-introduce Jewish thinkers and modernist artists as parts of a cultural tradition suppressed under National Socialism.[9] But as with the sociologist, Adorno saw the critic as an ambiguous figure. The semi-professional reviewer had appeared in bourgeois society to discriminate among its abundance of goods, but ultimately turned against the capitalist dynamic of commodification that required the development of connoisseurship in the first place. And yet even at his most critical and dismissive, Adorno continued to provide a kind of guidance in an economically booming and "americanized" West Germany a little overwhelmed by the proliferation of gadgets and stimuli.[10] He rejected broadcasted soccer games, paperback books, simplistic music appreciation records, but by doing so still brought them into his work, publicly modeling an informed but ascetic stance toward consumer society.

But Adorno did not solely write about art; he addressed modes of living. In his writings, Adorno could discuss situations of domesticity, hospitality, and sociability under conditions of modernity, and emerged as something of a sage or counselor who dispensed advice on how to negotiate everyday situations and even lead a dignified life under difficult circumstances. Numerous letters from readers and radio listeners in the Adorno archive testify to his peculiar role as an authority on modern existence in the Federal Republic: quite a few people of different ages and from different walks of life wrote to Adorno for a helpful word or two about their dilemmas and difficulties.[11] And yet as *Minima Moralia* shows, Adorno did not simply adopt a tradition of bourgeois self-improvement or offer reassuring consolations. Instead, he entered the postwar literary scene in 1951 by delivering bleak statements on the unavailability of any simple, innocuous ethical position in a compromised world. Adorno was precisely not a success-oriented life coach, but rather used the format of advice to remind his readers of the stifling grip of a totally administered world.

Adorno, then, was not a free-floating intellectual, but a professor, expert, critic, and sometime counselor. He did not simply comment on postwar Germany, but spoke from and reflected upon his various positions within this society. He knew that he was embedded in hierarchies, attached to disciplinary programs, active on a cultural market, and that his interventions were both enabled and constrained by the particular functions and limits of a series of societal roles.

Indeed, Adorno's interventions often took the form of critical performances of established scripts: he was a professorial authority who argued for dismantling authoritarian education, a sociologist who voiced skepticism on the discipline's mission, a critic who indicted the commodification of art, and a wise counselor who refused to provide easily usable advice. This type of paradoxical performance was rooted in his critical analysis of society. Adorno's unflinching detection of pervasive organized dependence under capitalism combined with his desperate wish to reform modern society led him to articulate a complex, even ostensibly contradictory program of practical enlightenment and education, simultaneously ambitious and despairing, which took the form of paradoxical, even self-subverting enactment of his multiple roles as a professor, expert, and counselor. This shaped many if not most of his public interventions in the 1950s and 1960s, but also *Minima Moralia*. His first work to reach the German literary market was a collection of counsels for individuals for whom autonomy had become an almost impossible project; it was a book of advice that openly declared its own impossibility, and aimed to bring this disheartening, even tortuous impossibility into the realm of individual's experience. It was as such that *Minima Moralia* anticipated and prepared many of Adorno's future interventions, although the demanding density of its style may have remained unsurpassed.

Autonomy and Postwar Enlightenment

In the postwar period, Adorno emerged as a proponent of an Enlightenment notion of individual autonomy. This aspect of his public interventions might surprise contemporary American readers of Adorno, who know him as a critic of the dialectic of Enlightenment, but his repeated commitment to a conception of freedom explicitly rooted in the Enlightenment is undeniable, at least at the level of public rhetoric. As an invited speaker at public events, discussant in radio conversations on current issues, and a writer for ambitious general-audience magazines in West Germany, Adorno consistently and without reservations called for a vigorous defense of Enlightenment principles, chief among them the idea of "maturity," or *Mündigkeit*. In a 1956 address at the annual conference of German adult education programs, Adorno declared that the objective of adult education must be "Enlightenment," defined as the struggle against entrenched irrationalities such as inculcated norms, unjustified principles, routinized and prejudiced assessments, traditionalist behaviors, and superstitions. In the same brief address, he approvingly invoked the liberal Prussian civil servant and linguistic researcher Wilhelm von Humboldt's ideal of a personality capable of independently forming judgments, developing individual faculties, and resisting commands from external sources that lack any connection to inner motivations or reasons.

For Adorno, the conceptual core of his repeated appeal to Enlightenment could be precisely defined. Enlightenment was synonymous with the individual's emergence from self-incurred immaturity, a definition that Immanuel Kant had delivered in his 1784 article entitled: "What Is Enlightenment?" In a series of three broadcasted conversations with Hellmut Becker, the Director of the Max-Planck Institute for Educational Research, held in 1966, 1968, and 1969, Adorno repeatedly returned to Kant's dictum as the loadstar of all pedagogical efforts, especially in the final interview, held only six days before Adorno's untimely death. The contemporary relevance of Kant's rousing call to exit self-incurred immaturity lied, Adorno claimed, in its crucial significance for a well-functioning, authentic democracy. The democratic rule to which West Germany aspired of course meant the rule of the people. But if the individuals who constituted the citizenry willingly submitted to authorities rather than truly committed to make informed and independent judgments, especially during election time, the rule of the people would be devoid of substance. The political system of democracy in West Germany and elsewhere was premised on the genuine autonomy of its members. In the series of radio conversations with Becker, the theorist's preoccupation with education dedicated to autonomy often took the form of quite specific and nuanced suggestions for early childhood socialization. For instance, Adorno wanted to eliminate brutalizing violence to children, but by no means make child-rearing indiscriminately permissive. Compliant children, he said, typically grow up to become more questioning adults, since they have successfully internalized authority, whereas completely undisciplined children may remain in need of external, repressive measures during their later lives. As in other venues, Adorno emerged as something of a counselor, even dispensing vaguely Freudian parental advice for the purpose of stabilizing a postwar civic order.

But autonomy was not an easily obtainable status. In his 1784 article, Kant had discussed the ever-present obstacles to the exit out of self-incurred immaturity. Humans, Kant noted, are all too willing to accept the commands and counsels of authorities out of fear or complacency—we are frequently too timid or too comfortable to make judgments and decisions for ourselves, to make the cognitive effort or take the risk of making independent judgments and live with the consequences. But the key message in Adorno's public interventions was a different and less encouraging one. He held that advanced capitalist society put pressure on individuals to adapt to its arrangements and induced acceptance of such dependency by means of the culture industry's modulation of everyone's internal lives. Modern individuals were compelled to be "well-adjusted"—Adorno used the English word in the conversation with Becker—to the point at which they no longer could emerge as specific, unique individuals but only functioned smoothly and flexibly in teams, groups, and organizations.[12] According to Adorno, oversocialization had produced a kind of frozen, perennial immaturity.

Adorno thus argued that the conditions for a process of Enlightenment had deteriorated since the era of Kant and Humboldt, because in the contemporary moment, actual heteronomy was being enforced by interlinked corporations, organizations, and bureaucracies on which everyone depended for their livelihood and social integration. The hindrances to genuine self-determination were no longer primarily the anthropological ones of timorousness or laziness pointed out by Kant, but the very conditions of existence in the society of total administration. Immaturity was not self-incurred, and could therefore also not be removed by daring self-assertion. Or it was self-incurred, but then at the level of the entire of human socioeconomic order with its automatized and autonomous functioning: "the experiences of real powerlessness" so common to individuals in modern society, Adorno wrote, were in fact "anything but irrational."[13] Adorno even admitted that people sought to rid themselves of the Enlightenment obligation to be autonomous, because it would simply be too torturous to try to achieve an ideal in a context in which every attempt to do so would be worn down by society. Adorno thus repeated Kant's call to autonomy while clearly conceding that responding to the summons of the Enlightenment—"be autonomous!"—had become harder than ever, perhaps even impossible.

Society as Organized Heteronomy: The Case of Germany

Adorno's bleak update of the obstacles to autonomy was informed by his sociological analysis of advanced capitalism. He conceived of society as a complex and distinctly modern configuration of functions that typically escaped the cognition of individuals and yet structured their lives by compelling them to assume roles and tasks in the whole, or else face social ruin in the form of unemployment, downward mobility, and ostracism. In the classical bourgeois era, Adorno argued, society had typically been imagined as an association of equals free to pursue their own interest in a market economy and cultivate their independence of mind and individual talents; bourgeois society had been the site of general autonomy. However, the constant volatility of the market, the starkly unequal distribution of resources, and above all the emergence of a large exploited class, the proletariat, had undermined the validity of the liberal-bourgeois imagination. Real autonomy had been the tainted privilege of a certain class.

When Adorno then turned to the contemporary moment and the Western nations, he saw a society that had neither made good on the liberal promise to promote individual autonomy, nor one that had been transformed by a revolutionary working class. Instead, he spoke of an administered society, in which economic power had been concentrated in a few corporations and conglomerates which planned their every activity and cooperated with large state bureaucracies. This new societal arrangement had raised the consumer opportunities of the population and eliminated much naked poverty and yet it was still a rigid class society without a fair distribution of goods, and most members felt caught and caged by a highly structured context they could neither understand nor escape. The mid-twentieth century was the age of the impersonal yet overbearing organization in which people's felt impotence made them frustrated or frightened, until they were forced to accept their powerlessness and indulge in escapist immersion in the products of the culture industry—or in authoritarian identification with existing powers. Society precluded autonomy and also erased individuality, because the tightly managed, profit-driven process of production ultimately rendered human beings fungible and superfluous, a fact that struck them with terror.

This sociological analysis of organized heteronomy also informed Adorno's identification of the pathologies exploited and stoked in and by Nazi Germany. Due to the somewhat belated modernization of Germany, a process often marked by reluctance and resentment in the population, Adorno saw Germans as having been significantly less comfortable in their interaction with the market and also the modern centralized state, and believed that they remained relatively alienated from both, in comparison with citizens of Anglo-Saxon countries. But with regards to political institutions, Germans had all too often sought to overcome this alienation from a modern centralized and bureaucratized state power by identifying with it even more ardently. Pained resistance to concentrated modern state power had tipped over into belief in the state's infallibility and rightful belligerence. Germans, Adorno wrote, had "deified the state in order not to hate it."[14]

For Adorno, a pernicious German tradition of state idolatry was a consequence of a harsh, less gradual confrontation with modernity. Similarly on the micro-level of the family, Germans had become known for being marked by authoritarian family structures, and yet this authoritarianism, which Adorno did not deny, was an outcome of a quickly destabilized patriarchal structure, which triggered a frantic search for surrogate authorities. Under the Nazi regime, Germans had fanatically worshiped Hitler and yet the image of the *Führer*, Adorno claimed, had possessed no particularly "fatherly traits";[15] the popular adulation for the fascist leader had not been a mere extension of conservative authoritarianism at the level of politics, but a symptom of destabilized family relationships in a country that experienced modernity as a shock.

More broadly, Adorno argued that German nationalism had served as a refuge for deeply anxious individuals who had sought to recover their eroded sense of agency. Interwar Germans made insecure by a succession of severe economic crises, including runaway inflation and high levels of unemployment, were attracted by the National Socialist vision of a deep ethnic community, a so-called *Volksgemeinschaft*, in which no members of the now racially defined German people would be allowed to sink into destitution. This manipulative evocation of warm togetherness in the form of a national socialism that would neutralize class differences possessed a strong appeal in times of vulnerability.

By broadcasting stories of German superiority, the Nazi regime provided an antidote to perceived helplessness, but in the form of an organized collective narcissism. The consciousness of social impotence would be remedied, but only through willing subordination to a higher community—the German *Volk* as led by the *Führer*—that would secure the strength previously denied to the humiliated individual. In Germany, self-esteem would be restored through servility.

The end of the Third Reich and its promises of perpetual victory should have dealt a massive psychological blow to regime's many supporters and yet the absence of a process of reckoning suggested, Adorno thought, that the identification with the supposedly superior German collective quietly endured and only searched for other outlets. One such outlet was the immediate postwar economic boom, which put German productivity on display for the world but did not inspire much confidence in stability among a shaken population, haunted by the terror of imminent unemployment as raw evidence of individual disposability.

In his compressed retelling of the German twentieth century, Adorno thus argued that nationalist-racist belligerence reproduced the logic of the subject made insecure and suffering from damaged agency. Adorno viewed the modern history of German aggression as composed of a series of interlinked moments of wounded self-confidence. Individual Germans had embraced the Nazi party state in an effort to escape the insecurities of the interwar period and enjoy the pleasure of fraudulent collective invincibility, and the German nation had sought to prove itself to itself by ramping up the level of destructiveness. Millions of fearful and angered Germans had looked for protection and reassurance in a German nation with its own episodes of fearfulness and deadly rage.

It is against the backdrop of Adorno's conception of modern society and the delayed crystallization of market and statehood specific to Germany that one can understand his writings on the postwar situation in Federal Republic. For Adorno, West Germans lived in the shadow of total war and organized, industrial-scale mass murder. The symptoms of disavowed complicity with an unspeakable historical event infected almost every conversation. And Adorno himself worked to facilitate and maintain the public recognition of German guilt, unceasing attention to anti-democratic and latent fascist dispositions, and struggle against widespread xenophobic and anti-minority sentiments. The central imperative of the postwar period ought to be, Adorno believed, to prevent the reoccurrence of genocide; all societal institutions and efforts should be organized toward this end.

And yet Adorno also asserted repeatedly that the socioeconomic conditions conducive to a collective turn to fascism had not in fact changed. The "basic structure of society," he stated in 1966, "are the same as 25 years ago."[16] In conditions of advanced capitalism, individual autonomy was necessarily constrained and attenuated and people continued to face their helplessness and even dispensability, which inevitably triggered fear, dissatisfaction, and anger, in turn susceptible to exploitation by authoritarian groups. Mass identification with an aggressive regime and vicious targeting of minorities therefore remained possibilities. Adorno believed that he must work to avert the threat of fascist recidivism in a situation where there root causes of fascism had not and could not be eliminated. *Postwar* society was in a fundamental sense not different from *prewar* society and hence haunted by the same problems.

This explains Adorno's turn to socialization and education, and to his emphasis on individual autonomy, however precarious. Since Adorno believed that postwar and prewar society were similar with respect to the relations of production, and that fascist dispositions lingered on, Adorno joined an ongoing West German discussion of democratic education, democratic child-rearing, and even "democratic fatherhood" and called for a new, postwar educational system and a postwar moral culture meant to prevent authoritarianism.[17] In a series of essays and addresses, Adorno focused on the significance and design of pedagogical and therapeutic institutions as the principal component of postwar reform. Among his writings, one finds an address on adult education (1956), a theory of far from innocuous semi-erudition or semi-*Bildung* (1959), pragmatic guidelines for the neutralization of anti-Semitism delivered to pedagogues (1962), a radio essay on philosophy and teacher training (1962), a lecture on the status of the profession of the teacher (1965), and an essay that encapsulated his effort at de-barbarization and prevention through pedagogy: "Education After Auschwitz" (1966). The collection of essays and interviews entitled *Erziehung zur Mündigkeit* [*Education for Autonomy*], published in 1970, became one of his bestselling books.[18] Adorno's postwar anti-fascist program read: educate the educators. And yet judging by the logic of his statements on society, this persistent focus on education and pedagogy as a way to promote independence of mind and judgment still represented a compensatory program, implemented *instead of* a more fundamental reorganization of material relations. According to Adorno's own standards, educational reform was a second-best option. In an age crowded with workshops, training sessions, anti-bias education, and so on, we may have forgotten Adorno's insight that reform by education alone cannot eliminate political pathologies ultimately rooted in the socioeconomic organization of capitalist society.

Minima Moralia and the Problems of a Postwar Pedagogy

We now have the elements of Adorno's analysis of the contradictions in bourgeois society and the fatal way these contradictions had played out in modern Germany history. According to Adorno, autonomy was the fundamental requirement of a genuinely liberal democracy, and yet in his own analysis, advanced capitalism constituted a form of organized heteronomy, a veritable system of unfreedom. Facing curtailed independence and sabotaged self-worth, individuals were susceptible to the virulent, perverted fascist response to heteronomy in the form of mass subordination, as well as persecution, expulsion, and extermination directed as minorities. Once fascism had collapsed, the German population retreated into denial and disavowal, still lacking the sense of autonomy necessary for taking responsibility for past individual and collective action, and, one should add, still living under socioeconomic conditions that perpetuated precariousness. In light of this, Adorno then turned to a set of educational and therapeutic devices that might contain the aggressive symptoms of heteronomy and yet never quite eliminate the possibility of their reappearance. A postwar pedagogy grounded in Enlightenment principles of autonomy and maturity was a limited program of mitigation, and yet it was, Adorno thought, the only available option in the present, one to which he was nonetheless sincerely committed.

Adorno might have been one of the early Federal Republic's most prolific thinkers, with new texts and talks every year, but if one is to believe his own assessments, he was writing for an audience that was in danger of becoming a hollowed-out host of a "reified consciousness."[19] The strenuous publication strategy was seemingly contradicted by the uncompromising darkness of the diagnosis, which suggested its ultimate futility. But Adorno was consistent insofar as he believed that the work of Enlightenment could not count on engaging with already autonomous beings, but must instead begin by promoting an "education toward maturity [Erziehung zur Mündigkeit]." The contemporary intellectual, he believed, must first and foremost become a pedagogue intent on the construction of independent selfhood, although such autonomous selfhood would remain fragile absent a societal transformation, which seemed so remote as to be a near-impossibility.

Turning now again to *Minima Moralia*, we can begin to discern how Adorno's paradoxical combination of continued pedagogical advice and dispiriting sociological analysis, sustained over many years, was already on display in his 1951 collection of aphorism, the first of his books published in the Federal Republic and one of the most well-known. In the text itself, Adorno explicitly and immediately placed his collection the philosophical tradition of wise counsel, instructions in the ancient art of the "good life," to be imparted by the philosopher to lay readers understood as selves intent on caring for their own selves.[20] Colored by the American environment in which it was written, *Minima Moralia* at times also alluded to a specifically American tradition of bourgeois self-optimization, running from Benjamin Franklin's mid-eighteenth-century exhortations to be frugal and industrious to Dale Carnegie's upbeat lessons in smooth sociability and winning salesmanship from *How to Make Friends and Influence People*, which became a bestseller in the 1930s.[21] *Minima Moralia* thus was categorized itself as a text addressed to a subject willing and capable of directed self-improvement, and the passages sometimes even delivered explicit instructions, such as "[a]dvice to intellectuals: let no one represent you."[22] By virtue of its declared and performed membership in an established genre of counsel, then, *Minima Moralia* conjured the notion of the independent agent equipped to evaluate and implement ideas for action.

At the same time, Adorno chose to incessantly expose this very reader to the message of the individual's demise. "It is the signature of our age," Adorno wrote in one aphorism, "that no-one, without exception, can now determine his own life within even a moderately comprehensive framework."[23] This matter-of-fact attitude to the socioeconomically conditioned end of the autonomous subject was quite frequently summarized in pithy, uncompromising declarations such as "[t]here is no way out of entanglement."[24] This bleak, post-individual state of affairs was even announced at the very first page of the introduction, where Adorno immediately likened the aphorist writing about the good life to the novelists who absurdly make people "who are no more than component parts of machinery" behave as if they still possess "the capacity to act as subjects."[25] In this way, Adorno's aphorisms formally gestured toward the promise of life wisdom and good counsel on how to think and behave in a range of contexts while simultaneously stating that the "nullity" of the individual subject sure of his or her autonomy had been "demonstrated" once and for all.[26]

By means of its self-categorization and its style, *Minima Moralia* addressed its readers as recipients of advice and hence as self-directed beings, individuals capable of making judgments and taking action, but quickly and systematically negated the possibility of meaningful individual action. In a sense, the book fused the two strategies that would come to characterize Adorno's postwar stance: it coupled the call to autonomy with the analysis of organized heteronomy, and did so on page after page in the very same text. Adorno did not so much tell his readers to exercise autonomy as he exhorted them to be perpetually aware of its impossibility, an uncomfortable condition. The task given to the reader in *Minima Moralia* was thus not to implement any philosophically vetted and experientially tested plan of action but instead to remain vigilant about the denial or resignation that would almost invariably result from the societal nullification of agency: "the almost insoluble task," Adorno writes, "is to let neither the power of others, nor our own powerlessness, stupefy us."[27] Adorno's goal in *Minima Moralia* was less to cultivate politically necessary autonomy as to facilitate and sustain the difficult, almost punitive recognition of inescapable heteronomy.

But why insist on this negative experience of denied autonomy? The problem Adorno had identified already in the 1940s was that human beings battered by capitalist society and drugged by the industrialized cultural production on offer would simply want to relinquish the objectively unrealizable ideal of autonomy, so central to democracy and the prevention of fascist politics. And he understood full well that knowledge of society's workings, as he conceived of them, would be almost unbearable to individuals, since this knowledge only forced its bearers to confront their utter helplessness as an objective condition. Against this backdrop, the widespread psychological preference for ignorance was entirely understandable. In this situation, Adorno opted neither for false hope and reassurance nor for complete retreat and resignation, but for a prolonged exposure and perception of society's overwhelming force. Adorno's writings, and especially *Minima Moralia*, were meant to extend the readers' lucid encounter with their desperate situation, however painful such a confrontation must be.

The intellectual in the administered society could not speak to his readers in the Kantian fashion, as autonomous beings, but as beings who must, at least as a first step, be brought to experience the social conditions relentlessly working against the achievement of self-determination. Adorno's postwar writings absorbed the contradictions of late bourgeois-capitalist society by proposing serious and specific reforms for the pedagogical cultivation of independent selves in the Enlightenment tradition, all the while admitting the insurmountable obstacles to the formation and exercise of genuine autonomy. This may seem like a package doomed to unpopularity, but few thinkers were as successful in spreading their message, and Adorno's scrutiny of authoritarianism and fascism did inspire a student generation in West Germany.

But it was also radicalized groups of students who eventually expressed their dissatisfaction with Adorno's attitude of apparent resignation, and they protested against his message through episodes of organized rowdiness. Adorno's university lectures were disrupted on several occasions in the final years of the 1960s, until he suspended his teaching. The left-wing students wanted to break out of political passivity; Adorno thought they engaged in action for action's sake, which tended to spill into violence. For a moment, Adorno's insight into the present impossibility of emancipatory action was countered by an irregular and desperate "actionism" that it may have helped generate.[28]

2

"Breathtaking Leaps" or from Doorknobs to Fascism

Oshrat C. Silberbusch

People lose the ability to close a door "quietly, gently yet firmly," Adorno tells us in the aphorism entitled "Do not knock." Subjected to the "unforgiving, as it were ahistorical demands of objects," they slam the doors of their cars and refrigerators and do not even turn around to close those of the houses they enter, as the latter have the unfortunate habit "to snap shut by themselves" (MM 44/40,[1] Aph. 19). Result? Gestures have lost "all hesitation, all deliberation and all civility," becoming "precise and brutal," and humanity with them (MM 43/40, Aph. 19).

> What does it mean for the subject that there are no more wide opening casement windows, but only sliding panes to be shoved rudely, no more gentle door handles but only turnable knobs, no forecourt, no threshold before the street, no wall around the garden? And which driver has not been tempted by the sheer power of his engine, to squash the vermin of the street, the pedestrians, children and cyclists, reduce them to pulp? (MM 44/40, Aph. 19)

The dizzying jump from doorknobs and sliding window panes to bloody mass murder is no accident, as the sentence immediately following these dark musings makes clear: "The movements machines [which seems to include modern use objects more generally, OCS] demand of their users already contain the violence, the blows, the jerky repetitiveness of fascist torture" (MM 44/40, Aph. 19). When Rahel Jaeggi, in her 2005 paper "'No Individual Can Resist': *Minima Moralia* as Critique of Forms of Life," speaks of Adorno's "breathtaking leaps,"[2] these are the kind of jumps she has in mind. *Minima Moralia* is full of them. Behind America's "dismantling of ceremony" (MM 46/42, Aph. 20), the "hellos of familiar indifference" (45/41, Aph. 20), Adorno the exiled senses "naked brutality"; the "directness . . . has already the form and sound of the command under fascism" (MM 46/42, Aph. 20). In gift items and exchange vouchers, invented for people who have forgotten how to give, he sees a sign that people are "freezing to death" (MM 47/43, Aph. 21), spreading that very same coldness without which, as Adorno never tired to point out, Auschwitz would not have been possible. The fact that waiters no longer know the menu, and "no one hastens to serve the guest, however long he has to wait, if the person responsible for him is busy," proves that "concern for the institution, which culminates in prisons, takes precedence... over the concern for the subject, who is administered like an object" (MM 132-33/117, Aph. 75): in other words, your long wait for your scrambled eggs comes from the same tree as the inhumane treatment of prisoners, just as there is a straight line "from the civil servants and employees that have you wait in line" to the "torturers of the Gestapo and the bureaucrats of the gas chambers" (MM 208/183, Aph. 117).

These are just some prominent examples of these leaps, where Adorno passes from the observation of what would seem like a mundane, innocuous phenomenon, even a simple gesture, to a sweeping—and often damning—statement about the state of society and the individual. Far from outliers, they are, in more than one way, the quintessential minima moralia—not so much minimal ethics as ethics of the minute, the trivial, the seemingly insignificant—or as Adorno calls them, "micrologically deluded ethics [*mikrologisch verblendete Moral*]" (MM 206/182, Aph. 116). "There is nothing harmless left" (MM 26/25, Aph. 5), he writes, programmatically, early in the book, and draws the consequence. This idiosyncratic attention to the most minute defines *Minima Moralia*, and through it Adorno's work as a whole. For *Minima Moralia* reflects not only the experiential, emotional fundus from which the latter springs—it is, in Adorno's words, "the attempt to present elements of [his] philosophy from the standpoint of subjective experience," and as such, its aphorisms are "points of entry, models for future work on the concept" (MM 17/18, dedication). There is no doubt that *Minima Moralia*'s model, with its breathtaking leaps, in more than one way shaped—and prepared the way for—Adorno's theoretical work of later years.

Before I delve deeper into the role and significance of Adorno's breathtaking leaps, I want to reflect briefly on the philosophical sensibility at their root—and on their relationship with exile. Indeed, we cannot understand the affective core of Adorno's musings on refrigerator doors and room service without placing it in its context: the "most narrowly private domain of the intellectual in exile" (MM 16/18, dedication). In aphorism 13, Adorno writes: "Every intellectual in exile, without exception, is damaged (*beschädigt*)" (MM 35/33)—significantly, one of only three places where the word "*beschädigt*" used in the subtitle, *Reflections from the Damaged Life*, is used in the text (a fact lost in translation, as E. Jephcott translates this occurrence as "mutilated"). And Adorno goes on: "He lives in an environment that must remain incomprehensible to him, however flawless his knowledge of trade unions or car traffic; he is always astray" (MM 35/33).

Minima Moralia is infused with that damage, that incomprehension, the bewilderment of one who suddenly finds himself in a place where everything is unfamiliar. Those of us who have lived in different countries, different languages know this perplexity all too well: the feeling that you are slightly off, out of whack—that you are always astray, as Adorno puts it: *in der Irre*. One consequence of that felt discrepancy is that even the most mundane interactions, the most banal objects, are vividly experienced. By denaturalizing the natural, turning the quotidian into the foreign (think doorknobs and windows), exile leads to the kind of heightened sensibility that plays such a crucial role in *Minima Moralia*, where the incomprehension of the emigrant is turned into an epistemic tool. It is an incomprehension that will never completely leave Adorno—more, it will come to lie at the very heart of his philosophy. "The only true thoughts are those that don't understand themselves" (MM 218/192, Aph. 122), Adorno wrote in a famous monogram toward the end of *Minima Moralia*. Experiencing for twelve years a world he did not understand fundamentally shaped his approach to philosophy, and his idea of truth—and helped him edge closer to the latter as he understood it: as something that is not only by nature "floating" and "fragile," but that has in that openness its very essence.[3] As we will see, that very same openness and fragility, or rather, its lack, plays a fundamental role in Adorno's leaps from doorknobs to fascism.

With this context in mind, let us now return to Adorno's breathtaking leaps. There are many dimensions to them and I would like to highlight a few, without pretending to be exhaustive. In the paper from which I borrowed the expression, Rahel Jaeggi focuses on a central aspect:

> If the significance of phenomena is pursued "into the minutest ramifications of everyday life," this is because under the gaze of *Minima Moralia* everything ... can become a particular that stands for the universal of a form of life, in which the latter is mirrored and manifested. In this way every individual aspect stands for the whole; it can be deciphered as an instance of a context of social practices and institutions one can, with Hegel, call "objective Spirit."[4]

That is, Adorno directs his attention to the minute particular because he sees the universal reflected in it—and the leap is his expression of that reflection.

It is a philosophical method, a kind of radical induction in which the minute particular serves as a signifier for the universal. Adorno himself points to this epistemological aspect in the very first page of *Minima Moralia*'s dedication: "He who wishes to know the truth about life in its immediacy must scrutinize its alienated form, the objective powers that determine individual existence even in its most hidden recesses" (MM 13/15, Dedication). The individual life that is individual no more because "society is essentially the substance of the individual" (MM 16/17, Dedication) reveals in its behaviors, its objects and its language, its desires, its pleasures, and its fears, the truth not about any hypothetical subjectivity but about the objective powers that control it—capitalist society, or as Adorno liked to say: the context of delusion [*Verblendungszusammenhang*].

This methodological function plays certainly a crucial role in Adorno's breathtaking leaps. He directs his micrological gaze at his surroundings in a desire to understand "what life as such has become under the conditions of monopoly capitalism,"[5] as he writes in a letter describing *Minima Moralia* to his parents. As Andreas Bernhard puts it, *Minima Moralia* is "Adorno's attempt ... to think the decline into barbarism from the invention of doorknobs, gift articles and room service."[6] Claus Offe, less generously, speaks of a "methodological artifice" and chastises Adorno's "zealous excessiveness."[7] To the accusation of excessiveness, *Minima Moralia* has an answer ready: today, we read in the aphorism "Regressions," "reason can only endure in despair and excess; one needs absurdity not to succumb to objective insanity" (MM 228/200). The question remains, however, just how breathtaking Adorno's leaps from the micrological observation to the philosophical insight really are. To see the leap as an artifice, an intentional exaggeration, is tempting—not only because the jump from doorknobs to fascist torture, from long lines at the government agency to gas chambers, is indeed dizzying, but also because Adorno himself explicitly embraced exaggeration as a philosophical tool. He once told his students that he considered it his task as a philosopher to deliver "shocks"[8] that propel the audience out of their mental comfort zone and force them to think. At the same time, it is important to understand that Adorno's exaggerations are much more than a foil, more than a *Denkanstoß* meant to provoke reflection. In their glaring excess, they shine the light on the hidden underbelly of the mundane, on what the latter contains yet too easily conceals, and as such, they serve as a fundamental depositary of truth—possibly the only one: "Today," Adorno said in a lecture on confronting the Nazi past, "exaggeration is the sole medium of truth."[9]

Adorno's breathtaking leaps are thus neither methodological artifices whose sole intent is to grab the attention of the reader nor are they even primarily epistemological—or rather, while their epistemic role is undeniable, it is but one of multiple, interconnected dimensions. We have to look beyond their epistemic function and examine what it means that they take it on in the first place. What is philosophically implied when sliding doors and gift vouchers, casual hellos and waiters that don't serve you take on such an outsized importance?

First, it is crucial to understand that Adorno's breathtaking leaps don't just *create* shocks—they respond to one. And in the process, they reveal something crucial about Adorno the philosopher. In his *Lectures on Negative Dialectics* given in 1968, Adorno told his students: "I must confess, I cannot help it: In my thinking, I react first of all idiosyncratically, that is to say, with my nerves, and the so-called theoretical thought is to a large extent but the attempt to follow these instinctive reactions with my mind."[10] Adorno's strong reactions to American windows, to gift shops, and to doors that snap shut by themselves are more than just quirks of an exiled intellectual, more than methodological tools—they are the starting point of his philosophy. It is impossible to overstate the importance of what he here calls the nerves—impulse, instinct, idiosyncracies, emotions—in his thought. That they lead the way, and thought follows, in other words: that Adorno thinks with his nerves, is an impression one can never quite shake when reading his work, far beyond *Minima Moralia*. I have shown elsewhere the intimate connection between that prominence of impulse in Adorno's thought and the millionfold suffering he witnessed in his lifetime, the importance of the Ur-impulse that lies at the root of them all: solidarity with what he calls, in an allusion to a Brecht poem on Benjamin, the torturable body, [*quaelbare Leib*].[11] Auschwitz, as he would later metonymically call it, convinced him that philosophy needed first and foremost "to give a voice to the pain of the world, the suffering of the world"[12]—a need that he saw as the "condition of all truth."[13] Henceforth, he told his students, one had to "philosophize in such a way as not to have to feel shame in the face of the victims"[14]—a necessity that did not impose itself through reasoning, but through what he called "pre-philosophical experience."[15]

Crucially, Adorno turned the realization that his insights spring to a great extent from "pre-philosophical experience" itself into philosophical knowledge, incorporating it into a theory where the role of the so-called irrational, the somatic in reason, is ever more forcefully asserted. *Minima Moralia* not only emphatically performs that validation of the non-rational in rational thought but also contains Adorno's first attempts to theoretically reflect on it. "Knowledge comes to us through a web of prejudices, opinions, innervations, self-corrections, presuppositions and exaggerations, in short through the dense, firmly founded but by no means uniformly transparent experience" (MM 90/80, Aph. 50), he writes in the aphorism "Gaps," and a bit later calls the nerves "the tactile organ of historical consciousness" (MM 111/99, Aph. 62). In the aphorism "Intellectus sacrificium intellectus" (the intellect is sacrificed to the intellect), he writes that "because even its remotest objectifications are nourished by impulses, thought destroys in the latter the conditions of its own existence," asserting quite unambiguously that "once the last trace of emotion has been eradicated, nothing remains of thought but absolute tautology" (MM 139/123, Aph, 79).

Adorno will hold all his life that reason, in order to protect itself against tautology and coldness, in order to actually *know*, cognize, must open itself to what itself is not, the non-rational, must let itself be affected by the things, objects, beings around it—as Adorno puts it, quoting Friedrich Hebbel, it must lose itself to find itself again.[16] Reason must throw itself into "live contact with the warmth of things" (MM 47/43, Aph. 21), as Adorno writes in the aphorism on gifts—rather than subsuming the particular under categories, squeezing it into conceptual molds and thus turning it into just another instance of the ever same, it must take its cues from the unique object in front of it, nestle close to it [*anschmiegen*],[17] experience it as what it (most likely) is: something never encountered before. Once more, what Adorno will develop extensively in his later work is already outlined in *Minima Moralia*—in theory and practice. "Knowledge can only widen horizons by lingering so insistently on the particular that the insistence breaks up its isolation. This admittedly presupposes a relationship to the universal, though not one of subsumption but almost its reverse. Dialectic mediation is not a recourse to the more abstract, but a process of dissolution of the concrete in itself" (MM 83/74, Aph. 46). As he will put it more succinctly in *Negative Dialectic*: "Not about the concrete one must philosophize, but out of the concrete."[18]

Adorno's breathtaking leaps do just that: They philosophize out of the concrete. They linger insistently on the particular until it breaks up and says more than itself—or rather, says itself in a way it has never been heard before. They reveal the cracks, the ungrasped, and the damage. In the aphorism "Finale," the last aphorism of *Minima Moralia*, where the debt Adorno's micrological approach owes to Walter Benjamin is most apparent, he reflects on "the only philosophy that could still be answered for in the face of despair" and writes: "Perspectives must be created that displace and estrange the world, reveal its rifts and crevices, as it will appear one day, indigent and distorted, in the Messianic light. To gain such perspectives without arbitrariness and violence, solely from close contact with the objects, this alone is the task of thought" (MM 283/247, Aph. 153).

Through infinitely close contact with his surroundings, Adorno's micrologically deluded ethics create such perspectives. He displaces and estranges, forcing us to see things we've never truly seen in a way we've never seen them before. He looks at refrigerators, cars, married couples, at highways, and gift items, and sees the world indigent and distorted—the rifts and crevices, with all the suffering that entails. His minima moralia shine a glaring light on those rifts, force them out in the open, "solely from close contact with the objects." If this contact inspires breathtaking leaps, it is because, true to the messianic idea, Adorno believes that small differences make all the difference: "In the right state, everything would be, as in the Jewish theologumenon, only very slightly different than it is now, but not the slightest can be imagined as it will be then,"[19] he writes in *Negative Dialectic*. One day, in the right life, things will all be only very slightly different. Until then, conversely, very slight differences make things what they are, damaged and damaging, rather than what they could be. Negatively, Adorno's idiosyncratic reactions to the mundane and trivial register the right life that is not, the minute differences that stand between us and redemption. It is the philosopher's task to bring these to light—to make the leaps that expose them for all of us to see. In fact, philosophical thought hinges on the ability to make those leaps. As Adorno tells his students in a lecture on *Negative Dialectic*: "The ability to think philosophically is essentially the ability to experience the crucial differences [*Differenzen ums Ganze*] in the minimal differences [*Differenzen ums Kleinste*]."[20]

As we have seen, to be able to experience the minimal differences that make all the difference matters not just when it comes to exposing the bad, but also when it comes to the possibilities of the good. In a time where there is no right life in the wrong one, and where, as we read in *Negative Dialectic*, "true praxis," which could transform the wrong life that paralyzes us, is "indefinitely postponed,"[21] survival of the humane may very well hinge on those minimal differences. In an essay on the artist in the administered world, Adorno writes: "The minimal differences from the ever same that are open to him represent, however helplessly, the *Differenz ums Ganze*. It is in difference itself, the deviation, that hope has retreated to."[22] This is the flipside of the wrong life's invasion of the most minute. The singular particular is not just the objective powers' first victim, but also the locus of resistance against them. The infinitesimal difference, the ungraspable and ungrasped nonidentical, as Adorno will come to call it, contains within it the promise that things could be other than what they are. Freedom, he writes in *Negative Dialectic*, is "the possibility of non-identity."[23] To save freedom, we need to save that possibility.

Let us now return to the aphorism I quoted at the outset and look at it again, with the things I touched on in mind. In between his musings about refrigerators and self-closing doors, doorknobs and windows, Adorno writes that "one cannot do justice to the new human type without awareness of what is constantly and even in his most secret innervations done to him by the things that surround him" (the torturable body, once again). And he ends the aphorism with the words:

> Not least to blame for the withering of experience is the fact that things, subject to the law of their pure functionality, assume a form that limits the contact with them to mere handling, and allows no excess, be it of freedom of conduct, be it of autonomy of things, that would survive as the core of experience, because it is not consumed by the moment of action. (MM 44/40, Aph. 19)

In other words, that difference, that vital remnant of freedom we just talked about, is smothered. The pure functionality of things predetermines the subject's interaction with them, limits the contact to mere handling—it is the design that imposes what you do with them, not you (and as Adorno points out, it rarely invites gentleness). The close contact with the warmth of things that he intuits as the locus of undamaged experience, that dialectic between subject and object, is precluded by the purpose-driven nature of the thing: there is only so much you can do with a sliding window pane. The in-built limitation of subject-object interaction eliminates the "excess," the possibility of non-identity that Adorno sees as the precondition for freedom, and as the first bulwark against the coldness inherent in pure functionality. The same applies to human interactions: In the ones that Adorno's nerves react most strongly to, human beings are handled like objects—in keeping with the commodification of all relationships that capitalist society is built on.[24] The hostess that leads you to the table you did not choose and the waiter that cannot serve you because you are not in his service area are both limited in their freedom by the function assigned to them. For the social security employee that makes you wait in line, you are just a number, literally—and those of us who have had the misfortune of spending any amount of time in a Medicaid office know that that is indeed how you are treated, most of the time. The jump to "the bureaucrats of the gas chamber" may be less breathtaking than we would like to think.

What ultimately connects the two poles of Adorno's breathtaking leaps, and what his philosophical impulse reacts so strongly to, is violence—on one side, the surreptitious—yet no less staggering—violence done to us on a daily basis by the mutilated members and objects of advanced capitalist society; on the other, the open fascist violence that is but the former come into its own. For Adorno, both forms of violence are at heart one and the same: violence of identity against non-identity, of that which is against that which could be, of the reified universal against the torturable particular—whether that violence be epistemic, social, or individual. To counter it, and create the possibility of its end, we need nothing less than an epistemic and social revolution—for Adorno, the two go hand in hand—a new Copernican turn toward the object, where the nonidentical shapes and transforms identity rather than being crushed by it. Adorno's two major works *Negative Dialectic* and *Aesthetic Theory* are attempts to theorize this turn: to rethink conceptual rationality so as to give the nonidentical a voice, to change how we think and thus open up the possibility of a different, non-damaged life. In *Minima Moralia*, the direction is reversed, as it were, as Adorno focuses on the "innermost innervations" of the damaged life in need of transformation: the "private" realm, and the nature of the objects and relationships that shape it. Throughout the book, and very explicitly in the aphorism I started out with, Adorno makes clear that it is not only that our thought patterns, the structures and concepts of identity thinking, affect what we think and how we treat the objects and beings around us—the reverse is also true: how we treat the objects and beings around us affects our selves, our thinking and being. The transactional and functionalist nature of capitalist society and its objects mutilates people, making them as "precise and brutal" as the interactions the latter impose on them. If you no longer know how to close a door gently because yours slam shut by themselves, that seemingly trivial loss stands for a much greater one, which it deepens, one gesture at a time: the loss of *Zartheit*, in the expansive sense in which Adorno uses it throughout his work: gentleness, delicacy, tenderness in our physical and cognitive interactions with the world and ourselves. In *Minima Moralia*, Adorno quotes Hume's assertion that "just reasoning [is always advantageous] to delicate sentiment." The argument, he writes, contains "implicitly and negatively the whole truth about the spirit of praxis" (MM 44/40, Aph. 20)—a praxis in which delicate sentiment [*zartes Gefühl*] leads to just reasoning. Late capitalism, however, has no place for *Zartheit*: "The practical orders of life, that profess to benefit man, lead in the profit-driven economy to the withering of everything human(e), and the more they spread, the more they cut off all *Zartheit*." And he continues: "For *Zartheit* between people is nothing but the consciousness of the possibility of relations without purpose" (MM 45/40-1, Aph. 20). Relations without purpose are relations without domination, without violence. In a world driven by efficiency, functionality, and calculation, the consciousness of that other, almost utopian possibility is lost, and violence pervades everything, from the handling (and even the design) of mundane objects, to our daily interactions with each other. While in the former, objects are reduced to purely functional tools, without "freedom of conduct" nor "autonomy of things," in the latter, "the ability to see the other as other, and not as a function of one's own will . . . withers, and is replaced by the appraising assessment of people [*beurteilende Menschenkenntnis*]" (MM 149/131, Aph. 85)—in other words, people become tools too. Identity thinking is the epistemic mirror, both source and fruit, of that violent, purpose-driven world, its concepts a way to turn the unwieldy richness of reality into a limited set of categories ready to be controlled and exploited. Unsurprisingly, the idea of *Zartheit* features prominently, if not always explicitly, in Adorno's attempt to counter the ravages of identity thinking and its societal counterpart through a new subject-object relationship. When he speaks of the need to "nestle up to the object" rather than subsume it, to recover "true contact with the warmth of things," the tenderness is palpable. In thought, *Zartheit* translates as a certain epistemic humility—not a relativism but rather a tireless groping for truth that fully embraces its frailty while holding on firm to the non-negotiable: solidarity with the nonidentical, with the torturable body, with what the violence of identity thinking crushes. In *Minima Moralia*, Adorno reminds us that the "irreducible" distance between mind and world that identity thinking wants to erase is "a field of tension: it manifests not in relaxing the concepts' claim to truth, but in the *Zartheit* and fragility that accompanies thinking" (MM 144/127, Aph. 82). To think with *Zartheit* and fragility means to refuse to bulldoze truth into a bite-sized identity. It means to never break off thought, to nuance and differentiate, to hold up the nonidentical as the minimal difference that makes all the difference—in the name of a transformed subject-object relationship in which the subject's apparent loss of certainty is in reality an immeasurable gain: "The inner depth of the subject consists of nothing else but the *Zartheit* and richness of the exterior world of perception."[25] As such, epistemic and physical *Zartheit* is not only the antipode of the violence of identity thinking and its societal capitalist counterpart, but also a form of resistance against the latter. In a world where the free one is he who "can grab a piece for himself," where we can at best get but rare, fleeting glimpses of an alternate reality, "what would be different is nameless"—but we can sense it in "what today stands in for it: solidarity, *Zartheit*, consideration."[26]

Advanced capitalism has not only no use for the latter, it feeds off their opposites: selfishness, ruthlessness, coldness. *Zartheit*, in the rare moments where it survives, is more than a reminder that things could be different than what they are: it undermines, however infinitesimally, the *So ist es*, the implacable status quo.

For Adorno, America as he experienced it in the 1940s represented the future. The United States, the most advanced capitalist country in the world, a step ahead of everybody else, made glaringly visible for all of us to see what the implacable capitalist logic had in store for human society. *Minima Moralia* is first and foremost a book about "life under the conditions of monopoly capitalism." The fact that some of the aphorisms treat of the dying bourgeois society in the Weimar Republic and others yet of early fascism, only confirm that for Adorno, these three social forms were closely connected. Capitalism could either fully collapse into fascism, as it did in Germany, or mask its fascist core and indefinitely postpone the outright collapse while steadily pursuing the same goal: total uniformization.

Capitalism's ruthless commodification of everything existing, its very lifeblood, "has permeated humans through and through, objectifying and making formally commensurable every one of their stirrings as a mere variation of the exchange relation . . . .. Its consummate organization demands the coordination of dead people." Dead because devoid of any true subjectivity, made fungible and expendable, like the corpses that fascism so readily produces. Capitalism has turned the will to live into a mere will to survive and thus into "the negation of the will to live: self-preservation annuls all life in subjectivity" (MM 262/229, Aph. 147). *Das Leben lebt nicht*, proclaims the epigraph by Ferdinand Kürnberger that Adorno put at the beginning of *Minima Moralia*: life does not live.

Capitalism shares with fascism what Adorno and Max Horkheimer identified in *Dialectic of Enlightenment* as the latter's "canon": "bloody efficiency."[27] Efficiency ensures the frictionless workings of the system: the smooth integration of fungible workers into the insatiable machinery of capital, just as the no less smooth integration of dehumanized victims into the machinery of extermination. "Genocide is absolute integration, which is being prepared everywhere where men are made the same [*gleichgemacht*], are ground and polished [*geschliffen*] as they say in the military, until they are literally annihilated as no more but deviations of the concept of their own nullity. Auschwitz confirms the philosopheme of pure identity as death."[28] Monopoly capitalism, as Adorno calls it, which is nothing but capitalism in its most advanced form, prepares people for fascism by turning them into replaceable and ultimately dispensable cogs, into pawns with neither the critical acuity nor the political will to oppose a system that holds them hostage and that they themselves perpetuate. How does it do it? By systematically preventing the emergence of any true individuality and stultifying the autonomous subject, thereby robbing it not only of the ability to truly experience the world and have human(e) relationships but even of the awareness of its own brokenness. In a capitalist society, "true contact with the warmth of things," the beginning of any meaningful knowledge of the world, is not only discouraged but violently prevented. From our handling of daily objects to our interactions with waiters and governments officers, from gift shopping to interoffice communications, from the tech industry to the culture industry, uniformity, efficiency, and functionality reign supreme, nipping in the bud any stirring of autonomy, any unregulated experience. Instead of individuality as the root of true solidarity, as the difference that would undo fascist-capitalist integration, we have individualism, its cheap ersatz, successfully reframed as consumerist "choice" and perverted to all-pervasive selfishness. As Adorno put it in the aphorism I quoted earlier: "The capacity to see the other as such and not as function of one's own will withers . . . and is replaced by the appraising assessment of people"—a pattern of engagement well known from "administration and HR policies," and which "tends of its own accord, even before any formation of political preference or any commitment to an exclusive party platform, to fascism" (MM 149/131, Aph. 85). By eliminating the "possibility of relations without purpose" (MM 45/40-1, Aph. 20), and through it the *Zartheit* that can only blossom in freedom, capitalism spreads coldness like the plague. "Coldness descends on all they do, the kind word left unspoken, the consideration not exercised." And suddenly, fascism is truly but a step away. The coldness of capitalism, the "treatment of the [other] as an object" instead of "thinking of the other as a subject" (MM 46-7/42, Aph. 21), is the same coldness that Adorno would later identify as the "fundamental principle of bourgeois subjectivity, without which Auschwitz would not have been possible."[29]

Minima Moralia was written almost eighty years ago, but its reflections from the damaged life remain acutely relevant today. With the monopolies (Amazon, Apple, Facebook, Google, etc.) taking on proportions that Adorno could not have foreseen even in his wildest nightmares, uniformization has been truly embraced by all, and experiences have become so standardized, so devoid of any "freedom of conduct . . . that would survive as the core of experience"— think emojis, Spotify playlists, or Starbucks—that soon there will be nothing left to wither. The corporatization of workplaces, of hospitals, nursing homes, universities, and prisons ensures that interhuman relationships at all levels are governed by the sole logic of profit, leaving ever less loopholes in the implacable uniformity, ever less space for the difference that is the refuge not only of hope but also of the humane. Coldness spreads, unfettered and uncontained. What makes reading *Minima Moralia* today so riveting is that while a lot has changed since the 1940s, while the capitalist grip seems to have immeasurably tightened, the logic remains fundamentally the same, and our present shines through at every turn in Adorno's dissections of the past. What is new is technological efficiency, harnessed by a neoliberal ideology that seems to have successfully quashed any residue of resistance that may still have lingered in rare places in Adorno's time. "The specific difference between the newest and what precedes it," Adorno wrote in 1946, reveals to us "the true identity of the whole: of terror without end" (MM 268/235, Aph. 149).

Adorno would not have been surprised at the latest face of the American right. Because of its crassness, its cruelty, its unabashed racism, because of the absurd spectacle of its public figures, it is tempting to focus on the specific difference between this newest form and what precedes it. But what reveals itself to the attentive observer is less the novelty than the true identity of the whole, terror without end. When thousands of immigrant children were forcefully separated from their parents at the US-Mexican border and put into cages, people recoiled in horror, and comparisons to Nazism were legion. What many of the rightfully horrified failed to see was that while the deliberate, systematic use of cruelty was new (at least as open government policy in the twenty-first century), its most terrifying aspect was not: the treatment of the other as an object, the complete lack of empathy, the utter coldness of it all. Even under Barack Obama, abuse and mistreatment at the border were rife, and it was under Jimmy Carter that children in cages first made headlines.[30] So once more, the leap was more of a hop, and when inhumanity was unleashed in its latest reiteration, the system was oiled and the actors were ready. Neither the cruel deception of the border officers taking five-year-olds from their mothers "for a bath" only to announce that they "won't be seeing their child again,"[31] nor the calculating coldness of the high government official stating matter-of-factly "We need to take away children,"[32] nor the indifference of the thousands of bureaucrats and other active and passive witnesses in-between had to be first constructed through ideology or coercion: they were already there. They are already here.

"Coldness," Adorno scribbled in his notebook sometime in the 1960s, "is the historical and psychological failure of the subject."[33] It is a failure that both capitalism and fascism rely on, that they feed and reward. "Whoever is not willing to talk about capitalism should keep quiet about fascism,"[34] Horkheimer famously wrote in 1939. Around the same time, Adorno, chased out of Europe by a murderous fascism, sat down to write a book about "life under the conditions of monopoly capitalism." In light of the genocidal violence he had fled, it could seem strange that it is to the violence of car doors and gift vouchers that he turned his attention. But to his mind, it made complete sense—more than that, it was critical. *Minima Moralia* is the fruit of Adorno's conviction not only that to talk about fascism, we need to talk about capitalism, but also to talk about capitalism we need to talk of the latter's trail of destruction in our own damaged lives: the "small" things, the objects, gestures, and interactions of our daily existence that nibble away at our individuality, our freedom, our experience, and our *Zartheit*, and inexorably spread the "truly unbearable coldness"[35] that paves the way for fascism.

In a time when coldness and violence have infiltrated almost every nook and cranny of our (not so) private lives, and have unabashedly and triumphantly taken center stage in the public arena, the continuing relevance of Adorno's micrologically deluded ethics is hard to deny. As an approach, an outlook on the world, a philosophical, sociohistorical sensibility, an *example* in the expansive Adornian sense, it models an intellectual and emotional alertness to what life under the conditions of monopoly capitalism is constantly and even in our most secret innervations doing to us—and what we, mirroring the violence, are doing back to the world. Are doorknobs the pits? Does slamming the refrigerator shut make you a protofascist? Maybe the precise answers to these questions are less important than the realization that the seemingly trivial things that make up our daily lives, shape gestures and relationships, and preclude other possibilities are not indifferent. It may just matter more than we think that people have lost the ability to close a door quietly, gently, yet firmly; that the possibility of a human encounter is decided these days by swiping left or right on a phone screen; that writing to someone without greeting and without signature, just like those "inter-office communications" Adorno abhorred,[36] has become the norm; and that American windows don't want you to stick your head out into the world.

The capitalist net has become so inextricable, so all-encompassing, that every attempt to push against it seems futile. *Minima Moralia* does little to lessen that impression, quite the opposite. At the same time, as we have seen earlier, it both implicitly and explicitly points to the flipside of capitalism's merciless integration of everything. Yes, the seemingly minute, the daily gestures and interactions have become an extension of the system, a locus of the crushing power of the whole. The little things are how they get you. But by the same logic, the little things are also (maybe, just maybe) how *you* can begin to get *them*. Coldness is the linchpin of capitalism. Every *Zartheit*, or to paraphrase Adorno: every kind word spoken, every consideration exercised, chips away at capitalism's indispensable foundation, undermines it, however infinitesimally.

Neoliberal hegemony is dependent on people's quiet acquiescence to, and active and passive participation in, its all-pervasive coldness. It thrives on that "profound indifference toward whatever happens to everyone else except for the few to whom [one is] closely bound, possibly by tangible interests,"[37] the same indifference that, according to Adorno, enabled Auschwitz eighty years ago. It gets all of the above because it produces them—capitalist damage spreads the coldness that creates it. To resist the latter, to hold up against it the *Zartheit*, the solidarity with the "torturable body" that would spell its downfall, may well be the first step toward ending the vicious circle made in hell. If that sounds too utopian, it may be worth remembering what all those that profit from the world as it is want us to forget: that the power of the few over the many, the iron principle of capitalism, can continue only as long as the many go along with it—be it out of fear, indifference, or, as in most cases, the inability of the mutilated self to see that things could in fact be otherwise. Yes, it is an undeniable fact that "society is essentially the substance of the individual." But rather than deplore this as fate, a stance that Adorno never tired of combating, a micrologically deluded ethics will insist on its corollary: that everything the individual does or does not do affects the society that has devoured her. It is a breathtaking leap, but one well worth taking.

Part II

The Effects of the Aphorism

3

Adorno's Senses of Critique

Gesture, Suffering, Utopia

S. D. Chrostowska

Gesture

Gestures: neither acts, nor attentive activity. A gesture of the head, voluntary or involuntary, can express disapproval or disagreement, without constituting an act of dissent or the activity of shaking one's head. A gesture of the hand, such as pointing, is not always an act of accusation or an activity, such as dancing the Travolta. It is proper to start with the head and hands when dealing with gestures, because "gesture" denotes behavior consisting in a bodily motion expressive of thought or feeling. And gestures originating in other body parts can be too subtle to even be legible. What unites these physical movements, however, is their appreciable *smallness* compared to acts.

The difference between gesture, act, and attentive activity is generally obvious (especially when tools are involved). "Mere" gesture does not enjoy the act's definition and distinctness. Yet neither is gesturing hopelessly ambiguous or confined to virtual mimicry, even when elaborate, as in pantomime. By default (when not qualified as "empty"), individual gestures can convey clear messages. Their carrying a message—a discrete communication—does not, however, make them *acts* of messaging. A raised hand only participates in the swearing of an oath. A gesture becomes a linguistic act only when it is first turned into a conventional sign.

What distinguishes gestures—their minority, or "immaturity," relative to acts—also holds for extensions of gesture beyond its concrete bodily manifestations. If a false promise—a commissive speech act—can be thought of as an *empty* gesture, it is only because such a gesture shares the meaninglessness of an act unfulfilled, not followed through, an act performed with insufficient investment or understanding of its entailments. A "gesture of friendship" and a "commercial gesture" describe formalities, requiring little physical and cognitive energy or cost, but counting as significant for the recipient, signifying particular attitudes. A gesture, whether physical or figurative, is meaningful despite being minor.

Writing, be it occasional or habitual, is commonly thought of as a solitary yet social *activity*, done in private to arouse a public reaction. "The *act* of writing": such magnification lends practical consequence to what is most often not performative, not markedly enactive (in the sense that the signing of a peace treaty or a declaration of war would be). Writing the last page of a book, momentous though it may be, is an attentive activity concluding a process. Putting a message in a bottle and setting it adrift counts as an act, if a self-consciously minor one, with writing as just one of its constitutive actions, along with the bottle's release into a body of water. Yet it is also true that composing such seaworthy messages is both less and more than attentive activity, even when multiple copies are produced: in it, thought both limits its expectation of communicating and rises to cast itself beyond the given and any foreseeable outcomes. Like inscription in the sand, such writing is better thought of as a *gesture*. Discontinuity and signifying beyond, as if to compensate for its minority, distinguish a gesture from an activity (and liken it to an act).

Developing a theory of gesture across several of his writings, Giorgio Agamben takes from the Roman savant Varro the idea of gesture as "a third mode of human activity," neither *poiēsis* (making) nor *praxis* (deliberate acting), and "open[ing] the ethical dimension for human beings."[1] *Poiēsis* and *praxis* are telic; gesture, by contrast, is a pure means, a "means without end." Agamben draws out the indeterminacy and (unexhausted) potentiality of gesture. This is its power of *negation*, deactivating the work (*opera, ergon*), and embraced by him as an alternative ethical and political paradigm. In the literary sphere, gesture is "a forceful presence in language," redeeming language from "outwardly-directed communication," emancipating it from established written works and meanings, placing it beyond interpretation, where it "oscillate[s] between reality and virtuality . . . the singular and the generic." Literary criticism in the "gestic" mode resolves a work's intention "into a gesture (or into a constellation of gestures)."[2] Agamben accounts for the "proximity between gesture and philosophy" by the latter's "mutism": every great philosophical text is "the gag that displays language itself, being-in-language itself," "the showing of what cannot be spoken of."[3]

A constellation of gestures is also at the center of this chapter: *Minima Moralia*, a literary as well as critical and self-consciously "minor" work of moral philosophy. At the start of it we learn that, in genre terms, it is a book of aphorisms. The word "aphorism" derives from the Greek verb *aphorizein*, which breaks down into *aph-/apo-* (off, away, de-) and *horizein* (divide or bound, -limit)—from *horos* (boundary), whence *horizon*. It is not hard to imagine Adorno being aware of the meanings of *aphorizein* when choosing to characterize the *Minima Moralia* texts as aphorisms. These meanings are *to delimit, to separate by or assign a boundary, circumscribe, mark off precisely*; *to determine rigorously one's proposition*, hence also, *to express in a concise form* (specifically, in the form of an aphorism). More broadly, *aphorizein* is *to determine or define conceptually*, for example, an art (such as the art of temperance, *sōphrosunē*), but also *to finish, bring a work to completion*, as well as *to separate or distinguish one thing from another*, and *to remove, to banish*. This brings *aphorizein* semantically close to *krinein*, meaning *to separate* (grain from chaff, in Homer) and *to distinguish* (good from evil, or the true from the false, in Plato), as well as *to choose, decide, interpret, evaluate, estimate*, hence *to interrogate, judge, resolve*, and *condemn—krinein* being, of course, the source of *to criticize* and *crisis*.[4]

The history of the word "aphorism" and its filiations reveal its dialectical character, which corresponds fundamentally to Adorno's project. Based on its semantic range, *aphorizein* involves negation *and* affirmation, while *krinein* is largely circumscribed by negativity, by sifting and contesting. The related senses of *determining* and *completing* ascribe to the aphoristic action a positivity; the aphorism is isolated and self-contained like a monad (or, to one German Romantic, like a "hedgehog"). When juxtaposed with Adorno's stated intentions and moral commitments, his choice of this genre thus belies—one could argue, deliberately—the *critical* approach adopted by him in *Minima Moralia*.

"[S]ome things have gestures, and so modes of conduct, inscribed in them," Adorno remarks here apropos of slippers, to be slipped on one's feet "without using the hands."[5] It is easy to apply his observation to physical books, unbound on three sides to fall open in the palm or invite manual opening, and whose pagination or other numbering indicates the intended order of their perusal. Our gaze "slips into" books, between their covers, accompanied by gestures and other expressions of focus and absorption. But could Adorno's insight concerning house shoes apply to something like a literary form? Might an aphorism also have modes of behavior written into it? What distinguishes the affordances of an aphorism from a poetic form (say, a sonnet) would have to be specific mental—rather than manual and bodily—motions that attend the reading or writing of one.

The semantic breadth of *aphorizein* gives us plenty of clues about the behavior that might be "inscribed into" an aphorism: a comportment that would consist in demarcating, discerning, determining, eliminating, completing, as well as making concise, which presupposes something larger or longer that is broken up, cut into smaller pieces; an economy of expression that implies verbally compressing one's proposition, which, once formulated, invites interpretation and judgment—*critical* operations, and even *acts* of criticism.

For an aphorism to be like a slipper, its behavioral affordances would also have to be gestic. The mental actions just named would have to qualify as gestures, rather than as continuous activities or discrete acts. They would need to be *minor* and *discontinuous*—which are, in fact, the formal requirements of aphoristic brevity, the succinctness of expression.[6] To come back to the basic definition of gesture with which we began, gestures are movements (bodily or mental) that are mimetic, expressive of thought and/or feeling. For the aphorism, as we have seen, these movements of thought and/or feeling are also dialectical, involving and expressing both affirmation and negation. Their presence lets us see an aphorism as *inscribed with specific gestures*.

What is assembled in *Minima Moralia*, however, is, for the most part, not aphorisms in the standard acceptation of the term, but texts ranging from the "long aphorism" to the "short essay."[7] They are too long to be aphorisms, and their individual sentences (propositions) can rarely be considered in isolation and understood. You will remember that *aphorizein* signifies also the action of finishing, of bringing to completion. This has nothing to do with it attaining a certain length. The aphorist is concerned with bringing their thought to a close in a concise way, usually in the compact space of several lines. *Finishing* may be true of *Minima Moralia* on the plane of textual composition, though not on the philosophical level. Each text, it is true, is brought to a desired end, rather than left unfinished for contingent reasons. Adorno's philosophical project, however, is presented as *resisting* closure. Identifying the genre as *aphorism* thus apparently contradicts his own moral, epistemic, and ontological commitments. The pieces in *Minima Moralia* transcend their generic identity as if by design: as a transposition onto the formal plane of his critique of identity thinking and philosophical reification.[8]

That these texts nonetheless consist of *gestures* has to do with their form: specifically, their *fragmentariness*. In his thoughts on literary genre in "The Essay as Form," Adorno speaks critically of the academic tendency to accept a work as philosophy insofar as "[i]t gets involved with particular cultural artifacts only to the extent to which they can be used to exemplify universal categories, or to the extent to which the particular becomes transparent when seen in terms of them."[9] The essay form, meanwhile—defined as "speculation on specific, culturally preformed objects"—accentuates "the partial against the total, in its fragmentary character."[10] The essay "has to be constructed as though it could always break off at any point." It does not actually break off at random; it is only prepared for the possibility of such breakage: the possibility of suddenly becoming a ruin, so to speak. Adorno suggests that an essay must seem accomplished at any particular moment, at the end of every sentence, without actually coming to a neat conclusion (identified as such) that ties everything together. The essay, thus, "thinks in fragments,"[11] or gestures. And it ends not with a grand finale, but with a gesture of farewell.

Reflecting on Max Horkheimer's essay "Art and Mass Culture," Adorno outlined the relevance of gestures for critical theory:

> you could almost say that the essay represents a gesture even more than a thought. Something like when, abandoned on an island, you desperately beckon a ship that is leaving, when it is already too far away. Our things will have to become more and more such gestures taken from concepts and less and less theories in the conventional sense. Except that this just requires the whole work of the concept.[12]

The Hegelian "work of the concept" to which Adorno refers involves the "grasping" and defining that constitute conceptualization.

There is no question that Adorno resisted the genre of the philosophical treatise, favoring instead the fragmentary form of the essay and the intentional "philosophical fragments"—this last being the original title, later the subtitle, of *Dialectic of Enlightenment*. My preference is to qualify most if not all of Adorno's *small* prose as "fragments"—rather than, and contrary to the indications in *Minima Moralia* itself, "aphorisms." As Friedrich Schlegel, a Romantic fragmentist and a contemporary of Hegel, writes: "Many works of the ancients have become fragments. Many works of the moderns are fragments as soon as they are written."[13] What remains of the writings of the ancients is fragmentary due to the destruction or deterioration of manuscripts, or to the censorship of medieval copyists. Modern writers, meanwhile, display a tendency to write in the form of a fragment. This *original fragmentation* of modern literature corresponds to a new experience of the world: increasingly complex, mediated, overburdened and distracted by the mass of knowledge and information. Texts that Schlegel might have had in mind—such as Erasmus's *Adagia*, the French moralists' aphorisms, or Novalis's *Pollen*—manifest this modern sensibility toward fragmentation. Pieces of thought are offered "as is," as if to convey the loss of universal mythical and religious coherence, experienced thereafter only in its imperfect, broken state and resisting attempts at restoration.

In his Dedication to Horkheimer that opens *Minima Moralia*, Adorno notes the tension between Hegelianism and aphoristic thinking: "Dialectical theory, abhorring anything isolated, cannot admit aphorisms as such. In the most lenient instance they might... be tolerated as 'conversation.' But the time for that is past. Nevertheless," he continues, a book of aphorisms like *Minima Moralia* "forgets neither the system's claim to totality, which would suffer nothing to remain outside it, nor that it remonstrates against this claim."[14] Adopting the *aphoristic* mode of discourse is, for Adorno, integral to his own project, which is both an extension and a critique of the Hegelian one. Thus, he practices what Hegel mostly only preaches. As Adorno explains,

> In his relation to the subject Hegel does not respect the demand that he otherwise passionately upholds: to be in the matter and not "always beyond it," to "penetrate into the immanent content of the matter." If today the subject is vanishing, aphorisms take upon themselves the duty "to consider the evanescent itself as essential." They insist, in opposition to Hegel's practice and yet in accordance with his thought, on negativity.[15]

They insist, that is, on "lingering" or "tarrying with" the negative and discovering truth in "absolute diremption."[16] Immanence, the content of experience, has been central to the aphorism ever since Hippocrates designated his lapidary medical observations "aphorisms," taken as launching the genre. Even so, the history of "aphorism" showed us negation serving determination and affirmation. In Adorno's practice, the opposite is true: positivity is subservient to negativity. It is not that Adorno made a mistake in naming his texts "aphorisms." What I read as their *generic non-identity* inscribes itself into Adorno's negative dialectical project, where determination, on the contrary, serves the work of negation. The texts in *Minima Moralia* break a formal mold whose relationship to systematic philosophy was already, by Hegel's day, oppositional. And it is this breaking of the aphoristic mold that turns them—regardless of their self-designation and the crucial work done by the term "aphorism"—into *fragments*.

Both the philosophical system and aphoristic "conversation" are telic modes of philosophical reflection or action. That is to say, they are a means to an end, that end being propositional. Adorno's small, fragmentary writings, consisting of gestures, seem to betoken *non-telic* philosophizing, in perpetual movement and thus provisional, while refusing its own instrumentalization. This is also what makes gesture distinct and superior for Agamben. There is a difference, however. Adorno's gestures are not "pure" in Agamben's sense; a "pure gesture" is—"as such—to the extent that it manages to remain a mystery and not inscribe itself in the apparatus of means and ends—unjudgable." For Agamben, a gesture directed toward "the good" is telic, thus impure, and disqualified as such.[17] Adorno was well aware of the difficulty of the end, the purpose: How do you orient yourself, your philosophical reflection, toward the good if your idea of the good, your conception of the right life, comes from, and is thus necessarily tainted by, *a wrong and damaged life*?

Suffering

Adorno's formal "choice of the small," in the words of Miguel Abensour, is inextricable from wartime experience. Also revealing in this respect is the Dedication of *Minima Moralia*, whose parts, we read,

> do not altogether satisfy the demands of the philosophy of which they are nevertheless a part. The loose and nonbinding character of the form, the renunciation of explicit theoretical cohesion, are meant as one expression of this. At the same time this ascesis should atone in some part for the injustice whereby one alone continued to perform the task that can only be accomplished by both, and that we do not forsake.[18]

This task was, of course, the development with Horkheimer of their "shared philosophy," begun with *Dialectic of Enlightenment*.[19] *Minima Moralia*'s formal ascesis is presented as likewise an ethical and spiritual choice. The disciplined indiscipline involved in denying himself the pleasure of theoretical cohesion, this productive self-restraint and self-imposed under-achievement by his own philosophical standards, also reflect the subjective desolation and objective destruction engendered by the war. Opting for deliberate smallness and incompleteness, for theoretical discontinuity instead of (false) unified wholeness, indicates in this context Adorno's embrace of his damaged experience, mutilated (*beschädigte*, in the subtitle of *Minima Moralia*) by the menace of extermination and the vicissitudes of exile. It is at once an empathetic attentiveness to present suffering and a refusal to accept it passively as *necessary*.

Abensour explains the aforementioned "choice"—appearing "against that total mobilization during the First World War, at its extreme opposite, . . . a figure of resistance"—not as some "nostalgic refuge," or longing for the *antebellum* world, but, instead, as an affirmation of individual experience against the totality that negates it. Resistance, for thinkers who made this choice, is "a turnaround, a change of direction," a "Saturnine" "refinement of vision," a "refusal originating from the body, the nerves," rendered fragile, minuscule, and mechanical by the latest advances in military technology.[20]

Fragments as pieces of *gestic* thought are tokens of damage wrought upon the individual. The damage is to a unified structure of thinking, rendering difficult a unified worldview. Smallness-as-resistance, as Adorno practiced it, precedes formulation; it pervades the very method of observation, which he called "micrological": an immersive analytical procedure that privileges the diminutive, the inconspicuous, to loosen the particular from the general. "The smallest inner-worldly markings would be relevant to the absolute," reads the penultimate sentence of *Negative Dialectics* (1966), "for the micrological glance demolishes the shells of that which is helplessly compartmentalized according to the measure of its subsuming master concept and explodes its identity, the deception, that it would be merely an exemplar."[21] In its optic

> Nothing absolute is to be expressed otherwise than in the subject-matter and categories of immanence... [This metaphysics] would receive [from the existent] its material, without which it would not be, would not however transfigure the existence of its elements, but would bring them instead into a configuration, in which the elements assemble into a script. To that end it must be good at wishing. That the wish would be a bad father to the thought has been since Xenophanes one of the general theses of the European enlightenment, and still applies undiminished to the ontological attempts at restoration. But thinking, itself a conduct, contains the need—at first, vital necessity—in itself. One thinks out of need, even where "wishful thinking" is dismissed.[22]

Micrology—literally, the study of the small, the minute—is a way of looking suggested by things that are already torn apart, one that takes advantage of this state of affairs to practice transformative critique. It teaches us to look differently, searching for faults, flaws, lies, to break out of the "objective context of delusion" via an immanent critique of particulars positing themselves as absolutes. Its negativity is so far-reaching that this dialectic finally turns *against itself* to critique its own claim to absolute knowledge. And it does not rest there, eschewing completeness. "[T]his is its form of hope."[23] Negative dialectics thus advances in fragments, in gestures—over the rubble of reality where the particular lies exposed and magnified as under a microscope. Metaphysics emancipated from the claim to absolute knowledge merges here with the individual experience of suffering and destruction.

Insisting on the truth of his statement from nearly a decade before, Adorno wrote:

> I have no wish to soften the saying that *to write lyric poetry after Auschwitz is barbaric*; it expresses in negative form the impulse which inspires committed literature. The abundance of real suffering tolerates no forgetting. Yet this suffering... also demands the continued existence of art while it prohibits it... [finding its voice in it] without immediately being betrayed by it.[24]

A seemingly unequivocal retraction of his famous dictum did not come until *Negative Dialectics*. "Perennial suffering has as much right to expression as a tortured man has to scream," he argues there; "hence it may have been wrong to say that after Auschwitz you could no longer write poems. But it is not wrong to raise the less cultural question whether after Auschwitz you can go on living—especially whether one who escaped by accident, one who by rights should have been killed, may go on living." At issue is the survivor's tortured experience of "drastic guilt."[25]

Philosophy's failure to change the world and thus forestall catastrophe puts into question philosophy's survival. Addressing this, Adorno opens his magnum opus with a reference to Karl Marx's "summary judgment that [philosophy] had merely interpreted the world, that resignation in the face of reality has crippled it." He sees Marx's thesis engendering "a defeatism of reason after the transformation of the world miscarried." Adorno's own dialectical alternative to such defeatism bears repeating: "Having broken its pledge to be as one with reality or at the point of its production, philosophy is obliged ruthlessly to criticize itself."[26] It is this double movement of "failure and promise" that characterizes negative dialectics: Philosophy's failure to forestall suffering calls for ruthless auto-critique, which becomes a condition of possibility for transformative praxis—hence also the promise of critical philosophy to become actuality.[27]

Adorno thus brings out a fundamental relationship between social critique and social suffering, which critique makes visible, and fails, and promises anew, to eradicate. The bridge between them is *critical suffering*, a species of philosophical melancholy. In Adorno, melancholy comes into its own as a method of critique. Rather than turning away from social suffering, his "melancholy science" (*traurige Wissenschaft*) turns toward it, assuming it like a burden that brings relief. It would be wrong to see in this thought-gesture nothing but a rationalized guilt-ridden affinity for suffering and resignation seen in Holocaust survivors. Instead, critical suffering flows from the fundamental affective disposition of radical social critique, from the empathic intimacy between it and negative emotional states. As Raymond Geuss noted, in post-Hegelian philosophy the "possibility of criticism and resistance, and sensitivity to suffering," hence also the susceptibility to it, "are closely connected."[28]

Adorno thematized this very connection when describing "the cognitive function of spleen." And he does use the English term "spleen," as if to distinguish it from the melancholy sadness, the *Trauer*, of critical theory. Critical spleen, then, which makes the critic naively and ridiculously "pounce[s] on barbarism at the nearest street corner" and, as a "defence mechanism," rebel against the "loss of experience" and "social estrangement," against the abstraction of immediate, "real suffering" in "general concepts" for a knowledge of the "oppressive social system" in which suffering originates.[29] Such knowledge is rejected by spleen, and the abstract general concept replaced by the critic's *idée fixe* to preserve their limited, particular experience.

But such splenetic "narrowness" can act, according to Adorno, as a critical corrective or "antidote" to "the all too broad overview." The spleen in Thorstein Veblen's critique of consumer society, for example, "stems from his disgust with the official optimism of the spirit of progress." The "negativity of society" becomes commensurate with Veblen's personal experience of it, which is "guided by spleen." At the same time, spleen, as negativity, is a "haven of potentiality," and has its counterpart in a prelapsarian "primitivistic utopia." Driving the "sharp insights of Veblen's social analyses," spleen, we are told, "dictates the particular character of Veblen's critique": that of "disenchantment," of "debunking," of denouncing society. His way of critically preserving "real suffering," "mak[ing] tangible the impenetrable and alien character of the whole," comes at the cost of grasping the said whole.[30]

Adorno's own critical melancholy is a somewhat different attitude. Dialectics, "an attempt to escape the either/or," becomes for him "the effort to rescue theory's trenchancy and consequential logic without surrendering it to delusion."[31] Linked into the mimetic/expressive and the aesthetic, it is an affective-reflective response to the suffering of the world that guards against moroseness and resignation. Melancholy sharpens both critique's ethical commitment and its utopian longing. Unhappy consciousness, Adorno points out, "reminds the mind, negatively, of its corporeal aspect." This somatic aspect, which survives in cognition as disquiet, "sets [cognition] in motion and reproduces itself unappeased in its progression." It is the capability of feeling such unrest that "lends the mind whatever hope it has" of abolishing suffering. "The incarnate [*leibhafte*] moment registers the cognition that suffering [—even 'the smallest trace of senseless suffering' and its 'inner reflection-forms'—S.C.] ought not to be, that things should be different."³² This, for Geuss, makes Adorno's "a philosophy of suffering spirit," driven to criticize the world for thwarting its utopian aspirations and anticipations.³³

The abolition of suffering, Geuss observes, is an "undialectical" and "undifferentiated" leitmotif of Adorno's philosophy, which lacks a constructive moment, or any "politics of 'alleviating suffering.'" The force of his thought lies precisely in its avowed "minority" and "weakness," in its "sensitivity" to pain and injustice, present and past—the, in Adorno's words, "lingering awareness of the ancient wound."³⁴ By sharpening the senses for a happiness that will not come,³⁵ it sharpens itself for the suffering that will not cease. "For nothing but despair can save us," Adorno declared in a 1969 interview.³⁶ Hope was to be found in it. "All pain and all negativity" were, for him, "the motor of dialectical thought." "The need to give voice to suffering is the condition of all truth," since suffering, subjectively experienced and expressed, is objectivity, being "objectively mediated."³⁷ Its expression is mimetic, gestic. Redemption can only come from a mind that does not avert its gaze from the world of pain. (The real, "objective hopelessness" was that of *Aktionismus*, the dogmatic "noisy optimism of immediate action," which at this historical moment was, in Adorno's view, "predestined to fail.")³⁸

The challenge facing critical theory is to dwell in despair, even at the height of despair, since, without this, critique cannot give reason to hope, just as it cannot give hope to reason. It is such critical suffering that drives the ruthless negativity of Adorno's critique, its dissatisfaction, as well as its negative-utopian aspiration, which is the release, from suffering, of nature.

Utopia

For Adorno, humans and animals are linked in bodily suffering and, through it, in happiness, which is more than the mere absence of suffering. "[T]he convulsive gestures of the tortured ... express what wretched life can never quite control: the mimetic impulse [which defies discipline—S.C.]. In the death throes of the creature, at the furthest extreme from freedom, freedom itself irresistibly shines forth as the thwarted destiny of matter."³⁹ Animals are damaged by us, and we (ourselves a piece of nature) are damaged animals. So how can we learn what happiness is from an animal, as Adorno maintains?⁴⁰ Adorno's dialectical maxim was *"falsum index sui et veri"* (the false is an index of itself and of the true): "the false, once determinately known and precisely expressed," he elaborates, "is already an index of what is right and better."[41] Thus, pure, animal suffering determinately known and precisely expressed becomes an index of itself and of pure, somatic bliss, which is to say also human bliss. "He alone who could situate utopia in blind somatic pleasure, which, satisfying the ultimate intention, is intentionless, has a stable and valid idea of truth," we read in the fragment entitled "This Side of the Pleasure Principle."[42] This iconoclastic utopian vision is reprised in remarks on the affection children have for animals. While animals are keepers of utopia in that they seem to live purposelessly, children "[u]nconsciously . . . rehearse the right life" by engaging in the purposive-purposeless, mimetic/gestic activity of play.[43] Adorno does not exclude the possibility of naïve *adult* play. But when six German political parties loosen the reins of their imagination to design each their own "utopia" in miniature, as happened in 2009 in Hamburg's Miniatur Wunderland, they are mostly politicking. Additionally, in Adorno's negativistic utopianism, only the "admission of falseness" on the part of such positive images of utopia can "cancel[s] [their] power and hand[s] [them] over to truth."[44]

The most sustained reflection on utopian desire in *Minima Moralia* comes in fragment 100, "*Sur l'eau*." Adorno highlights here, not the identity, but the correspondence, of utopia and animality. "Philosophy," he says elsewhere, "is really only there to redeem what lies in the gaze of an animal," in which "Utopia goes disguised."[45] What lies in the philosophical gaze of the *human* animal is a vision of harmony with nature, freedom from labor, and perpetual peace (*ewiger Friede*, an abstract concept that comes closest to fulfilled utopia and "find[s] expression, timidly, in the only way that its fragility permits"). "*Rien faire comme une bête* . . . 'being, nothing else, without any further definition and fulfillment.'" Baudelairean *luxe, calme et volupté*. The focus is on a minimal, moral happiness that does not come at the cost of another's suffering; where no one goes hungry or knows want; where all can be different without fear and shame.[46]

Adorno once described himself as a "martyr of happiness," suffering for utopia without losing hope for it.[47] His thought gestured toward the creaturely utopian "state" of *rien faire* from an experience of survival. The utopian imagination, the desire for the right or good life—among the highest human aspirations—can be alive without the objective conditions of leisure being met, outside of unoccupied time free of cares and concerns about subsistence. It can take root in a life radically pared down, exposed, distressed, and lacking, relative to before. As Abensour observed in relation to Adorno, "from catastrophe itself arises a new *utopian summation*, the 'never again' that immediately expresses, beyond the banality of the formulation, the exigency of utopia, as if catastrophe had *a contrario* revealed the necessity of utopia."⁴⁸ This supposedly base state of existence is also a source of one of the highest human desires. That it is so can be seen from utopianizing claims made by those who, materially or psychologically, are struggling to get by, to live on in the face of material scarcity, ecological degradation, political persecution, or social oppression. What makes individual or collective claims for happiness issuing from such circumstances and plight *utopian* is not so much the hope against hope they express as their *social* import, when they aim to improve the lot of many. They are, in this sense, *excessive* and can become political. *Dialectic of Enlightenment* and *Minima Moralia* both warn, however, that self-preservation can also excessively instrumentalize thinking for the domination of nature, our own and generally.⁴⁹ Yet when it does not do so, it points itself in reverie toward that which seems furthest from it: a utopia truer than those classically based on old and/or new relations of domination.

The truth of suffering bodies is that of utopia as somatic pleasure. When resulting from disability, illness, or incapacity, minor bodily movements, whether voluntary or involuntary, acquire greater significance. It is similarly with the gestures of thought, which, Adorno reminds us, arises from bodily needs and desires. The thinking in *Minima Moralia* issues from "damaged life" and is *meant* to be meaningful. Despite being gestic, and fragmentary, it is not devoid of intention or purpose. Its telos is *utopian*, which in this case means *open, iconoclastic, fragmenting* the bad, the false, totality to find in its "rifts and fissures" indications for how to transform it. "The utopian moment in thinking," Adorno writes,

> is stronger the less it . . . objectifies itself into a utopia and hence sabotages its realization. Open thinking points beyond itself. For its part a comportment, a form of praxis, it is more akin to transformative praxis than a comportment that is compliant for the sake of praxis. . . . Thought is happiness, even where it defines unhappiness: by enunciating it. By this alone happiness reaches into the universal unhappiness.⁵⁰

Moreover, such happiness is "the only aspect of metaphysical experience which is more than powerless needing."⁵¹

Adorno's critical-theoretical utopian gesture—pointing toward a horizon of true universality of emancipation, reconciliation, redemption—can thus no more be separated from suffering, nature, mimesis, or play, than it can be detached from the body, its needs and desires. Thought is in its "utopian moment" when it is experienced bodily. It opens a perspective that "displace[s] and estrange[s] the world"⁵² and plays on the horizon or vanishing-lines of desire, signifying that which to go beyond. For desire's (immanently self-critical) relationship to existing society is also dialectical.

Minima Moralia can at times seem like a nostalgic book. In fragment 19, we read that "[t]echnology is making gestures precise and brutal and with them human beings. It expels from gestures all hesitation, consideration, civility. It subjects them to the implacable, as it were ahistorical, requirements of things. Thus, one unlearns to close a door softly, discreetly and yet firmly."[53] *Dialectic of Enlightenment* diagnosed the contemporary consignment to oblivion of "the ineradicable mimetic heritage present in all praxis," in that "[t]hose blinded by [bourgeois] civilization have contact with their own tabooed mimetic traits only through certain gestures and forms of behavior they encounter in others, as isolated, shameful residues in their rationalized environment." Expressive of emotion, these "contagious gestures"—like "touching, nestling, soothing, coaxing"—become suppressed for their "immediacy" and repulsive in their "outmodedness."[54] Adorno's model of history calls into question Hegel's resolutely progressivist philosophy. The past, for the critical theorist, is never simply past, over and done with, nor is it something to be principally conserved, or compulsively recollected. It simply *is*, in traces bearing indices of possibilities of the right life—traces in the form of suffering and lost hopes awaiting redemption.[55] This fragmentary, trace-form of the past functioning as an index recalls the gesture of pointing (incidentally, pointing is among the gestures banished from common civility). In the Adornian dialectic of nostalgia and utopia, our utopian longing only for fragments of the bad past is negated on account of casting a particular image of utopia. Both of these telic orientations of thinking have, in Adorno, the open-endedness of the gesture—like fragments, suggesting some unprecedented new whole. Rather than envision *the whole as the true*, Adorno's own fragments see truth and being as fragmented.

The word "fragment" evokes something broken, incomplete, and, by implication, unaccomplished, imperfect. For technical reasons as well as those of cultural value, professional norm, and economic precarity, thought in our day finds itself in a period of nonfulfillment. Instead of going all out and to the limits of our critical and intellectual capacities, we browse and read in scattered, fragmentary, unsystematic fashion, and write in fragments—even if it is to link them to one another later on, piecing together an argument or a position in an effort to create the illusion of unified reflection. Reading and, indeed, thinking in fragments has become second nature.

In daily life, we distinguish gestures from *gesticulations*. The latter—as sets of animated and uncoordinated, exaggerated and convulsive, gestures—are incoherent, often obscurantist, a triumph of form over content. They can also, of course, be warnings, signs of genuine anger or of distress that should be heeded and, when possible, responded to. For Adorno, against the background of deceptive ideological silence in postwar West Germany, exaggeration could appear as the sole medium of truth, indeed, the form of all thinking.[56] For us, faced with a fragmented public sphere that forsakes ideological nuance for polarization and is host to a cacophony of indignation, resentment, paranoia, and conspiracy credence, exaggeration is the order of the day as the principal vector of verbal assault and disinformation. Calculated or hysterical, it can inflate a pack of lies into indomitable "realities," convert the diligent reporting of facts into "fake news," blowing out of proportion and, by so doing, blocking the truth. Reflective silence is then denounced as cowardice or guilt, the act of calling out hailed as activism, and the importance of an issue measured by its public amplification. Exaggeration in our day is inseparable from tireless competition for attention on social media and other online platforms, which thrive on it. If we must, nonetheless, make common cause with those who participate in the nuance-cancelling free-for-all out of a sense of civic duty, moral obligation, and woke solidarity, it is because their anger and spleen also convey real suffering, its accumulated quanta. When exaggeration lies in the very nature of things (as Walter Benjamin said), overstating the truth does truth a disservice.[57] In an environment where exaggeration takes its marching orders from mendacity and self-righteousness, magnified truth rings false.

Fortunately, magnification also exposes the fallacies, biases, and gesticulations that produced it. Gesticulation, no matter how full of pain, always appears incongruous next to gesture. It lacks the latter's composure and economy, its combination of affective attunement with reflectively productive restraint. Gesticulations are attention-grabbing; they exaggerate and caricature to elicit immediate reactions. Gestures are thought-provoking; they attend critically to the minima of suffering, to even microscopic pain. As such, they must take gesticulation seriously. As everywhere around us reflective gestures of resistance are mistaken, by their restlessness, for sheer pretentious gesticulation, and showy gesticulations routinely confounded, by their persistence, with intellectual investment and significance, keeping these two kinds of movement apart in our minds is as vital in verbal, especially written, communication, as it is indispensable to understanding the present.

Whether or not we engage in critical theory in Adorno's wake, we need to do more with less by multiplying meaningful, critical gestures, and by such small but elegant judgment (however trenchant), discerning fragments of genuine reflection from gesticulations of one kind or another, to lend our ear, not to noise and distractions, but to what really matters and urgently needs our attention. The manifold crises on our hands—climate, sanitary, economic, political—oblige us to try to sort things out, and quickly. We are morally called upon to practice immanent critique amid confusion, and to detect the hindrance of social contradictions in our own values and systems of ideas. A turning point, a moment of crisis, is by definition *decisive*, and activates the critical bones in one's body, keeping alive in thought despair, hope, and the desire to make things right. If this is thought in a utopian register, so much the better for thought.

4

Negative Dialectics, Negative Events
The Aphorism and Melancholy Historicism
Wyatt Sarafin

The aphorism is a technology of knowledge, a mediation of social life, and a poetic object. As a form, a genre, and a technology, the aphorism occupies a space in both the past and present. Of course, these mediated effects are the by-product of book production and design: the material life of the book is imbricated with the evolving realities of the present. Aphorisms—and the books that contain them—were never in the past, because they were always temporally situated in the *here and now*.

In Theodor Adorno's *Minima Moralia* (1951), epigraphs, aphorisms, and other classicizing modalities militate against a modernist fragmentation even while simultaneously incorporating that aesthetic onto the composition. While Adorno has been accused of being Eurocentric and universalist, stylistically *Minima Moralia* shares non-European counterparts. On the occasion of *Minima Moralia*'s seventeenth anniversary, I choose to reexamine the aphorism alongside non-Western examples. My argument runs counter to the post-Sedgwick, postcritical orthodoxy, a once dominant turn in the early to mid-2010s but has since waned in the wake of the Covid-19 pandemic.[1] (I take postcritique to be an academic brand distinct from Eve Sedgwick's queer feelings and José Muñoz's queer of color critique.) In many respects, my intervention is situated in the wake of Adorno: an epilogue haunted by aphoristic remains scattered across genres, performances, archives, and sites.

This chapter reexamines figural and literal representations of historical duration in the aphorism. Aphoristic form is transportable across national borders and disciplinary boundaries, and theorists and artists from the Global South have appropriated the aphorism, because of the compression of information inherent in the form. The aphorism is utilized to aggregate historical events or discreet frames of sensory information. Placed in a narrative succession, the end result is a collection of frames of world-historical events as they are being registered through a fractured subjectivity. This implicit engagement with fictionality is not simply an iteration of self-reflexive and critical metafiction, nor is it characterized by a self-reflexivity that might call to attention a text's ontological status as fiction. Rather, the formal engagement with literary and narrative tropes functions to systematically homogenize and incorporate elements of capitalist production—simultaneously disrupting the linear periodization of history and refracting that sociopolitical disjuncture through poetic aphorism.

I am keenly interested in teasing out aphoristic potentiality alongside a broad range of critical applications. Stephen Best has provocatively argued against Benjaminian "melancholy historicism": "history consists in the *taking possession* of such grievous experience and archival loss . . . a kind of crime scene investigation in which the forensic imagination is directed *toward the recovery of a 'we' at the point of 'our' violent origin.*"[2] *Minimal Moralia* famously begins with a dedication on melancholy and sorrow, which serves as a basis for a critical historicism (but importantly not method): "The melancholy science from which I make this offering to my friend relates to a region that from time immemorial was regarded as the true field of philosophy, but which, since the latter's conversion into method, has lapsed into intellectual neglect, sententious whimsy and finally oblivion."[3] I would like to think myself somewhere between the poles of surface (Best) and depth (Adorno). Best offers a compelling alternative to the paradigms of recovery. At the same time, I do not want to reify a corrosive politics of consumption via a return to attachments and surfaces. Here I find Adorno to be a productive foil, because "contemplation can do no more than patiently trace the ambiguity of melancholy in ever new configurations," in spite of the imperative to produce positive knowledge.[4] Frustrated but invested in the methods of historiographic re-description, I implicitly test the limits of Best's (and others) weak theory in reexamining the aphorism as something *immutable but transportable* across historical time and space.

There is a kind of spatial fix to the aphorism, and figurations of the planet, the world, and the globe have been the catalyst for the postcritical turn.[5] While I take a skeptical view of the critical tendency to relegate the environmental as a figural and not literal concern, I harness that critical potential to rethink the aphorism: as a poetic technology that refigures national borders, sustains the possibilities of fictive world-making, and moves across time and space and history. To clarify, I am suggesting certain material artifacts and generic forms—

the aphorism, for example—should not be regarded as static historical objects delimited by their social, economic, and book-historical contexts. My gesture is to reclaim Adorno's aphoristic modality as central to a materialist project of *reparation through negation*.[6] To engage the aphorism as a site and as an ecology is to acknowledge our shared mortality and connectivity across modernity's competing timescales.

Aphoristic Assemblages and the Wound of History

If melancholy historicism is in an interpretive bind, then the aphorism embodies the recovery problematic. The aphorism retains the wreckage of a forgotten history; the remains shimmer in the present time of a reader's first encounter; the form is not a de-materialized fragment but instead an archaeological composite.[7] The artifact must be put back into the historical dialectic: as a product of a complex, interconnected set of social processes. Critical theory—as a set of methodological generalizations and not a monolithic presentation of abstractions—is certainly viable in a history of modernity that is increasingly being characterized along the lines of economic and ecological catastrophe. The aphorism problematizes any easy unity of parts and wholes, but if aphoristic knowing has been accused of being willfully detached from history, materiality, and factuality, then to what extent is theory *conditioned* and *restricted* by *narrative* (historiographic; fictive) and *temporality* (sequentiality; simultaneity)?

Handling the traumatic and often submerged archives of Atlantic slavery, African Americanists have cultivated the practices of recovery and reparation. The tools of archival discovery uncover a lineage effaced—the populist detritus of Black cultural and intellectual production. The narrative of discovery, rhetorically paraleptic and pathetic, is framed as being particular to the Afro-American historical experience. Furthermore, Black art takes refuge in the fugitive practices of critique, but also the minor forms of expressive culture like the aphorism. Whether it is the Harlem Renaissance in New York, *négritude* in Paris, or *negrismo* in Cuba, Pan-Africanism of the twentieth century represents the formation of a Black identity and an emerging consciousness. It follows a certain logic of dynamism—of transformation and transplantation, change and cancellation. In their engagements with modernity, the African subject becomes a cosmopolitan figure. That subject is tied to a collective rather than an individual identity, and as such I will examine how transnational migration as an *aphoristic form* has come to produce the pan-African metropole—latent in Caribbeanist and Africanist theories of transnationalism, as well as the temporal possibilities that have been produced in cityspace.

Two years after his return to Cuba, the surrealist painter Wifredo Lam had completed his most celebrated work, *The Jungle*, in 1943. Making its debut at the Pierre Matisse Gallery in New York, *The Jungle* was later acquired by the Museum of Modern Art (MoMA), where it remains to this day. Lam's composition is an original but shocking synthesis of European and Caribbean styles—fusing an African "primitivism" with Western cubism.[8] Lam had aspired to capture the "black spirit" of the Cuban people or give expression to "the beauty of the plastic art of the blacks," creating that one "true picture" with the "power to set the imagination to work."[9] Or, as Adorno might describe it, Lam exhibits a fleeting and captive beauty which "still flourishes under terror . . . strives at once to reject happiness and to assert it."[10]

Standing at over ninety-three feet in length and ninety feet in width, *The Jungle* is aesthetically dominating. Its Africanist sensibility is embodied in the composition—with crescent-shaped masks, round breasts and buttocks, and ritualistic dances prominently situated in the foreground. The four masked figures are rendered as highly abstracted, elongated human-animal hybrids. The event that *The Jungle* bears witness to is amassed and weighed down by the sheer proliferation of masks, bodies, and sugarcane. The stark geometrical abstractions contrast with the composition's color palette of gently muted mixes of greens, yellows, and reds on the masked figures. These in turn contrast with the rich blue and black primary colors on the sugarcanes. These contrasts announce the magnitude of an African spirituality while ironically negating its transcendence. In that respect, the internal binaries convey a fundamental ambivalence toward modernity and reflect the complex aesthetic iterations that Lam utilizes to destroy it. It all starts to come together: Lam privileges the centrality of an organizing spatial function, militating against a modernist fragmentation even while simultaneously incorporating that aesthetic onto the composition.

How might we come to classify Lam's de-colonial, multicultural form? As the masked figures stand parallel to sugarcane, Lam is immediately responding to the island's collective history of colonialism and slavery. Cuba's sugarcane and tobacco industries began to flourish in the late eighteenth century; as the North American colonies had begun importing more sugar, more slaves were transported from Africa to the port of Havana. Consequently, Havana was transformed into a global metropolis, and yet to sustain Havana's commercial prowess critical resources were diverted from the countryside to city. As *The Jungle* yearns rather wistfully, nostalgically for the time of Cuban independence, it shares a sensibility with the modernist tradition of Cuban letters, *negrismo*. Spanning the 1933 Revolt of the Sergeants to the *Revolución cubana* of 1959, *negrismo* came during a decisive shift in the island's social and cultural life. Its contributors included the poets Nicolás Guillén and Emilio Ballaga, two mixed-race poets from Camaguey; the fiction writer and ethnographer Alejo Carpentier; and the anthropologist Fernando Ortiz. These artists and writers were inclined toward revolutionary and anti-imperialist politics—an impulse that, once again, stems from a collective anxiety surrounding the legacies of US-Spanish imperialism and the desire for liberation. The result is a program of artmaking standing between dialectical and undialectical thought—a negative dialectic.[11]

Cuba's imperial legacy is of particular concern to Fernando Ortiz, and in *Cuban Counterpoint* (1940) he theorizes the "transculturation" of Afro-Cuban people: "a steady human of African Negros coming from all the coastal regions of Africa . . . snatched from their original social groups, their own cultures destroyed and crushed under the weight of the cultures in existence here, *like sugar cane ground in the rollers of the mill*" (emphasis mine).[12] A work of economic nationalism, *Cuban Counterpoint* was published in 1940—three years before *The Jungle*, and moments before a new constitution was ratified. But, as Erico Mario Santí observes, Ortiz suggests something far beyond that, situating himself as part of the national debate regarding Cuba's economic dependence on sugar: "for precisely that reason, it is a polemic, indeed heretical book, going so far as to suggest that sugar is *not* Cuban, in a reaction against the scandalous wealth the sugar industry had produced exclusively for a certain class, particularly during the Geraldo Machado years."[13] Knowing this political context, how do we talk about the aphorism, and how is the aphorism mediated in *Cuban Counterpoint*, *The Jungle*, and other pan-African texts? In the case of *Cuban Counterpoint*, Ortiz is analogizing the temporalities of capital production to the temporal progression of music.

Aphoristic Anthropologies and Cultural Production

Ultimately, the pan-African engagement with cityspace could be read as prophetic of the Revolution and an early iteration of Marxist humanism—a scholarly sub-discipline that comes to be embodied, more recently, in the works of David Harvey, Doreen Massey, and Henri Lefebvre.[14] In *Theory from the South* (2012), Jean and John L. Comaroff classify the Black avant-garde as part of the same Marxist "rhetoric" that is asserted in the "alterities of Pan-Africanism, Ethiopianism, Negritude, and Afrocentricism; in musical genres, Nollywood movies, and surrealist art that spell out profoundly local aspirations; in . . . the call for a generically 'African humanity,' and, even more ambiguously, the 'African Renaissance.'"[15] I find the distinctions made by Comaroffs restrictive here, as it fails to account for the radical, even revolutionary undertaking of literary and political world-making. Time is especially salient in Cuban letters, and the Cuban commitment to alternative world-making offers a response to the negative temporalities that the Comaroffs seem to suggest. The metropole is wistfully cast as a city "not here yet"—and not just merely existing in the "here and now" or the "then and there." Indeed, the Cuban intellectual José Esteban Muñoz goes so far as to argue that the aesthetic "contains blueprints and schemata of a forward-dawning futurity": for the "here and now" of modernization is

> a prison house. We must strive, in the face of the here and now's totalizing rendering of reality, to think and feel a then and there. Some will say that all we have are the pleasures of this moment, but we must never settle for that minimal transport; we must dream and enact new and better pleasures, other ways of being in the world, and ultimately new worlds.[16]

Muñoz's utopic hope is embodied in the aphoristic form, wherein the sublimation of an imperial teleology accounts for a modernist fragmentation and diasporic splattering that is so fundamental to it.

There is also a bit of a catachresis. Time does not accelerate in aphorism's rendering of the cityspace but lorries, pedestrians, and various other objects do when rushing toward one another. The temporal disjuncture of the contemporary Afropolis, then, is how we can come to appreciate the bodily and temporal hybridity that characterizes the composition of *The Jungle*. Indeed, Lam's stylized form of geometrical abstraction seems to capture what the Comaroffs describe as "modernity in Africa," which is at once "a re-genesis, a consciousness of new possibilities, and a rupture of the past—a past that, in the upshot, was flattened out, detemporalized, and congealed into 'tradition.'"[17] As Lam renders individual elements of his composition indistinguishable from one another, the viewer has no choice but to take in the whole sensory experience. And as the picture unfolds, the viewer also registers the evidence as it is being presented, relating them back to a finished product. But more fundamentally, Lam's pictorial anti-narrativity represents a revolt against *modernization*, against the strongly "normative teleology, a unilinear trajectory toward a future-capitalist, socialist, fascist, African, whatever—to which all humanity ought to aspire, to which all history ought to lead, toward which all the peoples ought to evolve."[18] Lam's four masked figures represent colonialism's disadvantaged subjects, whose existence may ultimately be redeemed through *modernity's* "variably construed and variably inhabited *Weltanschauung*, to a concept of the person as [a] self-actualizing subject . . . to a vision of history as a progressive, man-made construction . . . to a restless impulse toward innovation whose very iconoclasm brings a hunger for things eternal."[19]

Lam internalizes modernization's "unilinear trajectory" but seeks to destroy it. Meaning making is actualized through the multi-focalized product of the aphorism, encompassing the full range of temporal flux. Lam's aesthetical strategies are traditionally associated with that of an anti-narrative, which, as Jann Palster observes, depend upon the "expectations of a narrative, but frustrate it through continual interruption of a work's temporal process and proceed by change without narrative transformation."[20] A formal engagement with narrative temporality can establish the conditions of possibility for an anti-assimilationist aesthetic, as Lam inverts the temporal depth of space to suggest the negative dialects upon which aphoristic knowledge is produced. But with the masked figures integrated into that broader aesthetic, the viewer cannot help but recognize the artist's disadvantaged subject position.

In *The Jungle*, the pictorial elements are logically sequenced according to the thematic connections and resonances between objects. How this aphoristic form internalizes a loss to represent the potentiality of alternative futurities is evident in how Black artists respond to collective and traumatic histories, even when identity complicates the subject's claim to that traumatic history. Lam, for example, is the product of multiethnic parentage: he claims African, Chinese, and Spanish ancestry, and thus a *disidentification*—the fundamental indeterminacy of multiracial filial belonging—is displaced onto an aesthetic of fullness. True to the surrealist fascination with psychoanalysis, racial amalgamation becomes a return of the repressed: a material and melancholy trace, the ghostly remainders of a colonized subjectivity simultaneously erased from and manifesting itself from within the material fabric of the canvas.[21]

To uplift the spirit of "black folks," W. E. B. du Bois had famously advocated for a classical education of Greek and Latin, but to what extent is the Greek construction of rhythm mediated onto Pan-Africanism? In Lam's refiguration of aphoristic form, the cosmological order of elements, or *kosmios*, is of aesthetic importance. In ancient philosophy, a "counterpoint" is a concordance (*philia*) between opposites. According to the Platonic dialogs, as a clear distinction must be made between what is "good" and "best," rhythmical concordance creates the "best" results because they establish the literal harmony of music. A natural world is conceived as orderly, like the cadences and harmonies in music, this notion of irrational numbers deeply unsettles this set belief, as it firmly "untunes" cosmological order.[22] Lam clearly rejects the essentialist idea that beauty is conceived as an encounter with absolute forms; his surrealist, aphoristic art refuses to acknowledge the existence of absolute love. Rather than simply exhibit the sensuality of Otherness, Lam is keen to demonstrate how dissimilar objects love dissimilar things: an *epithymia*, or love as desire. To further extend this comparison, *epithymia* as a desire and *philia* as a concordance constitute a "double-*eros*." And yet this double-*eros* should not be conceived as passively existing in its own element; instead, it should be understood as belonging to a discreet set of elements are actively re-arranged to whatever best suits the artist or theorist.

Frederic Jameson's critique of late capitalism as a "crisis of historicity" verbalizes a concern that is fundamental to both Caribbean futurism and strategic transformations of African literature.[23] If, under the dictates of neo-colonial and neoliberal capitalism, "the subject has lost its capacity actively to extend its pro-tensions and re-tensions across the temporal manifold and to organize past and future into coherent experience," the aesthetic must necessarily compensate for that epistemological loss.[24] In Fernando Ortiz's *Cuban Counterpoint* (1940), Havana's everyday spatialities arise from the alterity between the metropole's material infrastructure and the social interactions inside and beyond them. The transnational subject, then, is partially the product of the formal and informal modes of cityspace, and yet it is the networks of metropolitan mediation that set up the conditions of possibility for transnational self-making. In other words, the transnational subject has the capacity to mature from heteronomy to autonomy, even if that disadvantaged subject position is dependent upon the media of a culture industry. That position has much more political and social agency than what Jameson or others might suggest. And as such, the transnational subject has the capacity to make meaningful sense of or resist a neoliberal, neo-colonial environment.

Furthermore, in *Cuban Counterpoint*, Ortiz claims that Afro-Cuban music is the inspiring and structuring element of his work. The first section is a single essay subdivided into fifteen parts or aphorisms; the second section, in contrast, consists of twenty-five iterative sections. As both sections literally "counterpoint" one another, Ortiz is thematizing the aphorism as a sort of musicality situated in relation to Cuban culture—specifically through transculturation. At once, a "transculturation" implies more than a simple acquisition of cultural elements—

as the word "acculturation" suggests. Rather, a transculturation is the product of "extremely complex transmutations of culture," but it is a process, too, encapsulating the morphologies of the island's "economic . . . institutional, legal, ethical, religious, artistic, linguistic, psychological, [and] sexual" aspects that come into being.[25] In the same vein, Ato Quayson's *Oxford Street, Accra* (2014) maps out the discourse ecologies that undergird the spatial logics of the African metropolis. A vivacious observer of urban life, Quayson samples from disciplines as eclectic as history and sociology, but his method of interpretation is one that ultimately privileges the role of narrative storytelling. It is intimidating to approach Accra's wide variety of inscriptions, slogans, and advertisements, even with Quayson as our guide. These materials are of transnational and multilingual character. They incorporate oral and written devices. They are mobile and stationary. And they are seemingly everywhere in the city. In other words, the difficulty in interpreting these aphoristic materials is that it is simply a lot to comprehend simultaneously. Like Ortiz's transculturation, Quayson is positing that "the communicative complexity of human interactions" can surpass the networks of global capitalism that partially (and aphoristically) produce them.[26]

When approaching transculturation and its relation to urban history and aphoristic form, it raises several questions. Do the forms of mediation take precedence over the forms of representation? And, if a history of transnationalism becomes but a mediation of autobiographical experience, can such a method transcend the limitations of literary criticism and literary form? *Oxford Street*, in particular, is notable in that it suggests that the conditions of Africanness can find full expression through the forms of aphoristic and transnational mediation—counter to the previous interventions from Chinweizu and Ngũgĩ wa Thiong'o.[27] Quayson's "horizontal archaeologies" enables the close-reading of the contradictory spatial logics of Oxford Street; "horizontal archaeologies" is a process in which the rhythmic and spatial dimensions of cityspace are ascertained from "modulating our perspectives along diverse vectors of interpretation, sometimes sequentially, but often also regulated by different forms of simultaneity."[28] The process of "horizontal archaeologies" also describes the assimilation of Afro-Brazilians (Tabons) and Danish Euro-Africans (mulattoes). These migrant identities constitute "a version of Africanness"—a racialized hybrid of Blackness or Black ethnicity—that indeed "cannot be easily assimilable to a normative blackness."[29] Quayson focuses on "the simultaneity of identities" that are "severed from any locality and thus made *transnational*"; under the stress of the transnational, "the modalities of what constitutes an African or indeed black identity are increasingly being put under scrutiny."[30]

As Quayson demonstrates, images of this hybridized Africanness are indeed reinforced and mediated through the aphorisms in billboards, lorry slogans, and advertisements of the city.

Oxford Street, however, is ultimately hopeful in that they endow the transnational subject autonomy even when that subject would seem to be without it. Ordinary people are totally capable of resisting the totalizing mechanisms of global capitalism.[31] Quayson is critical of the *structural* changes that have been mandated under neo-colonial and neoliberal capitalism alike, and as such acknowledges a critical insight from Jean and John Comaroff's *Theory from the South*: That the production of Afromodernity is but a collaboration between settler colonialism and its colonial subjects. Accra was founded in the seventeenth century as a British colony, and under British colonial rule the "overlap between top and bottom" locations has since "constituted" the identity-formation of the African metropolis; moreover, the "intra- and interethnic relations" among city-dwellers and their "out-of-town counterparts" had meant that "contests over who owned the city were regularly defined along lines of autochthony, primogeniture, and first arrival, thus producing various hierarchical relations that were in turn exploited by the colonial administration."[32] And, as Quayson also acknowledges that transnational self-making was a historical necessity in the wake of the IMF programs of the 1980s and 1990s, the legacies of settler colonialism are built onto the structure of these programs and thus the very structure of the city.

Aphoristic Rhythms

Historical melancholy is an encoding force for social and aesthetic production; the postcolonial literary ethnography (Ortiz, Quayson) is often privileged as the exemplary case-study for literary historicist (and new historicist) praxis, because the genre points to a set of materially realized negations.[33] To understand the aphorism's peculiar iteration of music, perhaps another metaphysical model might ultimately be useful here.

In an influential passage on *art négre* or the *négritude* style, Léopold Sédar Senghor postulates that rhythm can function as a mode of documentation: "The ordering force that constitutes the Negro style is music," Senghor claims. "It is the primary condition for, and sign of, art, as respiration of life"—yet it is not "a symmetry that engenders monotony; rhythm is alive, it is free."[34] Rhythm is framed in relation to the visual arts—to sculptures, masks, paintings, and other material forms. It is the elusive architecture of the Black aesthetic—the "respiration of life" that is both "regular" and "spasmodic."³⁵ For Senghor, music is both being contained by and the container of material form, and this has everything to do with the disjuncture of art and rhythm. History leaves behind a material trace. Art is the singular evidence of the Black experience—of a consciousness irreparably split by exile and colonial subjugation.

Senghor's theorization on *négritude* here represents turning away from a Eurocentric metaphysics of the subject.³⁶ But in moving toward the ontological and psychic conditions of the African diaspora, Senghor aspires to the same epistemological mastery that has become a legacy of a modernist aesthetic. Tacitly enforcing the unity and cohesion of high-culture's aesthetic tradition, *négritude* has been accused as assimilationist since its inception.³⁷ Franz Fanon, in his rebuttal to *négritude*, criticizes Senghor's assertion that rhythm is in fact the grammar for Blackness. "Had I read that right?" Fanon mocks, "From the opposite end of the white world a magical Negro culture was hailing to me. Negro sculpture! I began to flush with pride. Was this our salvation?"³⁸ And yet far from simply universalizing a diasporic experience, Senghor has begun to theorize the aesthetic documentation of a double-consciousness as an ethical expression of trauma.³⁹

Jean-Paul Sartre has quite a different take on *négritude*'s political import and thus the import of the aphorism. Sartrean existentialism places the self in relation to the future, or at the very least our potential for futurity. Anything beyond that is absurd and anti-metaphysical. In his controversial "Black Orpheus," Sartre acknowledges that *négritude*'s "density of . . . words" and styles is incorporated to accommodate a revolutionary, anti-colonial project: "thrown into the air like stones from a volcano," *négritude* seeks to destroy "*white* culture" and bring to light "the revolutionary aspirations of the oppressed negro . . . a certain specific, concrete form of humanity."⁴⁰ Sartre mistakenly assumes that all philosophical systems must necessarily be metaphysical ones.⁴¹ Senghor's *négritude*—whether a textual product, a metaphysical system, an aesthetic form or a political philosophy—establishes the conditions of possibility for testimony. It conjures up the ghosts of slavery and xenophobia and genocide, allowing for an uncanny homecoming. It is both flesh and not, the ghost from the past and the ghost of the future, a carnal becoming of sorts. All of this goes against Sartrean metaphysics, and, as Martin Puchner observes, a Marxist phenomenology as typified in the manifesto is formally characterized as "an attempt to undo the distinction between speech and action, between words and revolution . . . one that describes a fundamental gesture or attitude orienting the manifesto toward the world it seeks to undo and redo."⁴² For Sartre, *négritude*'s "concrete form of humanity" is what ultimately redeems the project: it becomes the new metaphysical import that can replace the hegemonies of European colonialism or "*white* culture."

Indeed, the ontological foundation of the aphorism is less a matter of Sartrean existentialism than it is something more post-structural. Sartre fails to appreciate *négritude* because it is dissimilar to modernization's "unilinear trajectory." To be a subject within this spectral economy, as Achille Mbembe explains, is to have the past constantly encroach upon the present,

> repeatedly overcoming the limits of what can be expressed through language. Thus, writers use several simultaneous languages of time and the body. . . . The same process takes place in relation to the memory of the postcolonial potentate, that magnificent manifestation of time with no past or future tense, or of a fallen past that one ceaselessly tries to revive but whose meaning appears only as a fracture and dissipation.[43]

Modernity's ghost, or the "postcolonial potentate," is a strange return of sorts, an uncanny return and a come. In this context, the project aphorism could be said to bear witness to the status of the Black slave in the first phase of capitalism. The temporality it aspires to through music is paradoxical, resembling a *relever* or perhaps even an *aufheben*.[44] It is not so much a form as it is formless, the compilation of specters and remainders—"modernity's ghost." A "specter" and a "remainder" are equal parts "ruptures" and "eruptions": there is always a meaning located at the surface of a text that is erupting from the cohesive whole. Modernity then is the product of historical resonances—a "lurking meaning" that is expressed indirectly, echoed.

The aphorism's temporal position, like Derrida's "time out of joint," enables a politics of mourning. In *Disidentifications* (1999), José Esteban Muñoz theorizes the reparative function of collective melancholies and identifications: "Communal mourning by its very nature, is an immensely complicated text to read, for we do not mourn just one lost object or other, but *we also mourn as a 'whole'*—or, put it another way, as a contingent and *temporary collection of fragments* that is experiencing a loss of its parts" (my emphasis).[45] Music, as a spectral but singular form, becomes the ideal form for capturing the fragments and scattered elements of a diaspora. As Ortiz and Quayson have demonstrated, the metropole's spatial ecologies are actualized through multiple linkages and deferrals—similar to a *différance*. And Theodor Adorno, too, enacts a historical and epistemological reorientation that is enacted through the sheer materiality and totality of the arts. The cultural production of modernity is incorporated into the text, and that new aesthetic is suggested as verisimilitude to social content. As a discreet system of competing and interlocking networks, music can create an epistemological charge strong enough to cut across the colonial discourses of primitivism and assimilation, minority sexual and racial positions, isolated and linked communities.

The aphorism, then, enacts a set of transnational processes: diasporic gaps and networks are converted into a single entity. Ultimately, these mediated effects allow for a shared grieving: the commensurability of an incommensurable loss. In pointing the way from the margins to new center of cultural production, the aphorism achieves a redemptive but melancholy timescale, and traumatic experience is sublimated onto a utopic futurity.

Part III

A Labor Theory of the Present

5

"The Whole of Life Must Look Like a Job"

Minima Moralia and the Capitalocene

Clinton Williamson

> *But how can a time belong? What is it to have time? If a time belongs, it is because the word* time *designates metonymically less time itself than the things with which one fills it, with which one fills the form of time, time as a form. It is a matter, then, of the things one does* in the meantime [cependant] *or the things one has at one's disposal* during [pendant] *this time. Therefore, as time does not belong to anyone as such, one can no more take* it, itself, *than give it. Time already begins to appear as that which undoes this distinction between taking and giving, therefore also between receiving and giving, perhaps between receptivity and activity, or even between the being-affected and the affecting of any affection. Apparently and according to common logic or economics, one can only exchange, one can only take or give, by way of metonymy, what is* in *time.*
>
> —Jacques Derrida, *Given Time: I. Counterfeit Money*

We are producing our(selves to) death. This moment, our moment, necessarily embedded in (but crucially not yet entombed by) the Capitalocene, relies upon the perpetual ongoingness of a production fueled by a multitude of extractions.[1] Continuing to burn the midnight oil, capital drives our endless working-toward-death, toward extinction. Even the owl of Minerva works the night shift. This relentless production signals the grotesqueries of the logics undergirding capital's temporality, the 24/7 world of constant accumulation, what Jonathan Crary refers to as "a generalized inscription of human life into a duration without breaks, defined by a principle of continuous functioning . . . a time that no longer passes, beyond clock time."[2] Thus, we arrive at the cruel irony that the more of our time we have stolen from us by capital, the less time we collectively have to halt the steady death march of the Capitalocene. We find ourselves doubly *out of time*, at once displaced by a regime of labor which desires no off the clock and constantly harried under the duress of a deadline imposed by the increasing damages inflicted upon us by an ever-warming world.

The query posed to us, that which is always already an echo of an echo (a revenant of that spectral communism's haunting presence heralding an out of time futurity), of "what is to be done" can only be answered by reckoning with this collective condition of being out of time. This impasse simultaneously signals a condition of possibility, one in which revolutionary necessity dictates that we must be out of the time of capital, the workday that looks to be everyday (every day, ad infinitum), that the connection between time and the value form must cease to be. Time cannot be money. A crucial surplus accompanies this initial query, beckoning toward us, asking, in the form of an immanent supplement, "what is to be undone?" It is with this question that we can begin (again) to look not only toward what must be dismantled, demolished, excised, and abolished but also to what must be *not* done—halted, abandoned, escaped from, and, above all, refused. Idleness stems from this refusal, one that calls forth the scrivener's negation, the preference not to participate in the productive processes of accumulation. Bartleby's preference not to always contains the threat of a spillover, of a collectivized refusal to go on toiling, the lingering dream of the general strike which portends to starve capital's hunger for production so long as the producers can sustain themselves long enough in the communal form to outlast it, to communize social relations. It is this idleness as a utopian leisure time which refuses the disciplinary temporalities of productivity, growth, and accumulation. This is the idleness that Ernst Bloch contends to be the beginnings (and ends) of a communistic temporality: "The work of leisure (which is not comfortable or aristocratic, but the terminal concept of all emancipated labor) itself makes order in the gloom of existence; there it builds a house for another time."[3] Bloch issues the crucial caveat that the "work of leisure" is neither "comfortable" nor "aristocratic." We are not in the realm of Veblen's conspicuous forms of idleness, those which marks more than anything the conspicuous consumption of proletarian labor time stolen by the bourgeoisie; instead, Bloch casts this "work of leisure" as "the terminal concept of all emancipated labor," a work that is precisely the negation of the drudgery and pain of the metered hours of production. This heralds utopia, no longer just off the map but off the clock as well, located in the communal to come, the abandonment of the regime of wage labor. To usher in that time which is no-time, we must look attentively to the non-productive, the halting of perpetual growth which only ever foreshortened our collective possibilities, not only disallowing anything akin to a flourishing but also now an imminent threat to mere survival. Above all, this moment requires a return to and extension of the political traditions which sought the abolition of the value form, for it's only from this revolutionary uprooting and overturning that we can come to know this utopian ~~work~~ that is otherwise.

In Adorno's 1951 *Minima Moralia*, we find the analysis-*cum*-lament that "the whole of life must look like a job."[4] This chapter intends to form a brief, provisional sketch of what this statement entails for our present predicament, and what possible futures may be engendered by the dismantling of those processes which transmogrify the whole of life into the appearance of work. Within this text, Adorno crucially outlines the tensions between capitalism's extension and insertion of the production processes into all facets of the day and a mourning of the increasingly lost possibilities bound up in what Bloch had called "the work of leisure." We can identify that mourning of a utopian horizon in the famed dictum which diagnosed an inescapable illness at the core of the capitalist world-system: "Wrong life cannot be lived rightly."[5] Capitalism, in which the productive life masquerades as the good life, cannot be merely reformed, as this system itself produces that life which cannot be lived rightly. Central to this "wrong life" is that the whole of it "must look like a job," must bear the desultory resemblance to a labor process even in its purported rest. Adorno presents the utopian ideal of the "work of leisure" as having become warped, a site where it has been rendered via antimetabole as the leisure of work, an endless theatrical production of production, a work that cannot be shirked, cannot be slowed down, cannot be walked out on. Which is to say, wrong life has as its basis wrong work. *Minima Moralia* expresses the tensions between a production process monomaniacally oriented toward endless growth, spreading its tendrils into every waking facet of life, and the liberatory possibilities visible in those stolen, fugitive moments of idleness which still carry an excess potentiality despite all of capitalism's attempts to nullify it, that idleness which arises out of a deliberate attempt to strike back at the rigors of work, that idleness which grows out of refusal. In what follows, I attempt to delineate the ways in which Adorno's observation that "the whole of life must look like job" can point us toward what is to be (un)done and how the refusal to work, the collective absconding from the productive life that is fundamentally and irrevocably wrong life, can still offer up a viable pathway out from under the yoke of the Capitalocene's deadly enervations.

I

Adorno's claim that "the whole of life must look like a job" can best be situated as a kind of critical outgrowth of that section of *Capital* on the working day which had already so astutely addressed this underlying impulse of capital. In this section, Marx describes how capitalism's ideal of production manifests in its desire to have its producers never for a moment do anything but labor and never for a moment be anything but laborers: "Capitalist production therefore drives, by its inherent nature, towards the appropriation of labour throughout the whole of the 24 hours in the day."[6] This system of production tends toward this totalizing subsumption, desiring the indefatigable worker who can always continue to generate surplus value. Crucially, Marx notes that this tendency exists as the "inherent nature" of capitalism, a fundamental feature of its voraciousness, since in this section we too find that capital which hungers, its "appetite for surplus labour appear[ing] in the drive for an unlimited extension of the working day."[7] Unlike its producers, capital needs no rest. It does not correspond to a diurnal cycle. The rhythm of capital is a ceaseless one. Capital contends that "it is self-evident that the worker is nothing other than labour-power for the duration of his whole life, and that therefore all his disposable time is by nature and by right labour-time, to be devoted to the self-valorization of capital."[8] Capital's ideal is for the whole of a life to *be* a job. As Massimiliano Tomba remarks of this chapter:

> It is in production that absolute injustice is demonstrated. Materialism begins here. There is no wage that could compensate for the living corporeality of the worker constrained to work in a repetitive and injurious job. It is the assumption of the non-neutrality of the point of view of this part that is the perspective of *Capital* against capital.[9]

In outlining the devastations wrought by the production process, Marx turns "*Capital* against capital" in that he here must take up the struggles of laborers against the theft of their time: "The establishment of a normal working day is the result of centuries of struggle between the capitalist and the worker."[10] Only via the struggle of labor against the vampiric tendency of capital to drain the entirety of workers' time, the entirety of their vital energies, can the struggle for communism even begin. The limitation of the working day, the reclamation of a time stolen, exists as a prerequisite for revolutionary struggle. The idleness gained via this refusal becomes infused by the possibility of morphing into a time to plot, a time to strengthen and develop the movement which can seek the abolition of labor as such. Time spent not laboring always already carries a threat to a regime which imbues the constancy of work with the moral sense of rectitude. Idle time glimmers with the utopian shimmer of the communistic. And for this very reason, capital continually attempts to reclaim this time so as to defuse it and put it once again back to work.

The whole of life, however, does not merely look like *any* job in the general sense. I contend that it carries particular contours and traits which are of great importance to the specific terrain of our current struggle. The climate crisis continually reminds us that in fact, the whole of a job must look like a mine. The logics of capitalist production are inseparably linked to the techniques and strategies of extraction of the mine. Lewis Mumford in his 1934 work *Technics and Civilization* argues that the inhumanities of mining, the peculiar and particular cruelties inflicted upon the miner at the site of production, move outward from their underground provinces to ultimately infiltrate the broader *modus operandi* of capitalist production. According to Mumford, the drive of capital to encompass the entirety of the twenty-four hours of the day has its origins in the mine: "Day has been abolished and the rhythm of nature broken: continuous day-and-night production first came into existence here."[11] He contends that "the methods and ideals of mining became the chief pattern for industrial effort throughout the Western World," employing the "devilish and sinister" formula of "mine: blast: dump: crush: extract: exhaust." If "life flourishes finally only in an environment of the living," the world of the Capitalocene is an environment of the living dead, of the reanimation and reification of fuels to be extracted and devoured.[12] The telos of the mine, that which directs all work unbendingly toward the inevitability of exhaustion (both of self of environment) burrows its way into the deepest recesses of all labor:

> The animus of mining affected the entire economic and social organism: this dominant mode of exploitation became the pattern for subordinate forms of industry. The reckless, get-rich-quick, devil-take-the-hindmost attitude of the mining rushes spread everywhere: the bonanza farms of the Middle West in the United States were exploited as if they were mines, and the forest were gutted out and mined in the same fashion as the minerals that lay in their hills. Mankind behaved like a drunken heir on a spree. And the damage to form and civilization through the prevalence of these new habits of disorderly exploitation and wasteful expenditure remained, whether or not the source of energy itself disappeared. The psychological results of carboniferous capitalism—the lowered morale, the expectation of getting something for nothing, the disregard for a balanced mode of production and consumption, the habituation to wreckage and debris as part of the normal human environment—all these results were plainly mischievous.[13]

In this passage, however, we discern more than Mumford's critical insight that "carboniferous capitalism" became the primary modality of the form of industry itself. We also find a supplement to Marx's contention in "The Working Day" that "our worker emerges from the process of production looking different from when he entered it."[14] The worker now emerges from the process of production inured to the whole of a job looking like a mine and now seeing the whole of life looking like extraction. These "habits of disorderly and wasteful expenditure" ominously become part and parcel of capital's every day, calcifying into an epistemological relation in which the entirety of the circuit of production and consumption bends under the weight of a thermodynamic contradiction: all work tends toward eventual exhaustion even as an ever more mystified value seems to arise via a conjuration by which nothing appears to beget something. Mumford crucially notes how the form of extraction intensifies and accelerates capital's inclination toward immolation, time like money simply fuel to burn. Yet the possibility of renewal still looms, since the remedy of rest still marks a stopgap to the exhausted. The refusal of this work that is always degrading in how much it deteriorates still signals a utopian hope as it marks the material site from which something *can* in fact be gained from nothing, the difficult work of overthrowing this deadly work of the Capitalocene.

II

If Marx points us toward capital's desire to extend and maximize the production of the working day and Mumford demonstrates the contamination of the form of labor by the tainted remnants of mine runoff, then Adorno offers up a critique of work centered upon the growing absence of its antithesis, the fading dreams of work as central to the communistic project. In *Minima Moralia*, Adorno likens utopian idleness to a spacetime resistant to the "savage spread of the social under mask of universal, the collective as blind fury of activity," a halting of those socialist barbarisms that would cast the utopian in incessant, productive laboring under an alternative guise.[15] This critique of a reform which would keep the value form intact under the guise of state capitalism hits at the crux of the problem, noting that any so-called socialism which fails to take up the abolition of work as a primary tenet will fail to adequately undermine the capitalist production process, ending up merely at the dead end of a re-forming of the underlying structure, the stultifications of the working day still intact. From the vantage of the Capitalocene, this kind of reform exists as precisely that which leaves us in Jasper Bernes's formulation, "stuck between the devil and the Green New Deal," aware that climate change needs immediate redress but simultaneously knowing that nothing less than revolutionary communism can bring about the scale of the overturning we desperately require.[16]

Adorno's *Minima Moralia* highlights the problem of work as necessarily tied to the problem of leisure. Adorno portrays non-productivity as the utopian possibility which gives lie to all those former entertainments which were in reality but another kind of work, a so-called free time that in reality marks a time bought and paid for during the working day, a purchased time that increasingly comes to resemble labor itself. He astutely points to the reclamation of idleness as the reclamation of a collective opportunity to reimagine what is so intensively wrong with capitalist work:

> A mankind which no longer knows want will begin to have an inkling of the delusory, futile nature of all the arrangements hitherto made in order to escape want, which used wealth to reproduce want on a larger scale. Enjoyment itself would be affected, just as its present framework is inseparable from operating, planning, having one's way, subjugating. *Rien faire comme une bête*, lying on water and looking peacefully at the sky, "being, nothing else, without any further definition and fulfilment," might take the place of process, act, satisfaction, and so truly keep the promise of dialectical logic that it would culminate in its origin. None of the abstract concepts comes closer to fulfilled utopia than that of eternal peace.[17]

This passage, couched in a speculative modality, provides a dual movement, imagining futurity in order to analyze that which is amiss in the present's vantage of the past. Locating this vision of idleness in a communistic future devoid of want, Adorno imagines a leisure which will be able to illuminate the past, a messianic looking back at history that can see those ends of capitalist productivity as designed only to further amplify and heighten the need for needless production. This looking backward would also reveal how much enjoyment itself under capitalism comes to take on the characteristics of production, resembling the class conflicts of "operating, planning, having one's way, subjugating." The enjoyment which can only be had at the infliction of miseries down the entirety of the commodity chain can only be "delusory" and "futile" as it relies upon the retrenchment of a power relationship undergirded by violence. "*Rien faire comme une bête*" stands in then for all that harried, endless work denies, a time recaptured, a time that one does not need to spend. Adorno casts this idleness as a new ontology, a new being and a new time, developed after the fall of the house of capitalist labor.

The house in *Minima Moralia* recurs as a motif both for the capitalist decay of the present and for the place of rest and rejuvenation which we can hope to one day occupy differently. The home in this text is both the intolerable place and the no-place of a utopia to come. In the section which ends with the recognition that "wrong life cannot be lived rightly," Adorno appears to castigate the contemporary house as oppositional to anything like home: "The functional modern habitations designed from a *tabula rasa*, are living-cases manufactured by experts for philistines, or factory sites that have strayed into the consumption sphere, devoid of all relation to the occupant."[18] The house that is also the factory merely alienates. Even the home (that place which had already been a jobsite for all the unwaged labor of the domestic sphere) now comes to resemble the regimentation of the factory. In another passage, however, Adorno dialectically casts an encounter with the unrecognizable home that no longer resembles itself as a sign of what liberation may feel like. He describes this moment as a child returning home from holiday and finding the familiar trappings of home suddenly estranged from the routinizations of duty and work, a kind of ostranenie which will find its echo in how the world will look "when it stands no longer under the law of labour, and when for homecomers duty has the lightness of holiday play."[19] In this passage, Adorno suggests that the crumbling of the capitalist labor process can produce a re-enchantment of the everyday, a seeing of all the minutiae of anew, an invigoration by which the possibility of play will come to replace the inevitable, deadening reifications of work. In the overthrow of wage labor, a homecoming would be made possible.

Yet it is precisely the distance between Adorno's present and that utopian future in which ~~work~~ could be known which Adorno's *Minima Moralia* obsessively mourns. We find this in the text's opening dedication which alerts us to the grim declaration that "our perspective of life has passed into an ideology which conceals the fact there is life no longer."[20] He laments this era of capital as one which aims to swallow up all that remains of life, the processes of its growth reaching ever closer toward exhaustion, echoing Mumford's critique of the mine that "life flourishes finally only in an environment of the living." Adorno sees mid-century capitalism's fundamental quandary as one in which "reality debases [life] to an ephemeral appearance of [production]." The utopian undercurrents borne by idle time now mark only a "dim awareness" of a world which could be completely different, a liminal gap through which "reduced and degraded essence tenaciously resists the magic that transforms it into a façade." In this dire situation where "means and end are inverted," he positions the singular hope upon "opposition to production," opposition rooted in hanging on to that life which is not a job despite capital's intentions to make it appear to be so. Only striking out against endless work and developing the utopian element still clinging to its negation can "the monstrosity of absolute production" be kept from triumph, a triumph which we can from our vantage apprehend as the totalizing exhaustion of the Capitalocene.[21]

Marx's famed lines from *The German Ideology* regarding a communistic system of production have in Adorno's analysis found themselves perversely integrated into the capitalist world-system's labor regime. If for Marx, communism's social organization held out the promise of creating a space "where nobody has one exclusive sphere of activity but each can become accomplished in any branch he wishes, society regulates the general production and thus makes it possible for me to do one thing today and another tomorrow," Adorno posits a capitalism which has negatively integrated this vision as its underlying *raison d'être* of expansion.[22] The monstrousness of absolute production arises out of its twinned Gothic precursors, its vampiric drainage of the well of idleness and its Frankensteinian reanimation of this once free time as now in consonance with the time of the workday, an extending and spilling over of the hurried rigors of Taylorist movement and the dull, blank repetitions (repetitions always with a difference engendered by the extension of exhaustion) of the Fordist manufacturing line:

> The haste, nervousness, restlessness observed since the rise of the big cities is now spreading in the manner of an epidemic, as did once the plague and cholera. In the process forces are being unleashed that were undreamed of by the scurrying passer-by of the nineteenth century. Everybody must have projects all the time. The maximum must be extracted from leisure. This is planned, used for undertaking, crammed with visits to every conceivable site or spectacle, or just with the fastest possible locomotion.[23]

Extracting the maximum from leisure ensures that if one now hunts in the morning, fishes in the afternoon, rears cattle in the evening, and criticizes after dinner, each activity becomes infected by what Adorno refers to as "pseudo-activity," the imposition of professionalization on every particular activity, ensuring that even if one is not a hunter, fisherman, herdsman, or critic, they must still perform as if they were, always engaging in the simulated playacting of the production process.[24] If, "the whole of life must look like a job, and by this resemblance conceal what is not yet directly devoted to pecuniary gain," it is in this obstinate resemblance that the monstrosity of absolute production appears.[25] When free time always already wears the mask of productive time the carnivalesque no longer detours but rather prepares for a coming eventuality in which idleness has been excised in lieu of the working day's capitalist utopia, a funhouse reflection of all time as worktime.

Since "nowadays most people kick with the pricks," the pretenses of appearing productive, of the whole life looking like a job, have been trafficked in by capital under the guise of a productive idleness, the work of mass consumption wearing the appearances of the good life.[26] In a capitalist system in which "the dreams have no dreams," the capacity of cultural objects to spirit away the spirit of utopia becomes null.[27] Adorno marks the expurgation of the utopian possibilities of leisure from the predominant strains of Marxism as indicative of its failures to adequately account for the perniciousness of the production process, an imaginary of the world rooted in redistribution of labor's ends but leaving its means firmly intact: "Since Utopia was set aside and the unity of theory and practice demanded, we have become all too practical."[28] This practicality fails to attend to those dreams in which work itself has been abandoned, those visions of a terminal refusal. Instead, "the unity of theory and practice" demonstrates the foreclosure of an imagination once bent toward a kind of jubilee, those radical impulses which would ask not for a longer break from work but which would break with the capitalist form of work altogether. Adorno posits that in fact, no rest has ever been the right one: "The *nostalgie du dimanche* is not a longing for the working week, but for the state of being emancipated from it; Sunday fails to satisfy, not because it is a day off work, but because its own promise is felt directly as unfulfilled; like the English one, every Sunday is too little Sunday."[29] In those idle idylls of the temporary absence from the scene of labor, we acutely recognize our free time as never really having been free, as only ever a brief stopover built into an accumulation cycle synchronized upon our perpetual return to putting idle hands to labor.

III

In the Spring of 1956, five years after the publication of *Minima Moralia*, Gretel Adorno took a series of notes recorded over three weeks of conversation between her husband and Max Horkheimer toward the goal of eventually creating a postwar iteration of *The Communist Manifesto*. In these fragments of conversation, we find Adorno expanding upon these threads he had previously begun to weave amid the fragmented reflection from damaged life, those visions of utopia still alight (however dimly) amid the nightmares of the monster of absolute production. Though the actual text remains unwritten, its possibilities continue to linger as a brief extension and amplification of what *Minima Moralia* did not (or perhaps could not) finish. In this text we can clearly discern how the utopia of ~~work~~ still holds out a promise that neither Adorno nor Horkheimer can seem to either put down or put to use, always just out of grasp somewhere on the horizon line of the commune. Their inability or unwillingness to complete this twentieth-century re-rendering of the manifesto seems to arise from the uncertainty regarding the omnipresent question of what is to be done about the whole of life looking like a job. They do not seem certain if they are waiting for Lefty or Godot.

Adorno returns once again to his critique of a Marxism sans utopia but herein expands it to thought itself as an impossibility without it: "The general stultification of today is the direct result of cutting out utopia. When you reject utopia, thought itself withers away. Thought is killed off in the mere doubling process."[30] He casts utopia as essential, for without it thought remains content with the mere positivistic, the empty, contented of rationalism of what is rather than what is to be: "Renunciation of utopia means somehow or other deciding in favour of a thing even though I know perfectly well that it is a swindle. That is the root of the trouble."[31] Yet once again, Adorno casts the absence of utopian thought as connected to the inability to imagine a world beyond work:

> How does it come about that work is regarded as an absolute? Work exists to control the hardships of life, to ensure the reproduction of mankind. The success of labour stands in a problematic relationship to the effort required. It does not necessarily or certainly reproduce the lives of those who work but only of those who induce others to work for them. In order to persuade human beings to work you have to fob them off with the waffle about work as the thing in itself.[32]

Work guarantees nothing for the exhausted, only for the extractor, and thus the problem of production resides in the treatment of work as its false appearance. When Horkheimer claims that "nowadays there is a false abolition of work," Adorno responds that this false abolition "amounts to production for its own sake," highlighting that all the schemes which promise to lessen the drudgery of labor in fact merely mimic a work increasingly useless to actually reducing the grueling work elsewhere down the production line.[33]

It ultimately, however, falls to Horkheimer to give utterance to the closest thing to an adequate slogan on behalf of utopia *sans* labor that these notes for another manifesto give rise to. After Adorno states that "animals could teach us what happiness is" (a recalling of his reveries upon the communistic idleness of "*rien faire comme une bête*"), Horkheimer issues a response that draws out a thesis which had been underlying so much of Adorno's critiques of production within *Minima Moralia*: "To achieve the condition of an animal at the level of reflection—that is freedom. Freedom means not having to work."[34] The unfreedoms engendered by the production process, all those rigors and restrictions which make the whole of life look like a job, had in *Minima Moralia* lurked in the analytical register which deduced the problem of an extractive labor regime which seeks only to lay waste to what our lives could be; Horkheimer expresses the possible solution, that we can only know freedom through the true abolition of work. Only then could the whole of life look like the good life and freedom come to be encountered. Yet, even so, it would seem the problem of how to explicate this political project, the actual route by which we could come to move once again toward utopia that this collaboration could not expound, for as Adorno states: "We are not proposing any particular course of action. What we want is for people who read what we write to feel the scales falling from their eyes."[35] At last, the clarity of sight granted in ideology critique remains a place to daydream again about what could be attained in the establishment of the commune, but that is only ever the condition of beginning. Actually moving toward that collective freedom of never having to work is another task altogether.

In conversation with Bloch in 1964, nearly a decade since his conversations on the new manifesto with Horkheimer, we once more hear an echo of all that remains unfinished, though now the impetus for seeing the project through falls squarely upon us. We find Adorno reiterating his mourning of the absence of utopian thought, here rooting its missingness in a collective inability to conceptualize the world turned upside down which necessarily relied upon the impermanence of capitalist totality in order to glimpse other worlds in the estrangement from this one: "It seems to me that what people have lost subjectively in regard to consciousness is very simply the capability to imagine the totality as something that could be completely different."[36] However, it is in our shared present moment of the Capitalocene, wherein the "monstrosity of absolute production" arcs toward its own consummate negativity, that an opportunity arises to conceptualize utopia as itself having now become an all too practical unification of theory and practice. When we no longer find that void apposite death in our idleness but rather in our ongoing work, the development of a laborless theory of value offers up an imagining of the totality as something that *must* be completely different. The abolition of work invites us first and foremost to simply stop, to embrace the work of leisure as the work of the general strike which sabotages both the extraction of our time and the extraction of capital's fuel, to let the fields lay fallow and ourselves lay still, to see in one another's refusal of the productive life that is the damaged life the utopia of mimetic inauthenticity that allows us to relearn the temporalities of our repose. We are out of time, but we are not yet exhausted. We know what is to be (un)done. In our here and now, the no-place of no-work found in collective idleness is mere necessity, "the question of the reality or unreality of redemption itself hardly matters."[37] To (re)encounter Adorno from the precarious precipice of our present is to see that no work can be the right one.

6

Life Still Doesn't Live

Adorno's Guide to the Realm of the Dead

Caleb Shaoning Fridell

Capital is dead labour which, vampire-like, lives only by sucking living labour, and lives the more, the more labour it sucks.
—Karl Marx, Capital, 342

Before the eighty-fifth birthday of a man well provided for in every respect, I asked myself in a dream what I could give him to cause him real pleasure, and at once answered my own question: a guide to the realm of the dead.
—Theodor Adorno, *Minima Moralia*, 190

Melancholy Science for a Dying World

Today we're in a time of catastrophe, as succeeding crises reveal a suicidal social system whose own slow death may leave in place structures of domination poised to sepulcher whatever is left of life. Though its legitimacy endures ever more degradation, still the living-dead capitalist order keeps its compulsions, necessities that no longer pretend to be necessary, enforced by ruthless social control to hold all in thrall. Political resistance seems only able to imagine wan appeals to the technocrats administering this prevailing evil, whether to tilt the oceanliner two degrees to the left or keep steering on the rightward path toward the iceberg; only able to muster competing nostalgia for a golden age of capitalism whose material basis no longer exists. The present tendency in the reproduction of capitalist social relations is toward the managed decline of social reproduction—living conditions deteriorate and work is reduced to the precarious performing servile tasks, exposed to deprivation, threatened otherwise to join the unemployed surplus population brutalized by the war machines of repressive state apparatuses. We may imagine that in the tranquility of the future liberated society we can reckon with all the wasted life in these many decades since communism has been possible, that when the shadow of this nightmare is past we can found an impossible archive to document the misery undergone for no reason but that capitalism subordinates the living to the dead, so sacrifices all potential it produces.[1] But the time now calls for more than lament.

The ongoing crisis of capitalism includes and defines particular contemporary crises: the transformation of environment that threatens the planet's habitability; the global wave of protofascist reaction (measured by authoritarian leaders, growth of police power, hardening of rife bigotry) already posing its eugenic logic as solution when denying survival to migrants and refugees; the fragmentation of a working class unable to mount resistance. If Theodor Adorno's *Minima Moralia* is a book for this time, its foremost relevance may be in grasping these distinctive destructive phenomena as bound by the same underlying logic. He understood the normal functioning of capitalist society to be a state of crisis, for its health, measured by economic growth, is maintained by an antagonism producing general unfreedom; "normality is death" because "underlying the prevalent health is death."[2] Once dialectical reason "has recognized the ruling universal order and its proportions as sick . . . then it can see as healing cells only what appears, by the standards of that order, as itself sick, eccentric, paranoia."[3] Though it feeds the caricature of the priggish scold wagging his finger at a debased society heading to hell because Schönberg can no longer be appreciated, Adorno's maxim that only in exaggeration is there truth is aimed at a condition in which images of happiness, desire, and liberation are knotted together with barbarous cruelties too easily disavowed. Judicious realism is deadly complicity. Facing barbarity, for Adorno, means recognizing capitalist society as a totality constituted by objectified social relations even as it mediates all that is individual, or more pithily, "the whole is the false."[4] All artifacts of and actions in society are implicated. Society's universal coherence is based on the general equivalence of the commodity form, which makes labor and its products directly exchangeable, everything with its price.[5] The commodity form's reign depends on a division of labor that "produces and reproduces itself precisely from the interconnection of the antagonistic interests of its members."[6] Reciprocal parts in apparent opposition reinforce the whole; individuals formed as objects of social domination as subjects reproduce domination, identifying with the means of subjection. "The world is systematized horror," yet "its unifying principle is division."[7] This dialectic between whole and individual guides all of

Adorno's thought, which must therefore always conclude that possibility of life depends on abolition of the whole, though that horizon seemed to him to be receding.

Adorno's characteristic deictic motif that today, now, these days, all is worse than ever—the thrust summarized by the aphorism title "Downwards, ever downwards"—doesn't imply that degradation of life is worsening (how could this be after the Shoah?) but that the probability of transforming the conditions that produced Auschwitz and could again dwindles. With the growth of capitalism as an integral organic system, its imperatives increasingly become the only rule. "Society, if it is understood as the functional context of human self-preservation," Adorno writes, should mean "that it aims objectively at a reproduction of its life which is consonant with the state of its powers."[8] That society manifestly does not, that it leaves hungry those it could feed with the overabundant food it would rather let rot, reveals the truth of its self-preservation. Only the modes of existence that sustain the system are themselves sustained. The economic order "renders the majority of people dependent upon conditions beyond their control," only able to live by submitting "themselves to the given conditions . . . they can preserve themselves only if they renounce their self."[9] That is, society has nothing to do with offering collective material security necessary for autonomous self-development, rather creating conditions in which people cannot but consciously and unconsciously adapt to capitalist imperatives.[10] "The necessity of such adaptation, of identification with the given, the status quo, with power as such, creates the potential for totalitarianism,"[11] or in other words, "the context which perpetuates life simultaneously destroys it."[12]

The following three sections of this chapter take one at a time the life-destructive forces of fascist calamity, proletarian labor, and domination of nature studied in *Minima Moralia*, showing Adorno's treatment of each to belong to his critique of capitalism, namely, the critique of the totalizing social mediation that characterizes commodity-producing society. The subsequent section presents his conception of self-preservation as the fate of the individual so dominated. Although Adorno's Marxist credentials have been alike disputed by those who would rescue him from such tarnishing ignominy and those who would kick him out of the club, this chapter will try to show his thought to be indispensable for the living Marxist tradition that carries on a legacy of emancipatory ideas and action by putting its own concepts into question. A definite political program is assuredly not to be found in the pages of *Minima Moralia*, but the last section of this chapter nevertheless attempts an answer to the question that waits to pounce at the close of every theoretical exertion, an address to the specter that lingers impatiently all the while. If Adorno doesn't tell us what is to be done, the consummate negativity of his work might offer the light "shed on the world by redemption," by which we can judge the effort to abolish social relations constitutive of capitalism.[13] "I do not believe that things will turn out well," Horkheimer tells Adorno in their desultory conversations planning a new manifesto for communism that lapsed into quietism. "But the idea that they might is of decisive importance."[14]

After the Avalanche

Minima Moralia's third part begins with an epigraph from Baudelaire, borrowing from the end of "Le Goût du Néant" a plangent call for the avalanche to take the poet with its fall. Avalanche, veux-tu m'emporter dans ta chute? The poem belongs to the first cycle of *Les Fleurs du Mal* called Spleen et Idéal, representing the former, the spleen Walter Benjamin describes as "that fatally foundering, doomed flight toward the ideal, which—with the despairing cry of Icarus—comes crashing down into the ocean of its own melancholy."[15] And the poem does find its speaker taking flight just before apostrophizing the avalanche, seeing the round globe from above and finding no hut for shelter;[16] from splenetic heights, the melancholic recognizes that "time is reified," so is left to grasp at "the scattered fragments of genuine historical experience," tempting glimpses of the ideal illuminated precisely by his melancholy.[17] Then with the avalanche he falls. But the memory of times lost bears pathos because of the reified time its retrieval opposes—revenge against the loss of history.

The theme of subjective surrender to an overwhelming objective tendency, and the consequent stakes of political resistance, struck Adorno as Benjamin's bequest to dialectical thought. In their famous correspondence over the preparation of a draft for publication in the *Zeitschrift für Sozialforschung*, stringent arguments over Baudelaire to clarify this analysis (Adorno admits to "insistent carping") jar with anxious reports on pogroms and looming war.[18] Benjamin sends "heartfelt and elegiac greetings from a part of the world that seems to be falling apart," feeling "entirely surrounded by fascism" in Paris, to Adorno, escaped to New York and unable to help Benjamin follow.[19] Brief reminders of the catastrophic present seem to intrude on their critical immersion in the dreamworld of late-nineteenth-century lyric poetry until Benjamin's emigration overtakes all other concerns, but the theoretical dispute at the heart of their exchange was intimately related to an analysis of their present. Adorno writes of the connection between the "tendency to transfigure capitalist alienation into 'sense'" he sometimes sees in Benjamin's writing and fathoming the most symptomatic spectacle in Barcelona after Franco's victory and in Vienna after the Anschluss: "the masses who now rejoiced in the fascist conquerors were the very same which had rejoiced in the opponents of the fascists only the day before."[20] At stake in the theoretical understanding of the commodity form was an understanding of calamity.

Where Benjamin had broken ground on an understanding of commodity fetishism, Adorno thought, his excursions to "the crossroad of magic and positivism" threatened to obscure the essential insight.[21] Representative of magic was Benjamin's phrase about every epoch dreaming its next, of positivism were moments when he linked superstructural aspects of Baudelaire's work to an economic base through a kind of mechanical determinism. Both the idealism and vulgar materialism were untrue to the advancement of Marxist dialectics Adorno felt to be their shared project, which would understand that "materialist determination of cultural traits is only possible if it is mediated through the total social process."[22] Such hermeneutics of the commodity form in culture develops Marx's theory that the "expression of equivalence between different sorts of commodities... brings to view the specific character of value-creating labour," so revealing the basic organizing principle of the capitalist social formation in full.[23] Commodity fetishism should therefore be recognized as an "objective historico-philosophical category rather than as a 'vision' on the part of social characters," as Adorno reprimanded Benjamin, and magical imagery serves "only to divert attention from true objectivity and its correlate, alienated subjectivity," while concealing class distinctions.[24]

Benjamin himself recognized that those who see human learning tending toward progressive enlightenment and proclaim the hope of humanity find themselves helpless confronted by growing fascist spectacles, by the same crowds who had opposed them now cheering for Franco or Hitler. As long as the structural features that organize society make meaningless any notion of human nature, the individual conscience of its members will not explain anything. When the progress of history leads to fascism, its opponents can only be amazed "that the things we are experiencing are 'still' possible in the twentieth century," having not recognized that they too were marching along toward the catastrophe all the while.[25] Their theory of progress was an empathy for victors; historical consciousness that would escape the ruse of reason must take the standpoint of the vanquished and anonymous, for knowledge whose subject is "the struggling, oppressed class itself."[26] Inability to do so forestalls the necessary revolution, for, Benjamin writes, "nothing has so corrupted the German working class as the notion that it was moving with the current."[27] Adorno picks up Benjamin's critique of the materialist thought that aligns itself with "the laws of historical movement" and "awaits salvation from stage-by-stage progression" of capitalism developing toward socialism. Practicing the worthy method of immanent critique, thought lured by belief in progress identifies itself entirely with the logic of that which it would overcome. When "everything is subsumed under the principal economic phases and their development," belief that the engines of economic growth will make possible eventual liberation forgets, reminds Adorno, that "the calamity is brought about precisely by the stringency of such development."[28] Calamity names the objective trend of economic reason that overwhelms subjective capacity.[29] The sense might again be summarized by Baudelaire's poem, as time engulfs the poet minute by minute like immense snow does a stiffening corpse, and he calls out for the avalanche to cover him, as well.[30]

"Avalanche" is the title of a précis of fascism's electoral victory among the concluding notes and sketches of *Dialectic of Enlightenment*. The motion of the avalanche describes the rise of Hitler's vote, but it still cascades after fascism's apparent defeat as long as the inertial "present time is without turning points ... when, as today, calamity is at its height." As a few results came in from select districts "on the evening of the prefascist election day," small samples, "an eighth, a sixteenth of the votes already anticipated the whole."[31] That the fraction can readily herald the nation's fate reveals the depth of conformist menace that the organization of society poses to its members. To have to vote against anti-Semitism on the ballot is already barbarous; it means to be "absorbed into the preconditioned reflexes of the subjectless exponents of a particular standpoint," into the mechanism that turns all political positions into clichés removed from experience, to adapt to the reproduction of illusion through these means.[32] The mechanism of electoral politics gives to voters a false choice representative of dominant interests, then announces consent to domination. Each person casting a vote that day did not harbor special intolerance against Jews, but the will of the people was eventually identified with a program of mass murder. So Adorno considered "the survival of National Socialism within democracy to be potentially more menacing than the survival of fascist tendencies against democracy"—as long as according to capitalist imperatives it's necessary to mobilize "hundreds of millions of people for goals they cannot immediately identify as their own," drumming the leaden slogans of nationalism en marche to electoral victory is still "the most effective means of motivating people to insist on conditions that are, viewed objectively, obsolete."[33]

Again, the calamity is the fact of that necessity, the preservation of capitalism's fundamental social relations, and persists as long as the political-economic order ensures most people are unable to control their lives. In this view, fascism was not an unprecedented rupture into Europe's political history but defended the status quo when parliamentary democracy could no longer against the opportunity for transformation—an exceptional state to protect the rule. It was a contingent political formation that would grow into a monstrous evil, whose ideology was able to displace and absorb anticapitalist sentiment into a project of expanding capital accumulation while crushing its egalitarian opposition. In its German uniform, fascism promised a national unity that meant the economic unification of a contradictory social formation, through the creation of a state that would renew growth by combining the two factors Adorno emphasized: monopoly concentration of capital and catch-up imperial conquest. So was the Fatherland to be saved, in the massively deluded effort to recover dignity in competition against the imperialist powers who had humiliated Germany in the last war; the effort "bore from the first moment the expression of catastrophe that was rehearsed in the concentration camps while the triumphs in the streets drowned all forebodings."[34]

The mass psychology of fascism that induced unwavering dedication to the doomed venture and drowned forebodings was the means by which the avalanche continued its course.[35] Its enchantment had this trick: as long as the dominion of capital seems absolute, though its power derives from passive compliance, agency seems to exist only in kicking with the pricks. People took up as their own the logic of the totality National Socialism was to realize, which meant "equation of the dissimilar, whether it be the 'deviationist' or the members of a different race, with the opponent."[36] Persecution that bonded group cohesion identified many targets, but it was the anti-Semitic construction of the Jewish figure as eternal enemy that revealed the logic of fascist ideology for Adorno. Against the conception of anti-Semitism as an unfortunate holdover from ancient history, an unpleasant anachronism in modern life, Adorno argues that anti-Semitism is a thoroughly modern phenomenon with complex psychological investments.

In Nazi propaganda, Jewish people were at once identified with abstract financial capital suffocating the productive life of the social body, and with images of liberation that authoritarian rule must negate: "happiness without power, reward without work, a homeland without frontiers, religion without myth."[37] The propaganda relied on an opposition between productive and non-productive capital to excuse and distract from economic crisis. Attributed only to the Jew is "the economic injustice of the whole class" of expropriators, whose exploitation of the production process is covered by the "socially necessary illusion" that the "circulation sphere is responsible for exploitation."[38] Rebellion against domination is then placed at the service of domination. Born supposedly from popular revolt against liberal-bourgeois capitalism, "absurdly, the Fascist regimes of the first half of the twentieth century have stabilized an obsolete economic form, multiplying the terror needed to maintain it now that its senselessness is blatant."[39]

Adorno writes that a doomed sense of fate haunted from the beginning German imperialism under the Nazi regime, the march to self-annihilation evident in the desperate last days. "When no way out is left, the destructive drive becomes entirely indifferent to the question it never posed quite clearly: whether it is directed against others or against its own subject."[40] When the conditions produced by objectified human relations are received as fate, the only option seems to be following the course to its fatal end. There's a precise analogy in Marx's description of how capitalism cannot by its internal dynamics regulate despoliation of available resources. From the perspective of capital, "it is self-evident that the worker is nothing other than labour-power for the duration of his whole life, and that therefore all his disposable time is by nature and by right labour-time, to be devoted to the self-valorization of capital."[41] Following only the logic of surplus-value extraction, capital works its labor-power inputs to hasty death, taking "no account of the health and the length of life of the worker." Though knowing this movement will lead to collective ruin just as surely "as by the probable fall of the earth into the sun," yet unbothered so long as they are convinced the fall will come too late to matter for them, the "watchword of every capitalist and of every capitalist nation" is: Après moi, le déluge![42]

Where Is the Proletariat?

But Marx is careful to note that the secular tendency toward collective ruin "does not depend on the will, either good or bad, of the individual capitalist. Under free competition, the immanent laws of capitalist production confront the individual capitalist as a coercive force external to him."[43] The capitalist and worker play their roles wearing "character-masks," in Marx's phrase, under a compulsion that Adorno with Horkheimer argues in late capitalism becomes internal as well as external: "the economic mask coincides exactly with what lies beneath it, even in its smallest wrinkles. All are worth as much as they earn... They know themselves as nothing else."[44] Complete identification has the paradoxical effect, as Adorno furthers the argument, that "despite a historical development that has reached the point of oligarchy, the workers are less and less aware that they are such." This "grimly comic riddle" pondered by sociologists—"where is the proletariat?"—contains the question about why fascism's fetishized revolt against capitalism replaced the workers' revolution that was supposed to be inevitable in a country so developed as Germany.[45] It needs to be posed correctly.

Proletarians are defined by dispossession: separated from means of production, they can only reproduce their own lives by selling labor-power as a commodity, thus reproducing capital. They are victims of what Marx calls artificially produced poverty, as their any other means of subsistence but market dependence are destroyed. What makes the proletariat a potentially revolutionary class, then, is that this "wrong it suffers is not a particular wrong but wrong in general": that is, their dispossession is the precondition for the fundamental social relations constitutive of capitalist production. The revolutionary proletariat cannot emancipate itself without ending the regime of value-creating wage labor, thereby emancipating all; their self-abolition [Aufhebung] delivers the classless society. They "no longer lay claim to a historical title, but merely to a human one"—rather than a "one-sided opposition" to unequal distribution with demands for better compensation as proletarians, they stand in "all-sided opposition" to the very premises of the capitalist system.[46]

But the ideology that would come to see in proletarian revolutionary potential an automatic necessity was not always true to Marx's original formulations, which emphasized an objective and subjective side to class formation. While separate individuals are objectively subsumed under their class based on "conditions of existence predestined," they "form a class only insofar as they have to carry on a common battle against another class; otherwise, they are on hostile terms with each other as competitors."[47] Adorno concludes that in late capitalism—defined by automated machinery of large industry, monopoly concentration of capital, and total administration—the latter hostile competition prevails to undermine class formation. His analysis focuses on the decline of the bourgeoisie as the class antagonistic to the proletariat. Though late industrial society is "seamed with class distinctions," its members are "encompassed by the total structure, which first reduces the individual subjects to mere moments, in order then to unite them, impotent and discrete, in the collective." Therefore, "producers no more function as subjects than do their workers and consumers, but merely as components in a self-regulating machinery."[48] While in past liberal capitalism self-possessed bourgeois owners asserted arrogant personal control over production, under the petrifying compulsion of "anonymous laws," it is the "signature of our age that no-one, without exception, can now determine his own life within even a moderately comprehensible framework."[49]

Adorno names this development with Marx's terminology as the growing organic composition of capital: the increasing ratio of constant capital (machinery, fixed means of production) to variable capital (expenditure of labor-power)—a distinction between dead and living contributions to commodity production. In progressively automated production, humans, still categorically necessary to valorize capital, serve specialized functions; the technical process "designates subjects more and more exclusively as partial moments in the network of material production."[50] Adorno's "partial moments" [Teilmomente] intensifies Marx's frequent use of "moments" to introduce a temporal description of elements in the moving system; Adorno emphasizes that those subjected to the integration of society bear no subjective agency as only representations of labor time expenditure, as partial moments in the huge, alienated machine network that encompasses and constitutes people as parts for its self-sustaining growth.[51] If the machinery of constant capital represents accumulated human labor put toward increasing technical proficiency and capacity, it should promise liberation from work. Of course, "this immanently socialist element in progress has been travestied under late industrialism," as the "technical forces [that] might permit a condition free of privileges" lead instead to "an egalitarian threat."[52] All can be replaced, and fewer interchangeable workers necessary means those made expendable serve as a surplus reserve army to keep labor disciplined and precarious. So the incongruity noted by Marx: "the most developed machinery thus forces the worker to work longer than the savage does, or than he himself did with the simplest, crudest tools."[53]

Crucial to understand the relentless compulsion for labor is the tendential rule that the greater the development of constant capital, "the more does the continuity of the production process . . . become an externally compelling condition for the mode of production founded on capital." For "capital itself is the moving contradiction, [in] that it presses to reduce labour time to a minimum, while it posits labour time, on the other side, as sole measure and source of wealth."[54] In other words, if the immanently socialist element of reducing need for labor is still to serve private capitalist interests, profit-seeking production must continually expand to absorb more surplus labor. Swollen production for its own sake, having met existing needs, obliges new demands for consumption to be contrived, new markets to be discovered—as long as it grows. Adorno's close friend Alfred Sohn-Rethel identifies this tendency as a decisive factor in the rise of historical fascism, which offered capitalist firms the state's strong hand to keep a high level of production profitable and maintain social control over the surplus population.[55] Against the communist alternative, at least fascist repression keeps the gears grinding. Besides novel political-economic arrangements, a new subjective reason evolves to justify profitability. Adorno describes the mean self-sacrificing struggle to conserve bourgeois forms of existence: "Now objectively threatened, the subjectivity of the rulers and their hangers-on becomes totally inhuman. So the class realizes itself, taking upon itself the destructive will of the course of the world. The bourgeois live on like spectres threatening doom."[56] Old bourgeois virtues developed during a comfortable tide of profits spoil when their economic precondition falls away, to mutate into a new work ethic; the old "ruling class disdained to earn money other than by privilege or control of production," the new pretend to get their hands dirty too as self-making entrepreneurs, proving that the moral worth indexed by their bank accounts is only won by hard work. A certain democracy between ruling clique and subject class is then established, if merely the "democracy of the earnings-principle," to justify the persistence of generalized competition through market relations when the elimination of scarcity under a reorganized concept of work is technically possible.[57]

The sociologist searching for an amber image of the proletariat is deceived by the apparently fluid subjective class membership that marks bourgeois decline. But structural inequalities are as rigid as ever; "perpetuation of the real difference between upper and lower strata is assisted by the progressive disappearance of differences in the mode of consciousness between the two."[58] The central fact that capitalist wealth consists in the privilege of controlling other people's work—appearing as the concentrated ownership of the means of production by the few—is obscure to a sociologist gazing at modern life's complex dynamics, not usually reducible to the exploitation of a worker by his boss (his: rapid transformation of gender relations in the last decades also frustrates the search for a "proletariat" understood as a synonym for a group of roughneck men). The growing organic composition of capital produces a shrinking value-producing working class and the fragmentation of other proletarians into dispersed offices at the service of capital, if not into the position of a population surplus to the needs of capital's valorization and maintenance, therefore to be treated as scum. The vast difference in power and influence between the owning and working classes has survived this apparent transcendence of class society, which Adorno called a parody of classless society; so have the ratcheted compulsions to productivity survived the disintegration of the capitalist workplace from its old consolidated centers. The new spirit of capitalism offers a parody of freedom as well, giving workers, encouraged not to think of themselves as such, the flexibility to devote ever more of their time to atomized, meaningless activity. Marx had hoped that capitalist crisis, when it struck them hardest, would revolutionize proletarians already teamed together in factories, able collectively to see the fundamental injustice of the system when unable to satisfy needs through commodity exchange even though, if the products of their labor were to be shared equally, there would be no crisis at all. But when large groups of workers are no longer so conveniently gathered and their labor is no longer so straightforwardly necessary for social reproduction, the contingent formation of proletarians as a class able to upend the social relations fundamental to capitalism by recognizing a common enemy of expropriators to be expropriated demands new resources of imaginative class struggle.

In Adorno's analysis, the "decay of the workers' movement" stemmed precisely from an inability to reckon with the diffuse antagonism brought about by "the immovable consolidation of the capitalist world." The official proletariat still beholden to the Soviet party line, he writes, is "more and more becoming a mere reflection of the tendencies of capitalist development."[59] As long as the working class identifies with the historical title, to return to Marx's distinction, they cannot claim the human one. If they advocate as working class for a greater share of profits generated by existing production, the horizon of emancipation is lost, for to presume only ever to be a working class means to be "less aware that they are such," in Adorno's phrase—less aware that the position of the proletariat in the capitalist order could with organization bring about the end of the capitalist world. Where is the proletariat? For Adorno prevailing identification with the economic mask only affirms present tendencies of capitalist production and adherence to worn working-class dogma has only led to the integration of an official working class in collusion with the capitalist state. "Philosophy cannot realize itself without the transcendence [Aufhebung] of the proletariat, and the proletariat cannot transcend itself without the realization [Verwirklichung] of philosophy," writes Marx;[60] but "the moment to realize it was missed," writes Adorno.[61]

Caught Together, Hung Together

Adorno frequently figured the near-impossibility of transforming society organized "under the primacy of the autonomous production process" with the image of being caught in a web or net.[62] "One can speak of the claustrophobia of humanity in the administered world, of a feeling of being incarcerated in a thoroughly societalized, closely woven, netlike environment. The denser the weave, the more one wants to escape it, whereas it is precisely its close weave that prevents any escape."[63] The image may have been borrowed from Marx, who wrote that "the division of labour is an organization of production [Produktionsorganismus] which has grown naturally, a web which has been, and continues to be, woven behind the backs of the producers of commodities."[64] The word "naturally" expresses the central contradiction: capitalist production that mediates social metabolic interchange with nature itself develops not according to human intention but as if following natural laws. Autonomous production exists as "second nature," humanity having overcome domination from the first only by instituting a new structure of imperious domination. There's a subterranean recognition of this fact, writes Adorno, "a universal feeling, a universal fear, that our progress in controlling nature may increasingly help to weave the very calamity it is supposed to protect us from, that it may be weaving that second nature into which society has rankly grown."[65]

Marx's description of the web of labor woven behind the backs of producers points to the necessarily haphazard, spontaneous social order built through a tangle of market relationships. Producers make scattered decisions about what they imagine will be socially useful commodities to direct private labor that must manifest as directly social labor. Earth in its original state is the "universal material [allgemeine Gegenstand] for human labour"—all labor, if it isn't involved in direct extraction or appropriation from the earth, uses raw material filtered through a previous labor process of extraction.[66] Need for metabolic interaction between humans and nature will shape every society, but mediation of all such interchange by a form of labor whose measurement by duration is expressed in the value of commodities is historically specific to capitalist society. Yet those characteristics, Marx writes, "belonging to a social formation in which the process of production has mastery over man, instead of the opposite, appear to the political economists' bourgeois consciousness to be as much a self-evident and nature-imposed necessity as productive labor itself."[67] Essential processes of extraction from nature will never be consciously regulated, with devastating consequence, as long as humans remain spellbound, dominated by their own activity. The fetishism inherent to the socialization (Vergesellschaftung) of labor represented by money in commodity markets has a special significance for Adorno's critique of the domination of nature.

In the aphorism "Toy Shop," he quotes from Hebbel's diary reminiscence of boyhood play innocent of adult reality. The child, whose idol may still be the garbage collector, imagines all the adult occupations his figurines pantomime done "for the joy of doing so." From the childsick perspective, that we know the true reason for it all tastes bitter, "namely earning a living, which commandeers all those activities as mere means, reduces them to interchangeable, abstract labour-time. The quality of things ceases to be their essence and becomes the accidental appearance of their value." Children in play side "with use-value against exchange value" as "unconsciously they rehearse the right life" among their toy simulacra "not ensnared" by the commodity world. But their subterfuge purposeless activity can exist only in the sandbox; "under universal compulsion," to be "colorful and useful at once" cannot be reconciled.[68] The same fantasy in adults who imagine themselves to follow their own untrodden path looks pathetic, for "the individual owes his crystallization to the forms of political economy" and "even as the opponent of the pressure of socialization he remains the latter's most particular product and its likeness."[69] Such individuality is only a reaction formation to imbrication in the social weave.[70] Yet "the more tightly the world is enclosed by the net of man-made things, the more stridently those who are responsible for this condition proclaim their natural primitiveness." Against the background of industrial mass-production, they strive to be non-reproducible: that is, genuine. "But like gold, genuineness . . . becomes a fetish. Both are treated as if they were the foundation, which in reality is a social relation, while gold and genuineness precisely only express the fungibility, the comparability of things; it is they that are not in-themselves, but for-others."[71]

So can nature, existing to be appropriated under prevailing exchange relations, never be treated as Hebbel's child does his play objects—never appreciated qualitatively, according to its own self-determination. Nature in itself can only be thought of as that "amorphous thing under the net that society has woven over the whole of nature," for "the webbing is so thick and dense that remembrance of nature's uncovered state seems childish, sentimental."[72] Yet Adorno has a soft spot for animals, who "existing without any purpose to men" may too rehearse the right life when they hold out names that cannot be exchanged: "I am a rhinoceros, signifies the shape of the rhinoceros." He even suggests that to banish childish critter sympathy can lead to grievous error: "The relation of children to animals depends entirely on the fact that Utopia goes disguised in the creatures whom Marx even begrudged the surplus value they contribute as workers."[73] The rather cryptic remark receives some elaboration in a late lecture. Adorno mentions that to begrudge animals surplus-value production though their "costs of reproduction are lower than the time or energy expended" is "merely the crassest symbol" of a Marxian logic that seeks to overthrow domination between people without changing unconditional domination of nature, "so that we might say that the image of a classless society in Marx has something of the quality of a gigantic joint-stock company for the exploitation of nature."[74] Adorno is mistaken about Marx's theory of value, which grasps the immanent logic of the capitalist system; animals like machinery are considered as fixed capital incapable of generating surplus value not for being subjectively inferior to humans, but because they are not, like humans, paid a wage. But Adorno's real target, as often is the case with his gnomic asides, is the Soviet Union whose ruthless exploitation of nature to compete with Western powers in economic development he thought self-defeating and worse. The Bolsheviks, true to Marx or not, transformed the world but allowed transformation to follow blindly its own course of domination. Therefore must domination of nature be thought together with the lattice of domination among humans, cautions Adorno, in imagining a "seriously liberated vision of society . . . if it is not constantly to reproduce itself in the internal forms of society."[75]

Self-preservation unto Death

Avalanche, machinery, and web—the metonymies in which his understanding of fascist political triumph, late capitalist social organization, and domination of nature crystallize are the signposts of Adorno's guide to the realm of the dead. All three report the calamity of a social totality propelled onward by a dynamic beyond human intention; like the "gigantic images" of blockbuster films symptomatic of terrors from the "monstrous total State," perhaps, Adorno's critical concepts attempt recognition of "what defies all experience."[76] The signposts trace a connected path. When mastery over nature consolidates into an inescapable quasi-natural structure of domination, "society perpetuates the threat from nature as the permanent, organized compulsion which, reproducing itself in individuals as systematic self-preservation, rebounds against nature as society's control over it."[77] If self-preservation formerly meant bare survival in a war against all, now it means adaptation to the total compulsion of production. It means for humans to "make common cause with the world against themselves, and the most alienated condition of all, the omnipresence of commodities, their own conversion into appendages of machinery, is for them a mirage of closeness."[78] Once the production process characterized by an organized system of machinery generates its own automatic logic of self-expansion, extreme forms of political repression, like historical fascism, will multiply the terror needed to maintain capital accumulation. And self-preservation then, already having yoked humans as appendages to machinery, will also take its most extreme form in joining the drive toward destruction. In short, "life has become the ideology of its own absence."[79]

With the aphorism "Novissimum organum" Adorno elaborates his concept of self-preservation.[80] It begins with the long-demonstrated principle that wage labor has formed the modern masses and created the workers, who more than their biological bases are a "reflection of the social process," as "mere agents of the law of value." Adorno's analogy is that the "organic composition of man is growing" in correspondence with the organic composition of capital. Just as the latter signifies "dead" material processes following an independent logic that excludes the living concerns of the human, likewise within the individual dead elements rule over the living; determination of subjects as "means of production" marginalizes their "living purposes." But it's a mistake to call this the "mechanization of man," Adorno writes (refusing the easy characterization often ascribed to him), because that supposes the human to be "something static" acted upon and deformed by external influences. The "deformation is not a sickness in men but in the society," as there's no substratum of true human nature beneath some distortion of society.[81] Rather, commodification of labor-power as the prevailing social relation into which all are born turns out people in its image—objectifies "each of their impulses as formally commensurable variations of the exchange relationship." This "real subsumption," to call it by another name, in which what seems to be deepest human nature conforms from the beginning to the division of labor, is the necessary condition for capitalist life to reproduce itself. Again Adorno resorts to his customary chiasmus: "The will to live"—self-preservation molded by capital's will for self-reproduction—"finds itself dependent on the denial of the will to live"—of free will for subjective human life.[82]

It's important too that the verdict doesn't narrowly apply to factory workers whose tasks, having once been performed start to finish as a meaningful whole, are divided into segments, separated into narrow spheres of repetitive activity. The wrong these exemplary workers suffer represents the general wrong encompassing society. Adorno quotes Georg Lukács to demonstrate the reified consciousness of those who imagine themselves exempt, like the journalists selling opinions: "precisely subjectivity itself, knowledge, temperament and powers of expression," having been sold as commodity are in the same way "reduced to an abstract mechanism functioning autonomously and divorced both from the personality of their 'owner.'"[83] Everyone must earn and exchange money to survive, so under its fetish the predominant master morality, disobeyed at peril, exhorts blind self-interest. The successful feel they accomplish all on their own, "as a self, what the objective spirit, the truly irrational predestination of a society held together by brutal economic inequality, intends," while "social witchcraft inescapably turns him who does not play the game into a self-seeker."[84] Human effort at self-preservation under the prevailing capital form of social relations—the best attempt by humans to adapt themselves to their social world—refers only to the reproduction of capital while denying the possibility of a self at all. "Self-preservation annuls all life in subjectivity," or, "self-preservation forfeits its self."[85]

What seems most natural under these conditions, the supposedly instinctive reflexes tellingly called mechanical, reflects social objectification. With the "transition from firm characteristics to push-button behaviour-patterns," the more immediate the response, the "more deeply in reality mediation has advanced: in the prompt, unresistant reflexes the subject is entirely extinguished." The division of labor having established "the person as a measuring instrument deployed and calibrated by a central authority," ready to kick whenever their knee is tapped, becomes the "anthropological pre-condition of all totalitarian mass-movements." So violence from masses should be understood not as an outburst of primitive human nature, nor only as a misplaced reaction against an oppressive social system, but as the fullest expression of that social system. The destructive tendencies which found terrifying voluntarist expression under National Socialism, Adorno writes, "are not so much death-wishes as manifestations of what they have already become. They murder so that whatever to them seems living, shall resemble themselves."[86] The evil unleashed was never truly overcome. The callous attitude toward death still ascendant confirms as much, for Adorno: "What the National Socialists perpetrated against millions of people, the parading and patterning of the living like dead matter, then the mass-production and cost-cutting of death, threw its prefiguring shadow on those who felt moved to chortle over corpses. What is decisive is the absorption of biological destruction by conscious social will."[87]

Join the Inhuman Club

An ongoing absorption of biological destruction by conscious social will––what is to be done with such a morbid diagnosis? To an audience for his lectures on moral philosophy whom Adorno presumes came to hear the author of *Minima Moralia*, having anatomized the bad life, tell them now how to live a good one, he's not gentle: "So if I am going to throw stones at your heads, if you will allow the expression, it will be better if I say so at the outset than for me to leave you under the illusion that I am distributing bread."[88] Although there exists "the legitimate duty to provide bread, not stones" when people still, despite the real possibility otherwise, go hungry, the "illegitimate conviction that there must be bread because it must be" nourishes only self-defeat.[89] Unlike life-philosophers who pretend to liberate listeners while freeing them only from the possibility of recognizing their imprisonment, Adorno can hand out no hope for humanity. Nor would he join a humanist club, but he might join the "inhuman union."[90] For the positive expression already supposes an existent humanity that acts, with better or worse judgment, as a coherent self-determining subject; the negative sticks to assailing what it knows, the forms of domination that integrate social totality and breed inhumanity. But while refusing to join the parade cheering on humanity, the inhuman club must take care, in order to unsettle both virtuous postures, to reject further the pessimism that, "in open agreement or under crocodile tears, will prophesy dominion an infinite future, for as long as any organized society exists."[91]

In the foreword to *Minima Moralia*, Adorno writes that under dire necessity "part of the social force of liberation may have temporarily withdrawn to the individual sphere" despite its falsity.[92] It was to be more than temporary.[93] His political commitment for the rest of his life was to be shaped by the effort to salvage from the individual sphere what disobeys totality and promises a fleeting glimpse of liberation, especially art that attests to the possibility of something else "as the plenipotentiary of what is free from domination . . . no longer distorted by exchange, profit, and the false needs of a degraded humanity."[94] He believed that no delivery from class society would naturally arise from its own creations, from a class that could fulfill its own needs only through self-abolition. For the most ready means of self-preservation for the individual proletarian are those that preserve capitalist social relations; their needs "are oriented toward a fulfillment which at the same time betrays them precisely of this fulfillment."[95] To become a gravedigger would have to be a conscious insubordinate act, so

> a cathartic method with a standard other than successful adaptation and economic success would have to aim at bringing people to a consciousness of unhappiness both general and—inseparable from it—personal, and at depriving them of the illusory gratifications by which the abominable order keeps a second hold on life inside them, as if it did not already have them firmly enough in its power from outside.[96]

Unable to see any viable mass political strategy, Adorno strove with a pedagogical method to break down the individual self-preservation by which the whole is reproduced: raising consciousness into unhappiness while decrying the lures of compensatory direct action, for such "pseudo-activity is an insurance, the expression of a readiness for self-surrender, in which one senses the only guarantee of self-preservation."[97]

In a moving passage, Adorno describes what, contrarily, real solidarity capable of facing the calamitous present looked like:

> It was manifested by groups of people who together put their lives at stake, counting their own concerns as less important in face of a tangible possibility, so that, without being possessed by an abstract idea, but also without individual hope, they were ready to sacrifice themselves for each other. The prerequisites for this waiving of self-preservation were knowledge and freedom of decision: if they are lacking, blind particular interest immediately reasserts itself.[98]

The class formation necessary for abolishing the proletarian condition cannot be based on narrow identity as proletarians, but may be based on class-transcending non-identity that aims at the emancipation of all through collective "self-production of the living," which, by transcending atomized methods of self-reproduction, allows for the truly free development of the individual.[99] By real satisfaction of human needs, not by forceful imposition of an abstract scheme for a blueprint utopia, will we be emancipated. "There is tenderness only in the coarsest demand: that no-one shall go hungry any more." Keeping faith to coarse demands dodges spurious divination of real needs from those invented to sustain reckless growth of production in general, its penetration into every private recess, which leads society "storming under a confused compulsion to the conquest of strange stars."[100] Those knots can't be untangled in this world, but may fall undone in the next.

He couldn't have known with what disturbing resonances we hear today his account of nature avenging itself on a humanity forgetful of it even as society's control over it rebounds against nature—today when every hurricane or wildfire whose likelihood global heating has intensified seems like a vindictive judgment on the failure to free ourselves from hypertrophied repressive apparatuses that maintain the catastrophic way of things. He grasped the solution with equal indirect prescience: the "forms of humanity's own global societal constitution threaten its life if a self-conscious global subject does not develop and intervene," as "the possibility of progress, of averting the most extreme, total disaster, has migrated to this global subject alone."[101] Climate change threatens the possible conditions of life on earth, and its increase will pressure-cook every tension and contradiction of a political-economic global order whose immense repressive forces work to exclude all possibility of necessary transformation. The obsolete system whose imperatives drive the extraction and burning of fossil fuel according to a logic detached from human need, this "all-embracing constitution which virtually no longer needs its members," will face immense stress.[102] Just as historical fascism, according to Adorno, thrived on a compromised capitalist system's desperate struggle for survival by multiplying the terror necessary to preserve the old regime, so can we see harbingers of the authoritarians' plan to weather the coming storm in the practices of revanchist governments today—in the assertion of control over the movement of people seeking refuge and over the distribution of resources. The emergence, against all arrayed forces, of a global subject self-conscious of how the present arrangement threatens life everywhere, capable of winning an alternative world of and for everyone, seems impossible to imagine, too large and vague a hope. But to take one step at a time in the right direction, to follow the coarsest demand, that no one go hungry, may show the way out of the realm of dead, to begin life.

Acknowledgments

I'm grateful to Caren Irr for convening a symposium on the occasion of *Minima Moralia*'s fiftieth anniversary, and for making possible this collection. And I would like to thank Katharina Menschick for help with German and everything more. This chapter is one-half of a conversation with you.

Part IV

Adorno's Ecology

7

Adorno and Animality after Auschwitz

Andrea Dara Cooper

In this essay, I read Adorno's *Minima Moralia* through the lens of animality, illustrating the resonance of his work with contemporary political, ecological, and ethical crises. Many of his aphorisms show that human self-conception is bound up in how we perceive one another across and through species lines. As Adorno observes, identifying the human with the animal is essential to the antisemitic program, and the racialized thinking that inflicts the trope of animality upon certain groups of humans has dangerous consequences. In what follows, I outline my critical assessment of the tools Adorno gives us to engage with these issues. By addressing how both human and nonhuman animals are implicated together in ethical-political systems of exclusion, Adorno's reflections on damaged life join urgent twenty-first-century conversations.

Adorno wrote *Minima Moralia* between 1944 and 1947, while living in exile in the United States. Like Simone Weil's *Gravity and Grace*, *Minima Moralia* represents an attempt to write aphoristically during and immediately after Auschwitz.[1] The fractured method of writing mirrors the breakdown of societal structures that both Weil and Adorno witness and reflect upon. Adorno's unique style enables him to offer criticism without grounding it in the presuppositions of the traditional philosophical-cultural system that he views as illegitimate. Yet, as Gillian Rose points out, the fractured nature of Adorno's deliberately paradoxical and polemical work has made it "eminently quotable" and "egregiously misconstruable."[2] This can lead his critiques to become popular in the very social-cultural arenas that they intend to oppose.

Minima Moralia can be read as part of the genre of advice-giving, but not the kind that luxuriates in banalities or easy fixes. Rather, as Jakob Norberg notes, "Adorno packs a social-theoretical diagnosis into a generic form that is undermined by this very diagnosis."[3] This is the ironic style that Rose refers to when she suggests that to follow Adorno's injunction in reading his text "means both that we must sometimes not take it literally and that sometimes we must."[4] The enervating experience of reading this work is an accurate reflection of the state of alienation that Adorno wishes to describe.[5] Reading the text is meant to generate discomfort, because it aims to provoke an awareness of the intolerable conditions of daily life under late capitalism. There can be no easy or trite resolution to the dialectic of powerlessness highlighted by Adorno, and *Minima Moralia* seeks to make readers conscious of their precarious situation.

Central to this precarity is the inhumanity of humans toward other humans and toward other animals. For Adorno, observes Christina Gerhardt, humans' suppressed animality "is a symptom of modern society; its antidote is sympathy with the suffering of animals."[6] The non-ethical treatment of animals and that of humans are intimately related. While it can be tempting for humans to numb themselves to animal suffering, Adorno enjoins readers to pay attention to animals, which, he maintains, will lead them to pay attention to human injustices. In doing so, though, he slips between emphasizing animal welfare as its own end and highlighting the animal as a means to illuminate implications to the human. This approach foregrounds animals, but ultimately instrumentalizes them as a way to think more deeply about human injustice and suffering. Adorno thus both reflects certain limitations to discourses of animality while anticipating the contemporary possibilities of critical animal studies.

Adorno and the "Animal Question"

Adorno seeks to show how idealist and humanist traditions attempt to suppress the animalistic in the human, with murderous consequences.[7] Together with Max Horkheimer, he demonstrates how certain elements of Enlightenment thinking led to the unthinkable in the twentieth century. As they write in a section entitled "Man and Beast" in *Dialectic of Enlightenment*, "Throughout European history the idea of the human being has been expressed in contrasdiction to the animal. The latter's lack of reason is the proof of human dignity."[8] The Kantian hierarchy that elevates humans for their ability to reason buttresses the logic that suppresses or instrumentalizes others. This logic leads to the condition of possibility for Auschwitz to occur.[9]

For Adorno and Horkheimer, the domination of nature and other animals has historically been tied to interhuman domination, and the failure to address one leads to the perpetuation of the other.[10] In *Minima Moralia*, Adorno writes that, as a result of so-called enlightenment progress, humanity's "control of nature as control of humans far exceeds in horror anything humans ever had to fear from nature."[11] For Adorno, then, "the path to humanity leads toward animality, not away from it."[12] Adorno urges readers to reflect on ethical and cultural resonances of the animal-human.

In asking the "animal question," Adorno intervenes in a "millennia-old tradition" in which Jewish difference has been historically identified along the human/animal opposition, involving "the observation, description, categorization, and exhibition of the other-than-human."[13] Twentieth-century Jewish writers often appropriated the figure of the animal to subvert this history of dehumanization, challenging the humanist tradition and reassessing Enlightenment ideals.[14]

Both animal subjects and their place in the human imagination are critical sites through which humanity is constructed and conceptualized.[15] The human/animal binary extends from Aristotle to the twentieth-century thought of Martin Heidegger, who sought to define the border between animal and human. Thinkers like Jacques Derrida challenge the philosophical lineage which defines the human against the animal, pushing back on this dialectical opposition. Even the term "animal" can reify a separation between humans and animals, forgetting that humans are themselves animals.[16] Hélène Cixous employs the neologism "animot" to invoke animals in their plurality alongside their linguistic registers.[17] Derrida famously uses "animot" to homophonically combine the French plural for animal, *animaux*, with the French *mot* (word). The category of *animot* blurs the animal with the linguistic.[18] This is part of Derrida's critique of logocentric culture, which elevates the speaking subject. The category of *animot* blurs the animal (*animaux*) with the linguistic (*mot*). This term illustrates the problem with speaking about "the animal":

> There is no Animal in the general singular, separated from man by a single, indivisible limit. We have to envisage the existence of 'living creatures,' whose plurality cannot be assembled within the single figure of an animality that is simply opposed to humanity. . . . The animal in general, what is it? What does that mean? Who is it?[19]

Any time we refer to the category "animal," then, we efface actual animals.

Animality refers to a construction of difference that is applied to both humans and nonhuman animals. On the one hand, as Beth Berkowitz observes, the discourse of animality represents an effort to claim agency and subjectivity for nonhuman animals. On the other hand, animality uncovers attitudes which privilege humans over other species. Animality makes anthropocentric attitudes visible while exposing the constructed nature of species difference, as speciesist outlooks enact violence both to other species and to other humans.[20] Animality can be linked to "a human exceptionalism that privileges not only human beings over other species but also some human beings over other ones," and animality thus forces us to pay attention to "the ideological deployment of species difference."[21] The use of the adjective "animalistic" to criticize certain human behaviors "demonstrates the manipulability of the notion of the animal and the flexibility of the binary of human/animal. In the discourse of animality, a person can easily end up on the animal side," and vice versa.[22] Investigating animality thus has real-world implications to both actual animals and actual humans.

Animality also refers to the figuration of the animal. As Andrew Benjamin argues in *Of Jews and Animals*, philosophical systems create and sustain identities as figures "in which the construction has a specific function that is predominantly external to the concerns of the identity itself."[23] Benjamin considers how the "Jew" and the "animal" have been co-constituted as first the particularized other to the universal, and then the enemy. These figures have propped up philosophical and theological Christian universals by being excluded from those categories, and they have been related to one another as historical others in polemical rhetoric. The universal depends on the exclusion of the particular and its maintenance in order to reinforce the universal's very existence, regardless of whether that particular is figural or actual. The figures of "Jews" and "animals" have real-world consequences; they "can have an effect on the operation of institutions as well as the practices of everyday life."[24]

The discourse of animality is further developed by Zakiyyah Iman Jackson, who reframes the animalization of Blackness in *Becoming Human: Matter and Meaning in an Antiblack World*. Jackson presses on the logic of liberal humanism entrenched within animal studies scholarship that assumes a stable human center, defined against the liminal animal other. This logic forgets that the very category of the human is itself contingent, provisional, and nullified along racialized and politicized lines. As Che Gossett aptly puts it, "blackness remains the absent presence of much animal studies and animal liberation discourse."[25] Rather, for the fields of animal studies and posthumanism "to do accurate, fully theorized, and principled work, they must show how the question of the animal bears on the question of hierarchies of humanity."[26]

Drawing upon Gossett's observation, Bénédicte Boisseron insists on the need to include Blackness in reflections on animality. In attending to the "race-animal combination" and the afterlives of cross-continental colonial history, Boisseron explains, we can become aware of how animality and racialization have developed alongside one another and continue to inform one another, rather than viewing them as a succession which progresses *beyond* race toward the animal question. The progression narrative obscures the ongoing relationship between these two categories. Instead, the "animal turn" in the humanities and social sciences and the array of scholarship available on the animal question provide an impetus to "take an in-depth look at the modern impact of a historically grounded system of mutual racialization and animalization."[27]

By reading literary-cultural productions that disrupt this tradition, Jackson seeks to undermine the authority of the trope of "the animal."[28] The question of the animal incorporates human and nonhuman lives, illustrating how discourses on nonhuman animals and animalized humans are co-constituted as they "reflect and refract each other for the purposes of producing an idealized and teleological conception of 'the human.'"[29] Both humans and animals are animalized in an intersecting process. The construction of speciesism is mobilized to produce racial difference, reflecting multiple discourses, rather than one single narrative, on animality. Crucially, because the human and nonhuman figured as "the animal" are defined as deficient by liberal humanism, "animality disqualifies one from ethical consideration."[30] Animalization functions as a key othering mechanism in this legacy of liberal humanist ethics. Racialized animalization is an essential, convoluted feature of the historical institution of liberal humanism and its entrenchment within hegemonic regimes of knowledge.

The race-based thinking that inflicts the trope of animality upon both animals and certain groups of humans is explored by Adorno in aphorism 66 of *Minima Moralia*, titled "Mélange." He takes the notion of an abstract utopia to task by challenging the "familiar argument of tolerance, that all people and all races are equal."[31] This position, he argues, has been easily refuted: "the most compelling anthropological proofs that the Jews are not a race will, in the event of a pogrom [an organized massacre], scarcely alter the fact that the totalitarians know full well whom they do and whom they do not intend to murder."[32] In fact, utopian ideals are consistent with society's racializing tendencies. This is especially evident in the concentration camp, in which "racial difference is raised to an absolute so that it can be abolished absolutely, if only in the sense that nothing that is different survives."[33] Those who promote the ideal of universal tolerance may easily support one marginalized group, such as African Americans or Jews, while discriminating insidiously against another.[34]

Adorno points out that the exclusion of certain groups from the category of humanity both precedes and exceeds scientific-anthropological arguments.[35]

At the same time, he risks collapsing the distinct processes of animalization that occur in the racialization of different groups. The social context in which Adorno wrote *Minima Moralia*, as a European refugee writing in the United States, reflects his understanding of the interplay between racialization, animality, and human injustice. Contemporary theories of animal studies and race that foreground anti-Blackness and the limits of species thinking expand his European-shaped approach (what Jackson calls the historiographical-philosophical "precincts of fortress Europe")[36] by demonstrating how Adorno's insights on ideologies of racialization can be both drawn upon and challenged in the American context. For example, despite the common characterization of members of the Frankfurt School as "elitist, Eurocentric, and dismissive of popular culture, characteristics that come together in Adorno's infamous critique of jazz music," Joseph R. Winters shows how Adorno can be useful for thinking about race and racial history by illustrating affinities and differences between Adorno and the Black literary tradition.[37] Jackson's and Winters's approaches are instructive for offering critical assessments of animal studies and critical theory. Although Adorno universalizes the processes of animalized racialization to involve dehumanization and exclusion, the context of enslavement demands that these discourses be further nuanced. Drawing on Saidiya Hartman, Jackson moves beyond the exclusion framework to emphasize bestialized humanization, abjection, and criminalization of the enslaved person's humanity, rather than the denial of it.[38]

Animality at Auschwitz

The slide from the human to the animal is further illustrated by Adorno in aphorism 68, titled "People are looking at you." The translator, Edmund Jephcott, notes that Adorno is here modifying the title of a picture book by Paul Eipper, an author of the animal stories *Tiere sehen dich an* ("Animals are looking at you"). Since the subject of the passage is animals, it makes sense that Jephcott would view this as a likely source. In Jay Geller's view, though, Adorno is more likely ironically playing on *Juden sehen Dich an* ("Jews are looking at you"), the 1933 antisemitic natural-historical taxonomy of "the Jew" by Nazi ideologue Johann von Leers. This tract included inflammatory illustrated chapters on the Jew as liar, corrupter of morality, blood-spiller, financier, and swindler. According to Geller, although the aphorism echoes the title of Eipper's "Animals are looking at you," there is no overlap with the content of that text, unlike Leers's

"Jews are looking at you," which is invested in identifying "particular varieties of the species 'Jew'" so that they can be marked for eradication.[39]

While this is a largely convincing argument, Geller dismisses the connection between children and animals captured in the reference to Eipper's animal stories, which is further evoked in *Minima Moralia*'s aphorism 146, "Toy Shop":

> In his purposeless activity the child, by a subterfuge, sides with use-value against exchange value. Just because he deprives the things with which he plays of their mediated usefulness, he seeks to rescue in them what is benign towards men and not what subserves the exchange relation that equally deforms men and things.... The relation of children to animals depends entirely on the fact that Utopia goes disguised in the creatures whom Marx even begrudged the surplus value they contribute as workers. In existing without any purpose recognizable to men, animals hold out, as if for expression, their own names, utterly impossible to exchange. This make them so beloved of children, their contemplation so blissful. I am a rhinoceros, signifies the shape of the rhinoceros.[40]

In this moment, Adorno considers this particular rhinoceros in and of itself, anticipating Derrida's injunction to attend to specific animals rather than effacing them in the generalizing category of "the animal." This rhinoceros genuinely shows up and announces itself to the child, prior to any social-cultural construction of it. Here, Adorno aligns the lack of commodifiable value in children's work/play with animal labor that resists the value of exchange.[41] As Leigh Claire La Berge observes, Adorno evokes the figure of the playful child alongside the animal with suspicion: "children become unwitting critics of 'the law of labor,' in Adorno's words; in their play one is offered a glimpse of life beyond the commodity form."[42] In *Aesthetic Theory*, Adorno later refers to the "primordial world of animals" in describing the artistic, clown-like routines of apes in the zoo, which "adults drive out of them just as they drive out their collusion with animals."[43] In likening humans to apes, Adorno uncovers the cultural efforts involved in stifling the human-animal link that occurs so naturally in childhood: "Human beings have not succeeded in so thoroughly repressing their likeness to animals that they are unable in an instant to recapture it and be flooded with joy; the language of little children and animals seems to be the same."[44]

The child-animal link has historically served to legitimize imperial and genocidal impulses. Animality has deep ties to the colonial categorization of religion, in which religious traditions viewed as closely aligned with nature, particularly animals, were categorically dismissed as childish, primitive, and uncivilized. As Kimberly Patton observes, "[t]he equation of childhood with 'primitive' religions through the link of an ingrained affinity for animals logically leads to a developmentalist model, with this affinity serving as a kind of index of theological or philosophical sophistication,"[45] a logic that supplements violent displacement, exclusion, and elimination. In the reference of the title to aphorism 68, the figure of the child allows Adorno to draws upon the history of animality in its colonial registers.

Adorno's critique of consumption in "Toy Shop" relates to the conditions of persecution and alienation outlined throughout *Minima Moralia*. Indeed, his "Dedication" makes explicit the link between universal alienation and genocide: "The subject still feels sure of its autonomy, but the nullity demonstrated to subjects by the concentration camp is already overtaking the form of subjectivity itself."[46] The concentration camp has nullified the subject, implicating all forms of subjectivity. According to Ulrich Plass, Adorno makes explicit the link between Marxist alienation and the production of death: "the demonstrable nullification of the subject in the camps is only the coldly rational consequence of the subject's nullification by the social relations of production. The unleashing of production comes at the price of eliminating the essence of the subject."[47] These concerns frame Adorno's later observations in *Negative Dialectics* on the (im)possibility of living and dying after Auschwitz, once the human becomes an eliminable "specimen" whose individuality has been effectively destroyed:

> The administrative murder of millions made of death a thing one had never yet to fear in just this fashion. There is no chance any more for death to come into the individuals' empirical life as somehow conformable with the course of that life. The last, the poorest possession left to the individual is expropriated. That in the concentration camps it was no longer an individual who died, but a specimen—this is a fact bound to affect the dying of those who escaped the administrative measure.[48]

The consequence is that one no longer has possession of one's own life and death. "From the point of view of structural continuity, Adorno interprets genocide as the biopolitical realization of the ongoing, everyday socio-economic practice of making everyone the same," in which the subject has been dissolved.[49]

We can see the connection between the conversion of the individual to a mere specimen in *Negative Dialectics* and the elimination of the individual in *Minima Moralia* from the human species.[50] As Adorno notes in aphorism 68, antisemitic perceptions have been socially schematized "such that they do not see Jews as human beings at all."[51] He broadens this to include other racist attitudes toward humans who were exploited and/or exterminated at various points in history, pointing to the criminal animalization of Jews alongside "savages, blacks, Japanese."[52] Here, Adorno draws focus to the particular logic of colonial brutality in the United States. His temporary American wartime refuge is itself deeply implicated in a history of racialized violence, beginning with the massacre of indigenous peoples it deems "savage," and it cannot assume immunity from ongoing toxic effects. In doing so, Adorno anticipates Jackson's present-day observation that "the discourse on 'the animal' is formed through enslavement and the colonial encounter encompassing both human and nonhuman forms of life."[53] In Adorno's words, "[t]he constantly encountered assertion" that these groups are "like animals"—in particular, like apes—is "the key to the pogrom."[54]

This choice of atrocities is deliberate: a pogrom is an organized massacre characterized by a particularly intimate form of violence, directed by neighbor against neighbor, rather than the invasion of one country by another.[55] This type of violence requires deliberately looking away from the animal/human's subjectivity. But, crucially, the denial of the animal's suffering is just as unnatural as the denial of the human's:

> The possibility of pogroms is decided in the moment when the gaze of a fatally-wounded animal falls on a human being. The defiance with which he repels this gaze—"after all, it's only an animal"—reappears irresistibly in cruelties done to human beings, the perpetrators having again and again to reassure themselves that it is "only an animal," because they could never fully believe this even of animals . . . those in power perceive as human only their own reflected image, instead of reflecting back the human as precisely what is different. Murder is thus the repeated attempt, by yet greater madness, to distort the madness of such false perception into reason: what was not seen as human and yet is human, is made a thing, so that its stirrings can no longer refute the manic gaze.[56]

In this powerful passage, Adorno makes a number of important observations. He identifies the Nazi goal of rendering the human not only less-than-human, that is, (according to this typology), an animal, but less-than-animal—a thing. This is echoed by Hannah Arendt, who writes in her analysis of totalitarianism that the living dead in the camps are transformed "into a mere thing, into something that even animals are not."[57] According to this murderous logic, while the animal can look back, the parasite cannot, and the platitude of "after all, it's only an animal," which is difficult to believe even with animals, can then become the obligation to eliminate the pathogen.[58] The perpetrator refuses to recognize the human/animal gaze in the eyes of the victim, effectively transforming an unforgivable violation into a necessary act of violence.[59] In bearing witness, the animal indicts human barbarism.

It is notable that Adorno focuses on the gaze as a controlling metaphor, because it remains entrenched within an anthropocentric framework. Here we can recall Donna Haraway's critique of Derrida's similar focus in *The Animal that Therefore I am*, in which his cat stands in for the figural animal gaze throughout the text while serving as its real-life feline catalyst by subjecting the philosopher to an unrelenting stare. Haraway points out that the cat is not heard from again in his essay, and she argues that Derrida fails an obligation to his "companion species" by missing the cat's invitation to "an alternative form of engagement" that might presumably involve other more catlike affective modes, such as tactility or smell.[60] Echoing Derrida, Jackson limits her analysis to the animal's gaze in a reading of Mister the rooster from Toni Morrison's *Beloved*. In Jackson's analysis, Mister's disruptive gaze allows readers to recognize his opaque presence in the novel as an invitation to animal-human correspondence and alterity.[61] Morrison attends to the perspective of this particular animal, Mister, rather than merely the anthropomorphizing figure of the rooster. While Jackson's reading thus follows Derrida's move beyond the unitary, generalized "animal," it also remains fixed within his anthropocentric sphere of ocularcentrism.[62]

Adorno elsewhere emphasizes senses other than vision in comparing humans to animal others. *Dialectic of Enlightenment* includes a meditation on the snail's tactility:

> The emblem of intelligence is the feeler of the snail. . . . Meeting an obstacle, the feeler is immediately withdrawn into the protection of the body, it becomes one with the whole until it timidly ventures forth again as an autonomous agent. If the danger is still present, it disappears once more, and the intervals between the attempts grow longer.[63]

In this illustration, the snail is emblematic of the earliest stages of animal-human mental life. The examples of the animal gaze and the snail's touch highlight the affective nature of inter- and intra-species ethics. The body and its senses are intrinsic to ethical relationships. But even in the extended discussion of the snail, the focus comes back to vision: "Each time an animal looks out with curiosity a new form of the living dawns, a form which might emerge from the clearly formed species to which the individual creature belongs."[64] In *Towards a New Manifesto*, Adorno again emphasizes the faculty of sight in highlighting the importance of the cross-species encounter to thinking: "Philosophy exists in order to redeem what you see in the look of an animal."[65] The animal gaze reflects the ethical imperative back to the seeing human.

When read through the lens of disability, a focus on the gaze effectively limits a definition of the human to include the able-bodied who possess visual acuity.[66] This boundary-marking has particularly troubling implications in the context of the Nazi genocide, which began through the extermination of those with physical and mental disabilities. The ocularcentric focus makes explicit the link between racialization, animalization, and ableism, which operate together to buttress the logic and construction of the "human."[67]

Adorno's description of the human becoming less-than-animal is echoed by Hannah Arendt, who similarly documents the Nazi goal of rendering concentration camp inmates as subhuman, and the victims' struggle to retain the status of the human species.[68] Arendt offers a political interpretation of the main stages involved in the degradation of the human. The camps kill first the juridical person in the human, then the moral person, and, lastly, the individual, obliterating the possibility for spontaneity and rebellion, and relying on an atmosphere of permanent dying. In order for the first step to occur, in which the juridical person is killed, the concentration camp must first cease being a site of definable punishment for clear offenses. The destruction of the juridical person in criminals is not successful, because criminals understand why they are in the camp. But the innocent placed in the camps, who are the majority, have absolutely no reason for being there. Deprived of their juridical person by being thrown into camps as a kind of insane punishment for no crime whatsoever, the inmates struggle to retain any aspect of their juridical selves. They are a stateless entity deprived of civil rights.

The next step in the destruction of the individual within the camp involves the murder of the moral person, "done by making martyrdom, for the first time in history, impossible."[69] By robbing death of meaning and making death anonymous, the individual's own death is taken away. Any dignity in seeing beyond death is prevented. The death of the moral person—the destruction of their unique identity—leads inevitably to the death of the individual. When the juridical and moral person has been killed, the death of the individual is inevitable, and they are transformed into nothing more than a living corpse.

The erasure of individuality is realized in the mechanized system of extermination, which is designed for bodies in general, not for the individual.[70] Once the camp system triumphs and individuality and spontaneity have been destroyed, nothing remains. Uniqueness is suppressed by destroying the human in the body. The camps' destruction of human dignity demonstrates that human nature is in fact unnatural: "man's 'nature' is only 'human' insofar as it opens up to man the possibility of becoming something highly unnatural, that is, a man."[71] The human becomes "a specimen of the animal-species man."[72] Totalitarian ideology aims at "the transformation of human nature itself."[73]

Like Arendt, Primo Levi describe the "walking dead" concentration camp inmates as animalized. In his memoir *Survival in Auschwitz*, Levi describes the concentration camp as a laboratory conducting a massive biological and social experiment, examining "the conduct of the human animal in the struggle for life."[74] An anonymous, drowned mass, for whom death is imminent, "form the backbone of the camp."[75] They are characterized by their "faceless presences," laboring in silence and exhaustion, inhabiting an empty space between humanity and non-humanity.[76] Their lives are deprived of political meaning. The camps reduce the struggle for life "to its primordial mechanism."[77] Arendt and Levi show how the perceived silence and invisibility of these inmates, in particular, excludes them from the category of human life. To be interned, in these accounts, is to be reduced to subhuman animality.

Arendt and Levi describe the victims' struggle to retain their humanity. Sarah Kofman evokes this struggle in *Smothered Words*, her account of her father, Rabbi Bereck Kofman, who was killed at Auschwitz. He was buried alive for refusing to work on the Sabbath. Referring to Robert Antelme's memoir, *The Human Race* (*L'Espèce humaine*, which could also be translated as *The Human Species*), Kofman describes what she calls the "reduction to animality."[78] The detainees "were transformed by the SS into beings without faces, without 'self,' anonymous, grotesquely 'disguised,' reduced to the worst abjection; treated without dignity, as garbage, undermen, slaves, 'Jews,' animals, horses, cows, oxen, as the beasts of burden whose fate seemed enviable to them, for at least they were accepted for what they were."[79] In contrast to Adorno's vision in aphorism 146, in which the lack of commodifiable value in animal labor can resist the value of exchange, Kofman here describes the aim of the SS to transform Jews into commodifiable animals within the capitalist economic system. Kofman observes that "what was always at stake in their fight . . . was the final, absolute, and 'almost biological' claim to belong, unequivocally, to the [human] species."[80]

As Giorgio Agamben later explains, Auschwitz created a subject isolated from the animal, leading to "the Jew, that is, the non-man produced within the man . . . the animal separated within the human body itself."[81] Drawing on the thought of Levi, Arendt, and Michel Foucault, Agamben describes how the anthropological machine creates the modern human by eliminating what it considers to be nonhuman. Ancient political-philosophical categories shore up a system that produces "bare life," perishable life that can be killed with impunity.[82] For Agamben, the concentration camp is the paradigm of this biopolitical system, which excludes certain humans, alongside animals, from legal rights.

Agamben's model of the concentration camp as the epitome of modern sovereignty has been challenged by Alexander Weheliye, who points out that bare life usually manifests itself not in physical mortality but in other forms of social and political death. Weheliye seeks to demonstrate the "thick historical relation" between the Nazi death camp's legal state of exception and its colonial and genocidal antecedents.[83] Locating the death camps within an exceptional ontological category, both in origin and teleology, as the biopolitical nomos of modernity displaces "racial slavery, colonialism, and indigenous genocide as nomoi of modern politics," rather than viewing them all as constitutively relational.[84] While physical annihilation was the purpose of the death camps, racial slavery sought to physiologically subdue and exploit, revealing "the manifold modes in which extreme brutality and directed killing frequently and peacefully coexist with other forms of coercion and noncoercion within the scope of the normal juridico-political order."[85] Drawing on Hortense Spillers's distinction between body and flesh, Weheliye seeks to enflesh Agamben's comparatively disembodied *homo sacer* by illustrating the historical transmission of bare life as it affixes itself to certain minoritized bodies.[86]

The accounts detailed by Agamben and contextualized by Weheliye show how marginalized populations become subject to racialized animalization. For Levi, animality is a method of dehumanization, and he continually reiterates the state of animality inflicted in the camp: "We had lived for months and years at an animal level."[87] But in Levi's account, embracing animality is also necessary. To survive, one must take part in the battle of the human animal, to "throttle all dignity and kill all conscience, to climb down into the arena as a beast against other beasts, to let oneself be guided by those unsuspected subterranean forces."[88] Levi here invokes another side to animality—the aggressive clawing for survival. This double side of animality—the source of both despair and redemption—is evoked by Adorno, for whom humans' suppressed animality is a pathologized symptom of modern society.[89]

Entanglements

Adorno seeks to show how dangerous consequences follow the attempt to suppress the animalistic in the human. Recognizing animality is what allows us to recognize our humanity. While this approach is helpful, it risks shoring up the human-animal divide, because it ultimately keeps circulating back to the human. In *Towards a New Manifesto*, Adorno echoes this impulse in noting that "Animals could teach us what happiness is."[90] In this observation, the animal serves to reflect back to the human a more elevated state of emotional being. Later on in the discussion, Adorno notes of human rationality, "Human beings do things in a far more terrible way than animals, but the idea that things might be otherwise is one that has occurred only to humans."[91] This suggests that humans are less inherently ethical than animals, but that human intellectual capabilities uniquely allow them to imagine a more ethical world.

An alternative that reflects Adorno's approach and takes it one step further is offered by Hélène Cixous, in her autobiographical description of the "animal humanity" shared between her childhood self and her family's suffering dog in Algiers after the Second World War. She writes about her dog,

> I should have spoken to him ... I thought him perhaps incapable of understanding for I was not then capable of understanding the profound animal humanity ... Am I Jewish? he thought. But what does that mean Jewish, he suffered from not knowing. And me neither. And I did not make light in his obscurity, I did not murmur to him the words that all animals understand.[92]

Cixous identifies a Jewish identity crisis that crosses species lines. In illustrating the unmistakable animal humanity of her neglected canine family member, Cixous's powerful essay implicitly grants religious subjectivity to animal others.[93] For both Cixous and Adorno, only once we have recognized our animality can we become fully human. They lament the disastrous effects of excising the animal from the human, thereby recuperating a more balanced approach.

While Adorno's approach may not take us far enough, it points to new possibilities for re-imagining the potential of animality. Within post-Holocaust thought, the figure of the animal is usually presented in a negative light. Adorno offers a more nuanced view of animality, emphasizing its strengths and possibilities even while acknowledging its challenges. This can help bring our attention to the calamities that are perpetrated when animals, along with certain humans, are dismissed from ethical and political considerations.

In aphorism 74, titled "Mammoth," Adorno writes of an ancient hope "that animal creation might survive the wrong that man has done it, if not man himself, and give rise to a better species, one that finally makes a success of life."[94] In Adorno's view, public zoos and gardens aim to mimic this eternal hope, as a structural defense against impending calamity: "They are laid out on the pattern of Noah's Ark, for since their inception the bourgeois class has been waiting for the flood. The use of zoos for entertainment and instruction seems a thin pretext. They are allegories of the specimen or the pair who defy the disaster that befalls the species qua species."[95] According to this simple and persuasive logic, humans build cages to house animals not for entertainment or pedagogical value, but for something much more primal: to ensure that at least some creatures will survive the inevitable devastation of the Earth—except that this great flood will have human, rather than divine, origins.

Given that Adorno's method of writing reflects the collapse of societal structures, it is not surprising that the experience of reading this book can be both revitalizing and discouraging. Rose argues that Adorno should not be viewed as a pessimist, though, "because, in spite of the gloomy picture which he dialectically paints of society, he is always concerned in his own work and in the assessment of the work of others, to achieve a style which will best intervene in society."[96] That he does not specify a particular political goal of his interventions, Rose maintains, should not lead us to read them as inapplicable or meaningless. Proposing an alternative set of synthesizing dogmas would, after all, go against Adorno's critical dialectical project.[97] The text is not prescriptive, and yet neither is it nihilistic. Adorno enjoins readers to be confronted by the powerlessness of our situation, without turning away from it. The task is in recognizing our lack of power, and not allowing it to paralyze us, an "almost insoluble task."[98] The urge to anesthetize is strong, and it can be a necessary survival mechanism in order to continue from day to day. *Minima Moralia* seeks to puncture cultural-political numbness and wake readers up to our helplessness.

In the "Dedication" to *Minima Moralia*, Adorno writes, "The major part of this book was written during the war, under conditions enforcing contemplation. The violence that expelled me thereby denied me full knowledge of it. I did not yet admit to myself the complicity that enfolds all those who, in face of unspeakable collective events, speak of individual matters at all."[99] And yet, despite his concern with speaking of individual matters in the face of collective catastrophe, the framework of the text indeed begins from the standpoint of the individual, demonstrating how speaking of individual matters can amplify wider social issues.[100] This is the alternative to bourgeois subjectivity, which stays mired within the individual's self-enclosed and reflexive ties to "authenticity."[101] Invoking individual matters with an awareness of one's subjectivity, and refraining from attempts to be complete or definitive in such reflections, allows individual experience to speak to greater thematic, social, and philosophical issues by stimulating structural awareness.

Adorno cautions that "[t]here is no way out of entanglement," and it would be futile to try.[102] This speaks to the project of the entire book—not to indicate a false exit, but to grant insight into the unrelenting state of enmeshment.[103] Adorno collapses the myth of historical progress by identifying civilization's movement as a progression toward hell, as each new form of horror outdoes the old ones.[104] This vision of the future feels especially resonant in the contemporary moment, in which, as in the epigraph by F. H. Bradley to Part Two of *Minima Moralia*, "Where everything is bad, it must be good to know the worst."[105]

By recognizing that this progressive destruction is not a "technical mishap" but rather another step in "civilization's triumphal procession," readers can embrace Adorno's dialectical vision and its political aims to "hold ultimate calamity in check."[106] Adorno's aphorisms speak to contemporary concerns with environmental, social, and interpersonal damage, anticipating Haraway's later call to transcend in/human borders toward new methods of multispecies engagement and ecological reparation.[107] *Minima Moralia* ends, in the final aphorism, on a note of tempered redemption:

> The only philosophy which can be responsibly practiced in face of despair is the attempt to contemplate all things as they would present themselves from the standpoint of redemption. . . . Perspectives must be fashioned that displace and estrange the world, reveal it to be, with its rifts and crevices, as indigent and distorted as it will appear one day in the messianic light.[108]

This redemptive vision, which reveals the existing world in all its failures, is not purifying or dialectic-resolving. It does not seek to dissolve tensions but merely to illuminate them.

8

Adorno's Anthropocene

Caren Irr

The Anthropocene is a series of metabolic rifts, where one molecule after another is extracted by labor and technique to make things for humans, but the waste products don't return so that the cycle can renew itself. The soils deplete, the seas recede, the climate alters, the gyre widens: a world on fire.
—McKenzie Wark, *Molecular Red: Theory for the Anthropocene*

The concept of the Anthropocene as many have come to use it defines the current geological period as one in which humans have made an indelible mark on the strata of the earth and disrupted its primary processes. By altering the chemical composition of the atmosphere, raising the temperature of the planet, introducing tons of synthetic waste, proliferating our own species exponentially, and triggering extinction cascades in others, humans have arguably remade nature according to our own ill-advised plans. However rightly contested and adapted, the concept of the Anthropocene plants a flag on the spot where a new phase in the nature-culture dialectic began. With the Anthropocene, we name the prospect of not only the domination but also the imminent subsumption of "first nature" (the nonhuman world on which humans act) by "second nature" (the world of human activity, priorities, and desire). Absorbing first nature into the notoriously conflicted, short-term, and restless universe of human desire in this way radically transforms our understanding of human action and plunges us into new experiences of our own collective barbarity to the extent that we pathologically envision ourselves as a species without limits. If we read the trendlines of climate change in particular, the prospects for a world in which first nature has been entirely consumed by the second look dire. The world, as McKenzie Wark reminds us, is on fire. However, even if that fire were by some miracle to be put out or, alternately, to set off an explosion of technological innovation that slowed its progress, we can be confident that the Anthropocene names a development whose staggering consequences we are collectively only beginning to comprehend.

Fortunately for those faced with the enormous task of understanding the Anthropocene, the twentieth century's foremost thinker on the problem of damage is here to help. As early as 1932, the young Theodor W. Adorno was working on the problem of what he called natural-history. In a paper that was delivered at the Kant Society and then translated and published posthumously, Adorno sought "to dialectically overcome the usual antithesis of nature and history."[1] Nature, for Adorno's purposes in this paper, is the realm of myth; it signifies an imagined permanence, a zone posited as exterior to change. History, by contrast, is the zone where the new emerges. The "usual antithesis of nature and history"—Adorno's starting point—describes a conventional limitation of prospects for change or transformation. To assert the mythic permanence or eternity of nature in this way is, for Adorno, to contain humanity within a set of inescapable limits, limits that turn out (spoiler alert) to rest on idealist foundations projected by the human. From the perspective of the Anthropocene, we will also want to note that this ideal, eternal nature is one that forecloses the question of damage and subsumption. Its deep ahistoricism renders it all but useless for contemporary purposes.

The philosopher that Adorno wrestles with in this paper is Martin Heidegger. In his 1932 essay, Adorno displaces what he identifies as the tautological idealism of Heidegger's thought with his own historical materialist method of interpretation. This method requires two steps: it historicizes nature, and it "naturalizes" history. Historicizing nature is a project that anyone tutored in a poststructuralist suspicion of essentialism can perform in their sleep. Naturalizing history is a less familiar task, however, and this is the task that is particularly urgent in the context of the Anthropocene. To introduce "nature" into a history founded upon its domination is necessarily to introduce the questions of damage, labor, and limitation for Adorno. While an environmental historian might veer at this point toward an account of the dependence of historical developments on the phenomenon that Raj Patel and Jason Moore call "cheapening" (that is, toward an analysis of the food, land, uteruses, oil, and more whose exploitation provides the material ground of history), Adorno moves the problem in another direction.[2] For Adorno, following Benjamin, the naturalizing of history involves "awakening the enciphered and petrified object" that second nature presents (119). This occurs when a constellation of concepts takes shape around and through a historically specific symbol, perhaps one whose meaning feels distant or one that manifests its necessary aesthetic reduction. In any case, within a constellation of concepts, the opaqueness and inter-relations of concepts is what signifies, in excess of their particular and literal definitions, the essential transience of nature. Nature is transitional (ever-changing, one says in a different tradition), and in this transience it reveals its commonality with history, the collective human experience of temporality. Naturalizing history, then, involves opening up historical objects to their own malleability; by altering or estranging historical objects in this sense, one grasps their ontology in a special sense. Adorno goes to some pains to distinguish this naturalizing of history from the "bewitchment of history" or a hypostatization of an essence of a period (122). Instead, he understands history as the experience of a discontinuity between what has been and the new, and he asserts that "'the new,' the dialectically produced, actually presents itself in history as the archaic" (123). The archaic (which he also calls the mythic or the natural) is what produces senses of déjà vu, foreboding, recognition, and reconciliation in our encounters with the new. Such encounters reveal that "second nature is, in truth, first nature" (124).

Although provisionally separating first and second nature is a necessary step for Adorno's method, as is entangling the two via the naturalization of history and the historicization of nature, he ultimately concludes that ordinary encounters do not involve any isolated or pure entity but rather engage a "concrete history" comprised of fused objects. The "alienated, reified, dead world" of first nature is entangled with a second nature that he describes (following Lukács) as a world of "rotted interiorities"; we confront this mythicized history as an array of "ruins and fragments" (261, 263). The task of "radical natural-historical thought" (i.e., Marxism) is to restore dynamism, to bring a dead and fragmented history back to life by revealing its engagement with a contradictory and historical nature.

The central object to be illuminated by Adorno's method, in other words, is an already damaged and petrified world. He borrows Lukács's figure of the charnel house as a figure for culture. That is, the space where interiorities have rotted is the house of bones, the place where disturbed skeletons lie after being unearthed from their graves. In this strikingly Gothic figure for cultural memory, artistic canons record the disarray of the dead, the jumble of parts, that comprises second nature, that set of petrified fragments whose connections to each other in living form has been lost. The decayed flesh and ligaments of culture cannot simply be reanimated by some philosophical Dr. Frankenstein. Instead, Adorno's version of historical materialism takes flight precisely in a mapping of the discontinuities, ruptures, and psychic dislocations that arise in concrete experiences of damage. And, since second nature has already, as he's told us, permeated first nature, this engagement with the petrified bones of damaged culture leads us inexorably back to the damage of the Anthropocene.

While Adorno's brief 1932 essay does not undertake a detailed illustration of its own method, it does help us isolate elements that are crucial to his explorations of damaged life in *Minima Moralia*. The emphasis on concrete encounters, non-schematic constellations of concepts, the overcoming of provisional oppositions, and dialectical discontinuities rather than unities: these characteristic gestures all appear everywhere in the later text. They draw our attention to the implicitly natural-historical elements of *Minima Moralia*, suggesting ways in which the kind of damage that we now associate with Anthropocene underlies this series of aphorisms, even though the explicit content may not always highlight the problem of ecology.

That is, "The Idea of Natural History" demonstrates that the moment when the historical joins nature and the material meets the psychic is literally crucial to Adorno's dialectic. Natural-historical thought is the crossroads of his chiasmus; it provides the risky point of mutation at the center of the chi (or X). From this site, Adorno's philosophically powerful negations arise. As we have seen, Adorno's dialectic overcomes an antithesis between nature and history by entangling the superficially static or reified opposition and then separating out the terms anew as the contradiction of not-nature and not-history. Negative dialectics arises from the moment of deepest entanglement, and it is aligned with a deontological nature that can then emerge. While many readers of Adorno have recognized the powerful role of negation in his thought (it is hard to miss!), in this discussion we will develop Deborah Cook's important insight that "the idea of natural history provides the template for interpretive practice in philosophy," including especially interpretive negation, throughout Adorno's career.[3]

As Cook demonstrates, reflections on the domination of nature provide important anchors in *The Dialectic of Enlightenment* and a chapter on natural beauty *Aesthetic Theory* outlines some additional considerations. It is, however, in *Minima Moralia* that Adorno's natural-historical method is especially visible. These "reflections from damaged life" begin from the ruins, fragments, wounds, and scars of the historically situated subject. As a gift composed for Adorno's friend and interlocutor Max Horkheimer, they are centrally concerned with event and number. Adorno presented the first fifty aphorisms to Horkheimer on the occasion of his fiftieth birthday on February 14, 1945, and then another fifty as a Christmas gift.[4] Adorno's form, in other words, follows the beautiful arbitrariness of the calendrical event during wartime. It is into these dead numbers that the mobile loving and thinking subject inserts itself. This implicit hero works to overthrow the "rotted interiorities" of the era—poking holes, one might say, in order to allow their pus and bile to drain away. The complex negativity for which Adorno is so justly famous here reveals itself as the means for naturalizing history, and its site is damaged life—that early figure for the Anthropocene.

Although the dynamics of natural-history permeate *Minima Moralia*, to simplify the discussion we can focus on a single manifestly relevant instance— aphorism 28. Entitled "*Paysage*," this single paragraph appears just past the midpoint of Adorno's carefully organized initial set of fifty aphorisms, suggesting its centrality to the concerns of the entire sequence. The connecting thread of this middle portion of Book One the émigré's experience of linguistic displacement. Aphorism 25 describes the mechanistic compression of a whole lifeworld into the kind of "background" experience listed on a job or visa application. Number 26 recalls the "archaic passionate" presence that English words had in a German upbringing[5] (47), while number 27 invokes the breakthrough of "imprisoned passions" that arise when one reads a translation. These passions attach themselves to the "innermost cell of meaning" (48), and the concrete experience of both repression and its antagonist arise simultaneously in the sign. This explosive fusion permeates the "dwarf fruit" of aphorism 29, a string of apparent miscellany that concludes with the inversion of Hegel's dictum; "the whole is the false," Adorno succinctly posits (50).

On this journey from the personal story of impersonalization to the properly philosophical intervention that negates ontological unities, aphorism 28 provides the chiasmatic moment of reversal when history intervenes. "*Paysage*" employs the French word for landscape to flag its émigré perspective on the "American landscape." Naming the landscape as "paysage" not only recalls the explosiveness of language and desire mentioned in "*On parle français*" (aphorism 27), it also plants that language in a particular juxtaposition of nations and sites. In aphorism 28, Adorno's speaker inhabits a particular though alien land, one characterized by the absence of "traces of the human hand" (48). Adorno notes, "the lack of arable land, the uncultivated woods often no higher than scrub," and the "expressionless" roads (48). He observes "no marks of foot or wheel" on these roads, "no soft paths along their edges . . . no trails leading off into the valley," and in a remarkable leap of imagination he intuits a different kind of figurative absence: "It is as if no-one had ever passed their hand over the landscape's hair." The passage then concludes with a "corresponding" diminishment of perception: "what the hurrying eye has seen merely from the car it cannot retain, and the vanishing landscape leaves no more traces behind than it bears upon itself" (48).

Some readers of this passage have discovered in its catalog of absences "a kind of sullen longing for the decorous gentility of what the former US Defense Secretary Donald Rumsfeld called 'old Europe.'"[6] Others hear a condemnation, a charge that the United States is "tawdry, fallen, phony to its core."[7] Still others suggest that "as a European used to a densely populated countryside, he was obviously intimidated by exactly what Americans have always cherished—the wide-open spaces from sea to shining sea."[8] All of these readings correctly identify an excess of affect in this passage and attach it to a national/cultural difference in landscape aesthetics. The affect thought to be triggered by the land is, however, notably various—ranging from sullenness to outrage to intimidation. To this list we might add a kind of sublime appreciation. After all, Adorno's relation to the American scene is marked as well by his sense that the United States is a "country [that] displays capitalism, as it were, in its complete purity, without any precapitalist remnants."[9] The "absence of historical memories" that Adorno refuses to identify as the primary "shortcoming of the American landscape" coexists with the presence of the "complete purity" of capitalism. When Adorno perceives an absence of precapitalist conditions, he observes in the same moment—through his estranged émigré's eye—the way that capitalist relations are written into the land. He sees the historical naturalized in its apparent purity.

The opposition between the "gleaming track" of the road and "its wild, overgrown surroundings" that "*Paysage*" presents is, after all, an almost too perfect example of "the usual antithesis between nature and history." Adorno's reading of the absences of a European way of life historicizes this apparent wilderness by comparing its management to other forms of such a relation. In the process the violence and loneliness of capitalist form reveals itself. This is, as we noted earlier, his response to a Heideggerian ontological or "romantic" illusion, and in many respects this is the easier of the two steps in his natural-historical method.

The next, harder, and stranger thought arises in the leap to the mythic. Readily marked as analogic by the phrase "it is as if," the comparison of the landscape to a head with hair becomes surprisingly sentimental. It introduces an allegorical scene of recognition—that mythic déjà vu. In this lightly Freudian moment, Adorno invokes a kind of maternal caress, a comforting passage of a "hand over the landscape's hair," though of course he does so negatively, noting the absence of this hand (48). This remembered caress never occurred. The landscape he imagines as a child (or lover) experiences no comfort and therefore gives none. This is the "alienated, reified, dead" land of a subsumed nature that Adorno had imagined more than a decade earlier, and this is the zombie that he seeks to reanimate through myth.

Several submerged myths are called into service at this point of transition. As already suggested, the phantasm of maternal care seems crucial, and the French "paysage" also associates this fantasy not only with the Sadean libido of the preceding aphorism but also (perhaps) with Adorno's own half-Corsican mother, the mother whose name he adopted as his own. The desire for the mother's hand is embedded in the word and projected to the land, releasing a myth of the hardened machismo of the lonely son. This theme was of course crucial to Adorno's contemporaneous work on authoritarianism as well as his recurring investigation of bourgeois coldness. He reads in the land an allegory for the psychic losses experienced by the capitalist and the fascist subjects, worrying through their potential feedback loops. In other words, he encounters in the landscape something of his own urgent and historical fears as well as the mythic force driving the factitious historical reality of his circumstances.

At the same time, this analogy is slightly humorous. After all, we might ask, doesn't the sensory longing for a hand on hair perhaps register with a particular curmudgeonly chagrin for the bald man? In 1945, Adorno had a smooth, nearly hairless head. And perhaps it is the case that something of this embodied smoothness persists in his final reflection on the traceless smoothness of a land sliding away from its perceiver, a landscape that "leaves no more traces behind than it bears upon itself" (48). Smoothness is here configured as a relation between the "hurrying eye" in the car and the "vanishing landscape" that runs away in the opposite direction; they meet each other in the transient slide. That smoothness is an absence but also a sensation in itself—oddly ecstatic on its own terms even if also flecked with nostalgia for the eroticism of a touch of the hair that once grew. There is perhaps a piece of a new myth of joyous release intermixed with this confrontation with the longing for the absent mother.

At the very least, a fragment of repressed joy may provide a "cell of meaning" in *"Paysage."* Adorno's biographer Lorenz Jaeger suggests a way into this cell when he associates this aphorism *"Paysage"* with a passage from Adorno's personal writings. Recounting "a dream that Adorno had in the early 1940s," Jaeger suggests that "the dream may even have prompted him to write down his observations on the American countryside." In this dream,

> the scene is a mountain path similar to those found in the region of Amorbach. Adorno is out walking with his mother and aunt. But at the same time they are on the West Coast of America. "Below us on our left lay the Pacific Ocean. At one point the path seemed to become steeper or to stop. I set about looking for

a better one through the rocks and undergrowth to the right." The landscape seemed almost trackless and impenetrable and so Adorno, still dreaming, had to turn back, at which point he encountered two blacks whose laughter struck him as a symbol of relaxation—and then, once he had passed through a gate, he found himself standing "in the square outside the Neue Residenz in Bamberg, shaken by happiness."[10]

The imagery of this reported dream involves walking, not riding in a car, and its scene is a footpath not a roadway. But the combination of family feeling with a jarring juxtaposition of Pacific and German scenes supports the connection. How surprising, though, to find that the moment of magical swerving or joyous transmutation appearing in this dream is associated with "two blacks" laughing. This markedly symbolic moment leaves Adorno reportedly "shaken with happiness" as he passes from a trackless wilderness to a simultaneously familiar and new (Neue) home. His moment of myth and desire is permeated by racial fantasy. In several places in *Minima Moralia* Adorno takes pains to affiliate European Jews with racial minorities in the United States. So, it is notable that in this passage (if Jaeger's suggestion that it provided a germ for aphorism 28 is correct) such an association is repressed. Whispers of alienation from Black life as well as imagined affiliation arise here, so Adorno folds away that portion of the dream, and the aphorism as published retains a trace of the joyous affect without the phantasmatic Black bodies that produce it. This affect lingers even as he stresses the absence of traces in the land and the perceiver of the land alike. In other words, he "mythicizes" natural-history by discovering in it a layered fantasy of maternal care and something akin to a solidarity restricted by racial logic.

These traces of laughter and smooth speed do not serve then as the uncomplicated recovery of wonder at virgin nature. As readers of the famous "*rien faire comme une bête*" passage have reminded us, even when *Minima Moralia* recovers utopian visions it does so in a manner fully alert to damage. The intensity of the fantasy is an index to the severity of the damage. And, the ever-diminishing space of subjectivity preserves a trace for itself not in visionary excess but in the manifestation of its own passivity. Since Adorno did not know how to drive, he makes these observations from the passenger seat.[11] Some might also be tempted to hear echoes here of the dreadful clattering of trains and the horror of other passengers headed to the concentration camps. But what is certain is that the imagery of "*Paysage*" resurfaces swiftly in the next aphorism, where Adorno identifies the "beauty of the American landscape" with a paradox of scale: "even the smallest of its segments is inscribed, as its expression, with the immensity of the whole country" (49). Within the microcosm, the brief perceptions of a man whose ironic pet name was "hippo," an immensity opens. A sublime terror at hypercapitalist modernity and a strange exhilaration at its beauty result.

In the end, the dialectic of *"Paysage"* rests simultaneously on its historicizing of the American wilderness through an eco-cosmopolitan comparison and its naturalizing revelation of an embodied desire for comfort, relaxation, and joy. Adorno's encounter with American landscape registers the techno-modern machinery of roads, cars, fascistic purity, and terror; he grapples with the surging awareness of barbaric elements of modernity, and the extruded underside of Nazi cults of nature and health. He encounters those horrors indirectly from a position that is both "out of the firing line" and exceedingly transient.[12] The landscape presents this natural-historical dilemma once we learn to read it as a dialectical constellation, once we learn to reanimate its fragments of damaged life. In the later formulation of *Aesthetic Theory*, we learn to read this treatment of natural beauty as a melancholic salve that "rubs on a wound."[13]

The wound has, however, continued to fester. Since 1945, the network of North American roadways that Adorno describes has expanded many times. It has risen, as he anticipated, to a level of a damaging worldwide petromodernity. It is, thus, to the antagonism of natural-historical thought (the real hero of *Minima Moralia*) to stupidity that we must finally turn if we are to fully appreciate the value of Adorno's method for the era of the Anthropocene.

In a work that prizes the restless dialectical mobility of thinking as much as this volume (and in so doing resists prematurely "restorative elements" [246]), it is not particularly surprising that damage so often takes the form of stupidity. Although frequently excoriated, stupidity fascinates Adorno, and describing it drives him to rhetorical frenzies that it would not be out of place to call baroque. In moments of glorious vituperative outrage, Adorno makes sweeping condemnations of "the planetary stupidity which prevents the present world from perceiving the absurdity of its own order" (198).

Sliding up and down the rhetorical scale in this passage, Adorno links this "planetary" blockage to the stupidity of the individual's pursuit of self-interest and consequent "inability to link the power of prejudice and business" (198). Adorno asserts that such stupidity "consorts with moral deficiency" and yet cannot be understood as evil, because it results from an overapplication of the limited but entirely everyday rationality of technical, instrumental reason. Stupidity then involves a failure to connect, to explain, to perceive; it is ultimately a problem of social cognition not morality. Planetary stupidity as Adorno would have us recognize it results finally from damage to the intellectual apparatus and most especially from a non-dialectical fixation within the petrified terrain of the local. On the problem of environmental degradation, the "stupidity" of climate change denialism, for instance, results from both a blindness to the sheer exercise of power on the part of "the rulers" and a narrowing of horizons when one's own self-interest is in question. In the same vein, technological management approaches to climate issues would similarly represent, for Adorno, an extension of the problem not a solution.

Stupidity is, after all, a scar for Adorno and his implicit interlocutor, Horkheimer. *Dialectic of Enlightenment* concludes with this memorable aphorism—one that reminds us to interpret the etiology of damage rather than protest (or excuse) its existence. A scar results from and is the trace of injury, but it can just as easily result from an accidental error as from an intentional assault. Willful action does not define the scar. In the case of stupidity at the planetary scale and about the planet, then, stupidity's scar is a natural-historical sign that prompts the formulation of a constellation of concepts that naturalize history (e.g., by exposing and exploring our sense of apocalyptic déjà vu) as well as historicizing damage to the planet (explaining how we got here). Taken together in their dialectical tension, these paired moves pull us out to the long history of capitalist extractivism and exploitation, reading this volcanic history from the pieces of hardened lava it throws up and recognizing the tumult, endangerment, and otherworldly horror it involves. From the point of view of Adorno's natural-history, we might adapt Benjamin's famous statement about documents of civilization simultaneously being documents of barbarism to say that there is no document of nature that is not also and simultaneously a document of an excess of so-called (that is to say, capitalist) civilization.

The obdurate stupidity of a nature damaged by capitalism will not be (to use Adorno's verb) "dissolved" by indiscriminate connection or simple narrativization, though. "Love of the contemplated" (in ecological terms, an identification with or fixation on particular symbolic species) does not foreclose stupidity. Neither does an irrationalist embrace of the purportedly natural "forces" within the social (i.e., Heidegger's romantic ontology) disturb stupidity. For Adorno, only "self-conscious reflection on the element of wish" allows for the dissolution of the drives organizing stupidity and therefore allows an "impulse toward Utopia" in the form of thinking to emerge (199). That is to say, it is not the lateral expansion of a logical or affective network that signals Adorno's utopian moment. Neither full domestication of nature nor a willful rewilding of the social is adequate to a fully constellated reckoning with the stupidity of damage to the world. In the place of these reified projects, Adorno requires "self-conscious reflection" on the wish buried within or below the most readily manifest (although blocked to full recognition) forms of social reason. At its ultimate limit, the reflected-upon wish evaporates entirely, leaving no residue, allowing for a less or perhaps non-subjective "impulse" of a different order. For Adorno, a depersonalized thought (that occupies a formal but not psychic selfhood) presents itself as one of the few options for a corrosive corrective to the absurdity of stupidity.

One or two aspects of this passage on the overcoming of stupidity recall Adorno's later and somewhat plaintive reflections on zoo animals. Adorno's socialized animals exchange gazes with the observer through the bars of the cage—recalling human internment, encampment, and a refusal to be observed, but in their most utopian forms they "exist . . . without any purpose recognizable to men," and signify only themselves, becoming "utterly impossible to exchange": "I am rhinoceros, signifies the shape of the rhinoceros," he writes (228). Even when we remember that the rhinoceros is a figure from "fairy-tales and operettas" (i.e., when Adorno recalls an image associated with lost childhoods), these reflections on the animal prematurely restrict our pursuit to the ultimately sentimental path between a degraded domesticity and a fantasmatic wilderness.

As in the rhino passage, in fending off stupidity, Adorno sometimes valorizes the self-sustaining completeness of a pure object, one unplagued by "heteronomous residues" (199). The rhino signifies the rhino; the thought signifies the thought. These moments suggest that Adorno's ecological ideal would consist of an impersonal and homeostatic "nature" operating beyond the scope of the human, relatively unaffected by "damage" on our temporal and geographic scale. This quest for a post-subjective purity initially sounds rather a lot like an idealization at the level of thought of the determinist universe—precisely that static nature that he was concerned to overturn in the 1930s.

As the natural-historical method's resistance to ontology requires, though, such recurring images of nameless, inhuman nature in *Minima Moralia* ultimately turns out to depend on a more dialectical condition that we might designate the feral. In a brilliant 2017 book entitled *tree*, Matthew Battles differentiates the feral from romantic wildness, explaining that "the feral . . . could be seen as a realization of the baroque; for feral things act as monads, each one of them reflecting a world in itself, and yet they're happy to act in assemblages that are always provisional confederations rather than cybernetic systems."[14] The feral creature is a domesticated one that adapts to wildness; it is a weed, an invasive species, a species exile that finds itself in associations—a microecology, as it were, to complement Adorno's microsociology.[15] The feral creature assembles with other similarly displaced beings in sometimes surprising configurations. These feral disorders swamp the potentially fascist ecology of rewilding with bewilderment, displacing the blood and soil trope of fixed belonging to a place (a tradition ensconced in a particular sort of place-based nature writing as well)[16] with a baroque abundance of edges, wastes, median strips, and other familiar yet mysterious sites.

In *Minima Moralia*, the feral note often sounds when a swerve toward boundary-crossing movement or process takes place. In the passage on planetary stupidity, for example, it arises in the account of dissolution and "impulse." These electrified, liquified movements agitate the apparent fixity of rigid stupidity and the calcified positions that it occupies (self-interest, romantic love, irrationalism). The feral thought crosses the perimeter of the roadway, moving into and below the wilderness. The multidirectional, multiscalar motility of thought is essential to its utopian aspect, and in the terrain of the nature concept (about which we are so often so apparently so irreparably stupid) this mobile capacity releases not simply the image of an idealized perfection but rather an almost Deleuzian dynamism of tension and transformation. This condition, rather than some momentarily achieved purification, is the situation of thinking for Adorno. This feral release of domesticated, stupid "instinct" into another, objective terrain constitutes Adorno's utopian "impulse."

Bearing the feral in mind suggests that the items available to borrow from Adorno and transport to the problem of the Anthropocene, finally, are not restricted to the mournful or pessimistic treatment of the planet as a scarred and damaged life, although *Minima Moralia* certainly develops a rich vocabulary of images for such scars and the stupidity that arises from them. We can also turn to the animal and vegetal bodies that bear these scars. Instinctual, feral, joyous, and shot through with longing, those bodies have a presence in Adorno's reading of even the most deadened and alienated landscapes, as I have attempted to demonstrate. The mythic, archaic, and natural body lurks in Adorno's woods like a Sasquatch at the perimeter of vision, dwarfing the trees and holding out the prospect of another life—one that negates the negation evident in excess human domination of nature.[17] In the era of the Anthropocene, we can recover, in other words, from *Minima Moralia* an active animated body that hums and chirps with its own eccentric needs even as relentless mechanisms of control constrain its territory.

Or, to put the matter in a slightly different way, we can think from Adorno's body in the era of the Anthropocene by recovering its historico-mythic registers. In the introduction to the *Grundrisse*, Marx writes that "all mythology overcomes and dominates and shapes the forces of nature in the imagination and by the imagination; it therefore vanishes with the advent of real mastery over them."[18] That is, mythology is a force for domination—often one that compensates symbolically for an incomplete subsumption of nature. We might understand Adorno to be following through on this thought, as he reckons with the mythic life of nature in an era of vastly accelerated modern techniques of domination. Wresting the kernel of myth from historical nature, he reveals sites where domination has not yet contained the whole. In our own, later moment, to the extent that the yearning for the hand on the hair still arises, we retain a connection to the partially disruptive force that first nature exerts on second. But, furthermore, by extending our inquiry to the perhaps entirely different sites of mythic dissonance at the molecular, atmospheric, or planetary levels, we perpetuate Adorno's method while casting off as many of the traces of, say, a racial imaginary we do not require. What Adorno offers to life in the Anthropocene, finally, is a methodology for reading nature-history hybrids in terms of our own ongoing obdurate stupidity and the prospects of a feral thought.

This Adornian approach to thinking the Anthropocene contributes to the project of a socialist ecology. Adorno's mid-twentieth-century reading in *Minima Moralia* brings a sociological eye to the mapping of the Anthropocene, at the same time that he deeply engages subjective life within the constellation of concepts that manifest the Anthropocene. He builds a bridge that is often missing between the material and subjective, and he cultivates an ethics of response and adaptation—drawing out a subtle humor and joy that make living "small" tolerable and even occasionally beautiful. And, most importantly, Adorno always returns his engagement with concrete manifestations of natural-history to the dialectical treatment of capitalism. Damage, it turns out, is another name for the natural-history of capitalism.

Notes

Foreword

1 Theodor Adorno, "Dedication," in *Minima Moralia: Reflections from Damaged Life*, trans. E. F. N. Jephcott (London: Verso, 1978), 15–18. In this chapter all quotations are to Jephcott's English translation, hereafter abbreviated as MM. For their many helpful suggestions I am grateful to Martin Jay, Max Pensky, Benjamin Wurgaft, and Caren Irr.
2 MM, 21.
3 MM, Aphorism 133, "Contribution to Intellectual History."
4 Adorno, "Four Hands, Once Again," trans. Jonathan Wipplinger, *Cultural Critique* 60 (Spring, 2005): 1–4.
5 MM, Aphorism 128, English edition 199.
6 Martin Jay, "Taking on the Stigma of Inauthenticity: Adorno's Critique of Genuineness," in *Essays from the Edge: Parerga and Paralipomena* (Charlottesville: University of Virginia, 2011), 9–21.
7 MM, 193.
8 For Adorno's critique of Heidegger, see Peter E. Gordon, *Adorno and Existence* (Cambridge, MA: Harvard University Press, 2016); for the specific rejoinder to Heideggerian dwelling and the affirmation of exile, see Gordon, *Migrants in the Profane: Critical Theory and the Question of Secularization* (New Haven, CT: Yale University Press, 2020).
9 MM, Aphorism 19, 40.
10 MM, 247.
11 MM, 49.
12 For a defense see Alexander Garcia Düttmann, *Philosophy of Exaggeration*, translated by James Phillips(New York: Continuum, 2007).
13 Adorno and Horkheimer, *Towards a New Manifesto*, trans. Rodney Livingstone (London: Verso, 2019), 45.
14 It has been suggested that the idea of a negative dialectic first assumed a concrete shape in *Minima Moralia*. See Detlev Claussen, *Theodor W. Adorno: One Last Genius*, trans. Rodney Livingstone (Cambridge, MA: Harvard University Press, 2008), 138.

15 For a superb commentary on this theme, see Axel Honneth, "A Physiognomy of the Capitalist Form of Life: A Sketch of Adorno's Social Theory," *Constellations* 12, no. 1 (2005): 50–64.

16 Rahel Jaeggi, "'No Individual Can Resist': *Mimima Moralia* as Critique of Forms of Life" *Constellations* 12, no. 1 (2005): 65–82.

An Adorno for the Twenty-First Century

1 Lambert Zuidevaart, *Social Philosophy after Adorno* (Cambridge: Cambridge University Press, 2007), 6.
2 Gerhard Schweppenhäuser, *Theodor W. Adorno: An Introduction*, trans. James Rolleston (Durham: Duke University Press, 2009), 13.
3 Tyvonne Yvonne Sherratt, *Adorno's Positive Dialectic* (Cambridge: Cambridge University Press, 2002).
4 Martin Shuster, *Autonomy after Auschwitz: Adorno, German Idealism, and Modernity* (Chicago: University of Chicago Press, 2014).
5 Lars Rensmann and Samir Gandesha, eds., *Arendt and Adorno: Political and Philosophical Investigations* (Stanford: Stanford University Press, 2012).
6 Christopher Craig Brittain, *Adorno and Theology* (London: Bloomsbury Publishing, 2010).
7 Deborah Cook, *Adorno on Nature* (London: Taylor & Francis, 2014).
8 Shannon Mariotti, "Damaged Life as Exuberant Vitality in America: Adorno, Alienation, and the Psychic Economy," *Telos* 149 (2009): 169–90.
9 Brittain, *Adorno and Theology*, 7.
10 Cook, *Adorno on Nature*, 1.
11 Mariotti, "Damaged Life as Exuberant Vitality in America," 4.
12 Rensmann and Gandesha, *Arendt and Adorno*, 6.
13 Peter E. Gordon, *Adorno and Existence* (Cambridge, MA: Harvard University Press, 2016), 2.
14 Alexander García Düttmann, *The Gift of Language: Memory and Promise in Adorno, Benjamin, Heidegger, and Rosenzweig*, trans. Arlene Lyons (Syracuse: Syracuse University Press, 2000).
15 Fabian Freyenhagen, *Adorno's Practical Philosophy: Living Less Wrongly* (Cambridge: Cambridge University Press, 2013), 11.
16 Rensmann and Gandesha, *Arendt and Adorno*, 17.
17 Theodor Adorno, *Minima Moralia*, trans. Renato Solmi (Torino: Einaud, 1954).
18 Theodor Adorno, *Minima Moralia*, trans. Maurits Mok (Utrecht: Het Spectrum, 1971).

19 Theodor Adorno, *Minima Moralia*, trans. Norberto Silvetti Paz (Caracas: Monte Avila, 1975).
20 Theodor Adorno, *Minima Moralia: Reflections from Damaged Life*, trans. E. F. N. Jephcott (London: New Left Books, 1974).
21 Ibid., 15.
22 Redmond's sentence reads as follows: "The melancholy science, from which I make this offering to my friend, relates to a realm which has counted, since time immemorial, as the authentic one of philosophy, but which has, since its transformation into method, fallen prey to intellectual disrespect, sententious caprice and in the end forgetfulness: the teaching of the good life." Theodor Adorno, *Minima Moralia: Reflections from Damaged Life*, trans. Dennis Redmond (Kentucky: Prism Key Press, 2011).
23 Theodor Adorno, *Minima Moralia: stochasmoi apo tē pthharmene zōē*, trans. Basilēs Tomanas (Thessalonikē: Ekdotikē Omada, 1984).
24 Theodor Adorno, *Minima Moralia: réflexions sur la vie mutilée*, trans. Elaine Kaufholz and Jean-René Ladmiral (Paris: Payot, 1983).
25 Theodor Adorno, *Minima Moralia: relfexões a partir da vida danificada*, trans. Luiz Eduardo Bicca and Guido de Almeida (São Paulo: Ed. Ática, 1993).
26 Theodor Adorno, *Minima Moralia: Sangcheo badeun sameseo naon Seongchal*, trans. Yu-Dong Kim (Seoul: Ghil Publisher, 2005).
27 Theodor Adorno, *Minima Moralia: Kizutsuita seikatsuri no seisatsu*, trans. Sanko Nagaharu (Tokyo: Hosei Daigaku Shuppankyoku Verl., 2009).
28 Theodor Adorno, *Minima Moralia: reflecties uit het geschonden leven*, trans. L. Hüsgen (Nijmegen: Vantilt, 2011).
29 Theodor Adorno, *Minima Moralia: Reflexiones Desde La Vida Dañada*, trans. Joaquín Chamorro Mielke (Madrid: Akal 2004).
30 Theodor Adorno, *Minima Moralia: Reflexões a Partir Da Vida Lesada*, trans. Gabriel Cohn (Rio de Janeiro: Azougue Editorial, 2008).
31 Theodor Adorno, *Minima Moralia: refleksjoner fra det beskadigede livet*, trans. Arild Linnenberg (Oslo: Pax Forl. 2006).
32 Theodor Adorno, *Minima Moralia: refleksije iz ošećenog života*, trans. Aleksa Buha (Sarajevo: Veselin Masleša, 1987).
33 Theodor Adorno, *Minima Moralia: reflexioner ur det stympade livet*, trans. Lars Bjurman (Lund: Arkiv, 1986).
34 Theodor Adorno, *Minima Moralia: Refleksje z poharatanego życia*, trans. Małgorzata Łukasiewicz (Kraków: Wydawnictwo Literackie, 2009).
35 Theodor Adorno, *Minima Moralia: reflectii dintro viata mutilata*, trans. Andrei Corbea (București: Editura Univers, 1999).
36 Theodor, Adorno, *Minima Moralia refleksije iz poškodovanega življenja*, trans. Seta Knop (Ljubljana: Založba, 2007).

37 Theodor Adorno, *Minima Moralia: reflexe z porušeného života*, trans. Martin Ritter (Praha: Acaademia, 2009).
38 Theodor Adorno, *Minima Moralia: sakatlanmis vasamdan vansimalar*, trans. Orhan Koçak and Ahmet Doğukan (Istanbul: Metis Yayınları, 2012).
39 Theodor Adorno, *Minima Moralia* ([Bakı] Alatoran, 2018).
40 Thijs Lijster, *Benjamin and Adorno on Art and Art Criticism: Critique of Art* (Amsterdam: Amsterdam University Press, 2017), 12.
41 Peter Uwe Hohendahl, *The Fleeting Promise of Art: Adorno's Aesthetic Theory Revisited* (Ithaca: Cornell University Press, 2013).
42 Alexander García Düttmann, "Without Soil: A Figure in Adorno's Thought," in *Language Without Soil: Adorno and Late Philosophical Modernity*, ed. Gerhard Richter (New York: Fordham University Press, 2010), 10.
43 Neil Larsen, "The Idiom of Crisis: On the Historical Immanence of Language in Adorno," in *Language Without Soil: Adorno and Late Philosophical Modernity*, ed. Gerhard Richter (New York: Fordham University Press, 2010), 118–19.
44 Andreas Huyssen, *Miniature Metropolis* (Cambridge, MA: Harvard University Press, 2015), 273.
45 Larry Alan Busk, "It's a Good Life? Adorno and the Happiness Machine," *Constellations* 23, no. 4 (2016): 532.
46 Roger Foster, "Lingering with the Particular: Minima Moralia's Critical Modernism," *Telos* 155 (2011): 101.
47 Rahel Jaeggi, "'No Individual Can Resist': Minima Moralia as Critique of Forms of Life," *Constellations* 12, no. 1 (2005): 69.
48 Mariotti, "Damaged Life as Exuberant Vitality in America," 171.
49 Ibid.
50 Ibid., 177.
51 Jaeggi, "'No Individual Can Resist,'" 67.
52 Huyssen, *Miniature Metropolis*, 281.
53 Busk, "It's a Good Life?," 525.
54 Ibid.
55 S. D. Chrostowska, "Thought Woken by Memory: Adorno's Circuitous Path to Utopia," *New German Critique* 40, no. 1 (2013): 93–117.
56 Jaeggi, "'No Individual Can Resist,'" 66.
57 Huyssen, *Miniature Metropolis*.
58 Eric Jarosinski, "Of Stones and Glass Houses: *Minima Moralia* as Critique of Transparency," in *Language Without Soil: Adorno and Late Philosophical Modernity*, ed. Gerhard Richter (New York: Fordham University Press, 2010), 158.
59 Busk, "It's a Good Life?"
60 Jakob Norberg, "Adorno's Advice: *Minima Moralia* and the Critique of Liberalism," *PMLA* 126, no. 2 (2011): 398–411.

61 Louis Klein, "Minima Moralia in Project Management: There Is No Right Life in the Wrong One," *Project Management Journal* 47, no. 3 (2016): 12–20.
62 Sherratt, *Adorno's Positive Dialectic*.

Chapter 1

1 Theodor W. Adorno, *Minima Moralia: Reflectons from Damaged Life*, trans. E. F. N. Jephcott (London: Verso, 2005), 17.
2 Adorno, *Minima Moralia*, 15.
3 Noah Strote, *Lions and Lambs: Conflict in Weimar and the Creation of Post-Nazi Germany* (New Haven, CT: Yale University Press, 2017), 243–67.
4 Christian Schneider, "Der exemplarische Intellektuelle der Bundesrepublik," in *Adorno-Handbuch: Leben – Werk – Wirkung*, ed. Richard Klein, Johann Kreuzer, and Stefan Müller-Doohm (Stuttgart: J. B. Metzler, 2011), 431–5.
5 Detlev Claussen, *Theodor W. Adorno: One Last Genius*, trans. Rodney Livingstone (Cambridge, MA: Harvard University Press, 2008), 204.
6 Stefan Müller-Doohm, *Adorno: Eine Biographie* (Frankfurt am Main: Suhrkamp, 2003), 507.
7 Tony Judt, *Postwar: A History of Europe Since 1945* (New York: Penguin, 2005), 394.
8 Clemens Albrecht et al., *Die intellektuelle Gründung der Bundesrepublik: Eine Wirkungsgeschichte der Frankfurter Schule* (Frankfurt am Main: Campus, 1999), 278.
9 Jürgen Habermas, "Dual Layered Time: Reflections on T. W. Adorno in the 1950s," trans. Kai Artur Diers. *Logos* 2, no. 4 (2003): http://www.logosjournal.com/habermas.htm
10 Alex Schildt and Detlef Siegfried, *Deutsche Kulturgeschichte: Die Bundesrepublik – 1945 bis zur Gegenwart* (Munich: Carl Hanser, 2009), 181–203.
11 Philipp Felsch, *Der lange Sommer der Theorie: Geschichte einer Revolte* (Munich: C. H. Beck, 2015), 37–42.
12 Theodor W. Adorno, *Erziehung zur Mündigkeit: Vorträge und Gespräche mit Hellmut Becker 1959-1969*, ed. Gerd Kadelbach (Frankfurt am Main: Suhrkamp, 1970), 109.
13 Theodor W. Adorno, *Gesammelte Schriften*, edited by Rolf Tiedemann, vol. 8 (Frankfurt am Main: Suhrkamp, 1997), 73. My translation.
14 Adorno, *Gesammelte Schriften*, vol. 20.1, 291. My translation.
15 Adorno, *Gesammelte Schriften*, vol. 9.2, 377. My translation.
16 Adorno, *Gesammelte Schriften*, vol. 10.2, 675. My translation.
17 Till van Rahden, "Fatherhood, Rechristianization, and the Quest for Democracy in Postwar West Germany," in *Raising Citizens in the "Century of the Child": The United States and German Central Europe in Comparative Perspective*, ed. Dirk Schumann (New York: Berghahn, 2010), 141–64.

18 Clemens Albrecht, *Die intellektuelle Gründung der Bundesrepublik*, 388.
19 Adorno, *Gesammelte Schriften*, vol. 10.2, 457. My translation.
20 Michel Foucault, *The Hermeneutics of the Subject: Lectures at the Collège de France 1981–1982*, trans. Graham Burchell (New York: Picador, 2005).
21 Steven Watts, *Self-Help Messiah: Dale Carnegie and Success in Modern America* (New York: Other Press, 2013).
22 Adorno, *Minima Moralia*, 128.
23 Ibid., 37.
24 Ibid., 27.
25 Ibid., 15.
26 Ibid., 16.
27 Ibid., 57.
28 Wolfgang Kraushaar, "Autoritärer Staat und antiautoritärer Bewegung," *Frankfurter Schule und Studentenbewegung: Von der Flaschenpost zum Molotowcocktail 1946–1995*, ed. Wolfgang Kraushaar, vol. 3 (Hamburg: Rogner & Bernhard, 2010), 15–33.

Chapter 2

1 The in-text page numbers refer to Adorno, *Minima Moralia. Reflexionen aus dem beschädigten Leben* ((Frankfurt/Main: Suhrkamp, 2003), and to Adorno, *Minima Moralia. Reflections on a damaged life*, trans. E. F. N Jephcott (New York: Verso, 2005) for reference. The format is (MM German/English).
2 Rahel Jaeggi, "'No Individual Can Resist': *Minima Moralia* as Critique of Forms of Life," *Constellations* 12 (2005): 66.
3 Adorno, *Negative Dialektik. Gesammelte Schriften 6* (Frankfurt/Main: Suhrkamp, 2003). English translation: *Negative Dialectics*, trans. E. B. Ashton (London: Routledge, 1973), 45/33. For Adorno quotes, I use my own translations of the German original and indicate the corresponding page in the English translation (where available) for reference. The format of the page numbers is German/English.
4 Jaeggi, "No Individual Can Resist," 66.
5 Letter of October 31, 1945, in Adorno, Briefe an die Eltern (Frankfurt/M: Suhrkamp, 2003), 336.
6 Andreas Bernhard in Ulrich Raulff and Andreas Bernard (eds.), *Minima Moralia neu gelesen* (Frankfurt/Main: Suhrkamp, 2003), 8.
7 Claus Offe, *Selbstbetrachtung aus der Ferne. Tocqueville, Weber und Adorno in den Vereinigten Staaten* (Frankfurt/Main: Suhrkamp, 2004), 96.
8 Adorno, *Philosophische Terminologie, Vol. 1* (Frankfurt/Main: Suhrkamp, 1973), 82.
9 Adorno, "Was bedeutet: Aufarbeitung der Vergangenheit," in *Gesammelte Schriften 10* (Frankfurt/Main: Suhrkamp, 2003), 567.

10 Adorno, *Vorlesung über Negative Dialektik* (Frankfurt/Main: Suhrkamp, 2003). English translation: *Lectures on Negative Dialectic*, trans. Rodney Livingstone (Malden: Polity, 2008), 49/29.
11 See Silberbusch, *Adorno's Philosophy of the Nonidentical. Thinking as Resistance* (New York: Palgrave Macmillan, 2017), particularly 57–122.
12 Adorno, *Lectures on Negative Dialectic*, 158/108.
13 Adorno, *Negative Dialectic*, 29/17.
14 Adorno, *Philosophische Terminologie*, Vol. 1, 167.
15 Adorno, *Lectures on Negative Dialectic*, 35/19.
16 Adorno, *Ästhetik* (1958/59) (Frankfurt/Main: Suhrkamp, 2009). English Translation: *Aesthetics*, trans. Wieland Hobarn (Medford: Polity, 2018), 183/114.
17 See Adorno and Horkheimer, *Dialektik der Aufklärung. Gesammelte Schriften 3* (Frankfurt/Main: Suhrkamp, 2003). English translation: *Dialectic of Enlightenment*, trans. E. Jephcott (Palo Alto: Stanford University Press, 2002), 212/154.
18 Adorno, *Negative Dialectic*, 43/33.
19 Ibid., 294.
20 Adorno, *Lectures on Negative Dialectic*, 53/31.
21 Adorno, *Negative Dialectic*, 15/3.
22 Adorno, "Kultur und Verwaltung" in *Gesammelte Schriften 8* (Frankfurt/Main: Suhrkamp, 2003), 147.
23 Adorno, *Negative Dialectic*, 266/269.
24 The expansion of the *Tauschverhältnis*, the capitalist relation of exchange, to all of human life is a theme that Adorno encountered first in György Lukác's highly influential 1923 book *History and Class Consciousness*. It informs his entire work.
25 Adorno and Horkheimer, *Dialectic of Enlightenment*, 214/155–6.
26 Adorno, "Reflexionen zur Klassentheorie," in *Gesammelte Schriften 8* (Frankfurt/Main: Suhrkamp, 2003), 388.
27 Adorno and Horkheimer, *Dialectic of Enlightenment*, 106/68.
28 Adorno, *Negative Dialectic*, 355/362.
29 Ibid., 356/363.
30 Crewdson, "Border Sweeps of Illegal Aliens Leave Scores of Children in Jail," *New York Times*, August 04, 1980, https://www.nytimes.com/1980/08/04/archives/border-sweeps-of-illegal-aliens-leave-scores-of-children-in-jails.html, accessed October 12, 2020; Antonio Olivo, "ACLU alleges that immigrant minors were mistreated in custody during Obama years," *Washington Post*, May 23, 2018, https://www.washingtonpost.com/local/social-issues/aclu-immigrant-minors-routinely-mistreated-in-custody-during-obama-years/2018/05/23/b7cb31a8-5e00-11e8-a4a4-c070ef53f315_story.html, accessed October 12, 2020.
31 Emanuel Maiberg, "As Sadism Surges on the American Border, Our Collective Understanding of Cruelty Collapses," June 18, 2018, https://www.vice.com/en/articl

e/4358a9/as-sadism-surges-on-the-american-border-our-collective-understanding-of-cruelty-collapses, accessed October 12, 2020.

32 Michael D. Shear, Katie Benner, and Michael S. Schmidt, "'We Need to Take Away Children', No Matter How Young, Justice Dept. Officials Said," *New York Times*, October 06, 2020, https://www.nytimes.com/2020/10/06/us/politics/family-separation-border-immigration-jeff-sessions-rod-rosenstein.html, accessed October 12, 2020.

33 Adorno, "Graeculus (II). Notizen zu Philosophie und Gesellschaft 1943-1969," in *Frankfurter Adorno Blätter VIII* (München: text + kritik 2003), 29.

34 Max Horkheimer, "Die Juden und Europa," in *Gesammelte Schriften, Band 4*, ed. Alfred Schmidt (Frankfurt am Main: Fischer, 1988), 308–9.

35 "the truly unbearable coldness that, with the expanding relation of exchange, spreads over everything" Adorno, *Negative Dialectic*, 280/284.

36 "that, instead of letters, they send each other inter-office communications without address or signature, [is] a symptom of the ailing of human contact." MM 45/41, Aph. 20.

37 Adorno, "Erziehung nach Auschwitz," in *Gesammelte Schriften 10* (Frankfurt am Main: Suhrkamp, 2003), 687. Translation: "Education after Auschwitz," in Adorno, *Can One Live after Auschwitz? A Philosophical Reader* (Stanford: Stanford University Press, 2003), 30.

Chapter 3

1 Giorgio Agamben, *Infancy and History: Essays on the Destruction of Experience* (1978), trans. Liz Heron (London: Verso, 1993), 155.

2 Giorgio Agamben, *Potentialities: Collected Essays in Philosophy* (Stanford: Stanford University Press, 1999), 80, 77.

3 Agamben, *Infancy and History*, 156.

4 Anatole Bailly, 'κρίνω,' *Dictionnaire grec-français* (Paris: Hachette, 1935), 1137.

5 Theodor W. Adorno, *Minima Moralia: Reflections on a Damaged Life*, trans. E. F. N. Jephcott (New York: Verso, 2005), 110 (sec. 72). Translations of Adorno's texts modified in places based on Dennis Redmond's translations and the original German.

6 For Adorno's thoughts on this, see Theodor W. Adorno, *Negative Dialectics*, trans. E. B. Ashton (New York: Continuum, 1995), 18.

7 Detlev Claussen, *Theodor W. Adorno: One Last Genius*, trans. Rodney Livingstone (Cambridge, MA: Belknap-Harvard University Press, 2008), 143.

8 Identity is, for Adorno, "the primal form of ideology." Adorno, *Negative Dialectics*, 148.

9 Theodor W. Adorno, *Notes to Literature*, vol. 1, trans. Shierry Nicholsen Weber (New York: Columbia University Press, 1993), 3.
10 Adorno, *Notes*, 3, 9. "Its weakness testifies to the non-identity that it has to express, as well as to that excess of intention over its object, and thereby it points to that utopia which is blocked out by the classification of the world into the eternal and the transitory" (11).
11 Adorno, *Notes*, 16.
12 Theodor W. Adorno, letter to Max Horkheimer, August 21, 1941, in Marx Horkheimer, *Gesammelte Schriften*, vol. 17: *Briefwechsel 1941–1948*, ed. Gunzelin Schmid Noerr (Frankfurt am Main: Fischer, 1996), 153.
13 Friedrich Schlegel, *Philosophical Fragments*, trans. Peter Firchow (Minneapolis: University of Minnesota Press, 1991), 21, trans. mod.
14 Adorno, *Minima Moralia*, 16 (Dedication).
15 Ibid.
16 G. W. F. Hegel, *Phänomenologie des Geistes*, quoted in Adorno, *Minima Moralia*, 16.
17 Giorgio Agamben, *Karman: A Brief Treatise on Action, Guilt, and Gesture*, trans. Adam Kotsko (Stanford, CA: Stanford University Press, 2018), 83, 71. Cf. his discussion of "the good" in Plato on pp. 66–7.
18 Adorno, *Minima Moralia*, 18.
19 Ibid.
20 Miguel Abensour, postface, "Le Choix du petit," in Theodor W. Adorno, *Minima Moralia: Réflexions sur la vie mutilée*, trans. Éliane Kaufholz and Jean-René Ladmiral (Paris: Payot, 2001), 339, 340, 341, 340.
21 Adorno, *Negative Dialectics*, 408.
22 Ibid., 407–8.
23 Ibid., 406.
24 Theodor W. Adorno, *Critical Models: Interventions and Catchwords*, trans. H. W. Pickford (New York: Columbia University Press, 2005), 188, my italics.
25 Adorno, *Negative Dialectics*, 362–3.
26 Ibid., 3.
27 Gerhard Richter, introduction to Theodor W. Adorno, "Who's Afraid of the Ivory Tower?" in *Language without Soil: Adorno and Late Philosophical Modernity*, ed. G. Richter (New York: Fordham University Press), 227; Gerhard Richter, *Afterness: Figures of Following in Modern Thought and Aesthetics* (New York: Columbia University Press, 2011), 49.
28 Raymond Geuss, *Outside Ethics* (Princeton, NJ: Princeton University Press), 114.
29 Theodor W. Adorno, *Prisms*, trans. Samuel Weber and Shierry Weber (Cambridge, MA: MIT, 1981), 88–9.
30 Ibid., 88–9.
31 Theodor W. Adorno, "Messages in a Bottle," trans. Edmund Jephcott, *New Left Review* 200 (July–August 1993): 11.

32 Adorno, *Negative Dialectics*, 203, 204.
33 Geuss, *Outside Ethics*, 116, 115 (referring to *Negative Dialectics*, 17–18).
34 Geuss, *Outside Ethics*, 130, 111, 130, 128; Adorno, *Minima Moralia*, 66 (sec. 40).
35 "[A]ll happiness aims for sensual fulfillment and garners its objectivity in it." Adorno, *Negative Dialectics*, 203.
36 Theodor W. Adorno, "Who's Afraid of the Ivory Tower? A Conversation with Theodor W. Adorno," trans. Gerhard Richter, in Richter, ed., *Language without Soil*, 235.
37 Adorno, *Negative Dialectics*, 202, 17–18.
38 Adorno, "Who's Afraid of the Ivory Tower?" 235.
39 Max Horkheimer and Theodor W. Adorno, *Dialectic of Enlightenment: Philosophical Fragments*, trans. Edmund Jephcott (Stanford, CA: Stanford University Press, 2002), 151.
40 Theodor Adorno and Max Horkheimer, "Towards a New Manifesto?" *New Left Review* 65 (2010): 35.
41 Theodor W. Adorno and Ernst Bloch, "Something's Missing: A Discussion between Ernst Bloch and Theodor W. Adorno on the Contradictions of Utopian Longing," in Ernst Bloch, *The Utopian Function of Art and Literature: Selected Essays*, trans. Jack Zipes and Frank Mecklenburg (Cambridge, MA: MIT Press, 1989), 12; Adorno, *Critical Models*, 288.
42 Adorno, *Minima Moralia*, 61 (sec. 37).
43 Adorno, *Minima Moralia*, 228 (sec. 146).
44 Horkheimer and Adorno, *Dialectic of Enlightenment*, 18.
45 Adorno and Horkheimer, "Towards a New Manifesto?" 51, trans. mod.; Adorno, *Minima Moralia*, 228 (sec. 146).
46 Adorno, *Minima Moralia*, 157, 156 (sec. 100), 103 (sec. 66), 86 (sec. 51).
47 Theodor W. Adorno, *Dream Notes*, trans. Rodney Livingstone, ed. Christoph Gödde and Henri Lonitz (Cambridge: Polity, 2007), 45. The words came to Adorno in a dream dated March 24, 1946.
48 Miguel Abensour, "Persistent Utopia," trans. James Ingram, *Constellations* 15.3 (2008): 419.
49 Horkheimer and Adorno, *Dialectic of Enlightenment*, 43, 65; "self-preservation annuls all life in subjectivity," so that "there is life no longer." Adorno, *Minima Moralia*, 229 (sec. 147), 15 (Dedication).
50 Adorno, *Critical Models*, 292–3.
51 Adorno, *Negative Dialectics*, 374.
52 Adorno, *Minima Moralia*, 247 (sec. 153).
53 Adorno, *Minima Moralia*, 40.
54 Horkheimer and Adorno, *Dialectic of Enlightenment*, 149.
55 Adorno entertains "the idea of a constitution of a world that would not only abolish existent suffering but also revoke even the suffering that is irrevocably past." Adorno, *Negative Dialectics*, 403.

56 Adorno, *Critical Models*, 99, 108.
57 Walter Benjamin, "Conversation above the Corso: Recollections of Carnival Time in Nice," trans. Edmund Jephcott, in *Selected Writings*, vol. 3: *1935–1938*, ed. Howard Eiland and Michael W. Jennings (Cambridge, MA: Belknap Press of Harvard University Press, 2002), 29.

Chapter 4

1 In this respect, the timing of "The Ideology Issue" for *South Atlantic Quarterly* was eerie, insofar the special issue reintroduced ideology critique at the very moment it was making a resurgence in public discourse. See, in particular, Hortense Spillers, "Critical Theory in Times of Crisis," *South Atlantic Quarterly* 119, no. 4 (October 2020): 681–3; Caren Irr, "Ideology Critique 2.0," *South Atlantic Quarterly* 119, no. 4 (October 2020): 715–24; and Andrew Cole, "The Dialectic of Space: An Untimely Proposal," *South Atlantic Quarterly* 199, no. 4 (October 2020): 811–32; among many others.
2 Stephen Best, *None Like Us: Blackness, Belonging, Aesthetic Life* (Durham: Duke University Press, 2019).
3 Theodor Adorno, *Minima Moralia: Reflections from Damaged Life*, trans. E. F. N. Jephcott (1951; New York: Verso, 2020), 15.
4 Ibid., 130.
5 Moreover, Bruno Latour's Actor-Network-Theory (ANT) is quite useful for reexamining the aphorism and spatial form: space is created through the networks between individual actors and agents, vexing narratorial agency and deferring poetic meaning.
6 Adorno's and Bloch's conditioned hopefulness, the yearning for reparation in the midst of heartbreak, was the project of José Esteban Muñoz's *Cruising Utopia* (2009)—a melancholy drive that has been made central in recent editions on Muñoz's letters. See José Esteban Muñoz, *Cruising Utopia: The Then and There of Queer Futurity* (2009; New York: New York University Press, 2019); and José Esteban Muñoz, *The Sense of Brown* (Durham: Duke University Press, 2020).
7 Lisa Gitelman, *Paper Knowledge: Toward a Media History of Documents* (Durham: Duke University Press, 2014), 111–35; Paula MacDowell, *The Invention of the Oral: Print Commerce and Fugitive Voices in Eighteenth-Century Britain* (Chicago: University of Chicago Press, 27–60.
8 Paulette Richards, "Wifredo Lam: A Sketch," *Callaloo* 34 (Winter 1988): 90.
9 Max-Pol Fouchet, *Wifredo Lam* (Barcelona: Ediciones Poligrafa, 1976), 188–9.
10 Adorno, *Minima Moralia*, 129. I see *The Jungle* as distinct from kitsch, or the sort of concept-driven artwork Adorno discusses in the aphorism Art-object (239–41).

11 I am thinking, in particular, of aphorisms 97 and 98 in *Minima Moralia* (Monad and Bequest, 158–62), in addition to the Dedication.
12 Fernando Ortiz, *Cuban Counterpoint: Tobacco and Sugar in Cuba*, trans. Harriet de Onis (Durham: Duke University Press, 1995), 96.
13 Enrico Mario Santí, "Towards a Reading of Fernando Ortiz's *Cuban Counterpoint*," *Review: Literature and Arts of the Americas* 37, no. 1 (2004): 8.
14 David Harvey, *The Limits of Capital* (Oxford: Basil Blackwell Oxford, 1982); Doreen Massey, *Space, Place and Gender* (Minneapolis: University of Minnesota Press, 1994); and Henri Lefebvre, *The Production of Space*, trans. Donald Nicholson-Smith (Hoboken: Wiley, 1991).
15 Jean and John L. Comaroff. *Theory from the South: Or, How Euro-America is Evolving Toward Africa* (New York: Routledge, 2012), 8–9.
16 Muñoz, *Cruising Utopia*, 1.
17 Comaroff and Comaroff, *Theory from the South*, 8.
18 Ibid., 9.
19 Ibid.
20 Jann Palster, "Postmodernism, Narrativity, and the Art of Memory," *Contemporary Musical Review* 7, no. 2 (1993): 27.
21 Lam's particular mode of expressivity resembles what Phil Harper describes as "abstractionist aesthetics." "Astractionism . . . entails the resolution awareness that even the most realistic representation is precisely a *representation*, and that as such it necessarily exists at a distance from the social reality it is conventionally understood to reflect," Harper theorizes. "In other words, abstractionist aesthetics crucially recognizes that any artwork whatsoever is definitionally *abstract* in relation to the world in which it emerges, regardless of whether or not it features the nonreferentiality typically understood to constitute aesthetic *abstraction* per se. An *abstractionist artwork*, by extension, is one that *emphasizes* its own distance from reality by calling attention to its constructed or artificial character—even if it also enacts real-world reference—rather than striving to dissemble that constructedness in the service of the maximum verisimilitude so highly prized within the realist framework just sketched. In thus disrupting the easy correspondence between itself and its evident referent, the abstractionist work invites us to question the 'naturalness' not only of the aesthetic representation but also of the social facts to which it alludes, thereby opening them to active and potentially salutary revision." Phillip Brian Harper, *Abstractionist Aesthetics: Artistic Form and Social Critique in African American Culture* (New York: New York University Press, 2015), 2–3. Obviously, my argument shares much in the way of Harper's, insofar as I examine the aesthetic as an important site of Black cultural production.
22 Thomas McEvilley, *The Shape of Ancient Thought: Comparative Studies in Greek and Ancient Philosophies* (New York: Allworth Press, 2001), 86.

23 See Ato Quayson, *Strategic Transformations in Nigerian Writing: Orality and History in the Works of Rev. Samuel Johnson, Amos Tutuola, Wole Soyinka and Ben Okri* (Bloomington: Indiana University Press, 1997).

24 Frederic Jameson, *Postmodernism, or, The Cultural Logic of Late Capitalism* (Durham: Duke University Press, 1991), 25.

25 Ortiz, *Cuban Counterpoint*, 98.

26 Ato Quayson, *Oxford Street, Accra: City Life and the Itineraries of Transnationalism* (Durham: Duke University Press, 2014), 22.

27 Chinweizu, Onwuchekwa Jemie, and Ihechukwu Madubuike, *Toward the Decolonization of African Literature, Volume 1: African Fiction and Poetry and Their Critics* (Washington, DC: Howard University Press, 1983); and Ngũgĩ wa Thiong'o, *Decolonizing the Mind: The Politics of Language in African Literature* (Portsmouth: Heinemann Educational, 1986), 4–34.

28 Ibid., 30.

29 Ibid., 150.

30 Ibid.

31 See also Michael Rubenstein, Bruce Robbins, and Sophia Beal, "Infrastructuralism: An Introduction," *Modern Fiction Studies* 61, no. 4 (Winter 2015): 575–86.

32 Quayson, *Oxford Street, Accra*, 8.

33 Jonathan P. Eburne, *Outsider Theory: Intellectual Histories of Unorthodox Ideas* (Minneapolis: University of Minnesota Press, 2018), 85.

34 Léopold Sédar Senghor, "Appendix: What the Black Man Contributes," trans. Mary Beth Mader, in *Race and Racism in Continental Philosophy*, ed. Robert Bernasconi with Sybol Cook (Bloomington: Indiana University Press, 2003), 296.

35 Ibid.

36 Stuart Hall argues that the "problem" of the psychoanalytic critique of the subject "is that the manner in which this 'subject' of culture is conceptualized is of a transhistorical and 'universal' character: it addresses the subject-in-general, not an historically-determinate social subject, or socially determinate particular language." Stuart Hall, "Cultural Studies, Two Paradigms," *Media, Culture and Society* 2, no. 1 (January 1980): 70, quoted in Elizabeth Maddock Dillon, "Fear of Formalism: Kant, Twain, and Cultural Studies in American Literature," *Diacritics* 27, no. 4 (Winter 1997): 46.

37 See, for example, A. James Arnold, *Modernism and Negritude: The Poetry and Poetics of Aimé Césaire* (Cambridge: Harvard University Press, 1982).

38 Franz Fanon, *Black Skins, White Masks,* 1952, 2nd ed., trans. Charles Lam Markmann (London: Pluto Press, 2008), 93.

39 Hillary Chute, *Disaster Drawn: Visual Witness, Comics, and Documentary Form* (Cambridge: Harvard University Press, 2016), 2.

40 Jean-Paul Sartre, "Black Orpheus," *Massachusetts Review* 6, no. 1 (Autumn 1964–65): 33.

41 The error of Sartre's metaphysical assumptions is a particularly glaring misreading of William Faulkner's *The Sound and the Fury*. Sartre reprimands Faulkner for his absurd metaphysical or "un-novelistic" representation of time. Quentin Compson's breaking of the watch is symbolic of Faulkner's failed futurity—the destruction of the novel's "concrete form of humanity." And yet Sartre fails to distinguish between Faulkner and the Compsons, attributing to Faulkner's metaphysics a problem in Compson-family social psychology. It might seem that Quentin defies futurity— most flagrantly when he smashes his watch. But an alternative metaphysics suggests that the smashed watch is not a dualistic rejection of public time but a synthesis that entails the eternality of despair. Eternal despair is precisely what Quentin wants, as his father notes. It matches Quentin's ideals and his anxieties and perfects their temporality. It is a form of futurity after all, even if it does not have the quality Sartre thinks necessary to the future as such, and it amounts to a valid metaphysic—if a self-destructive one.

42 Martin Puchner, *Poetry of the Revolution: Marx, Manifestos and the Avant-Garde* (Princeton: Princeton University Press, 2006), 22.

43 Achille Mbembe, *Critique of Black Reason*, trans. Laurent Dubois (Durham: Duke University Press, 2017), 123.

44 See, for example, Lawrence Venuti, "Translating Derrida on Translation: Relevance and Disciplinary Resistance," *The Yale Journal of Criticism* 16, no. 2 (Fall 2003): 237–62; Jacques Derrida; *Monolingualism of the Other; or, the Prosthesis of Origin*, trans. Patrick Mensah (Stanford: Stanford University Press, 1998); Jacques Derrida, *Spectres of Marx: The State of Debt, the Work of Mourning and the New International*, trans. Peggy Kamuf (New York: Routledge, 1993); and Jacques Derrida, "What Is a 'Relevant' Translation?", trans Lawrence Venuti, *Critical Inquiry* 27, no. 2 (Winter 2001): 174–200.

45 José Esteban Muñoz, *Disidentifications: Queers of Color and the Performance of Politics* (Minneapolis: University of Minnesota Press, 1999), 73.

Chapter 5

1 Andreas Malm's presentation of the Capitalocene remains key: "If 'the Anthropocene' is an indefensible abstraction at the point of departure as well as the end of the line, might there be a more adequate term for the new geological epoch? Our suspicion that the interests once entering the locomotive are still inside it seems to have been confirmed: accumulation of capital through abstract space, abstract time and anarchic competition runs ever faster away from the flow, demanding a fuel of matching qualities in constantly growing quantities. Unlikely to gather anything like a consensus behind it, a more scientifically accurate

designation, then, would be 'the Capitalocene.' This is the geology not of mankind, but of capital accumulation." *Fossil Capital: The Rise of Steam Power and the Roots of Global Warming* (London: Verso, 2016), 391.

2 Jonathan Crary, *24/7: Late Capitalism and the Ends of Sleep* (London: Verso, 2014), 8.

3 Ernst Bloch, "The Spur of Work," *Traces*, trans. Anthony A. Nassar (Stanford, CA: Stanford University Press, 2006), 76.

4 Theodor Adorno, *Minima Moralia: Reflections from Damaged Life*, trans. E. F. N. Jephcott (London: Verso, 2005), 138.

5 Adorno, *Minima Moralia*, 39.

6 Karl Marx, *Capital Volume 1*, trans. Ben Fowkes (London: Penguin Books, 1990), 367.

7 Ibid., 346.

8 Ibid., 375.

9 Massimiliano Tomba, *Marx's Temporalities*, trans. Peter D. Thomas and Sara R. Farris (Chicago: Haymarket 2013), 97.

10 Marx, *Capital Volume 1*, 383.

11 Lewis Mumford, *Technics and Civilization* (Chicago: The University of Chicago Press, 2010), 70.

12 Ibid.

13 Ibid., 158.

14 Marx, *Capital Volume 1*, 415.

15 Adorno, *Minima Moralia*, 156.

16 "We cannot keep things the same and change everything. We need a revolution, a break with capital and its killing compulsions, though what that looks like in the twenty-first century is very much an open question. A revolution that had as its aim the flourishing of all human life would certainly mean immediate decarbonization, a rapid decrease in energy use for those in the industrialized global north, no more cement, very little steel, almost no air travel, walkable human settlements, passive heating and cooling, a total transformation of agriculture, and a diminishment of animal pasture by an order of magnitude at least. All of this is possible, but not if we continue to shovel one half of all the wealth produced on the planet into the maw of capital, not if we continue to sacrifice some fraction of each generation by sending them into the pits, not if we continue to allow those whose only aim is profit to decide how we live." Jasper Bernes, "Between the Devil and the Green New Deal," *Commune*, 1, Issue 3 (2019): 61.

17 Adorno, *Minima* Moralia, 156–7.

18 Ibid., 38.

19 Ibid., 112.

20 Ibid., 15.

21 Ibid.
22 Karl Marx, *The German Ideology, Collected Works of Marx and Engels Volume 5*, trans. W. Lough (London: Lawrence and Wishart Ltd., 1976), 47.
23 Adorno, *Minima Moralia*, 138.
24 Ibid., 139.
25 Ibid., 138–9.
26 Ibid., 109.
27 Ibid., 204.
28 Ibid., 44.
29 Ibid., 175.
30 Theodor Adorno and Max Horkheimer, *Towards a New Manifesto*, trans. Rodney Livingstone (London: Verso, 2019), 3.
31 Ibid., 37.
32 Ibid., 7.
33 Ibid., 36.
34 Ibid., 10–11.
35 Ibid., 37.
36 Ernst Bloch and Theodor Adorno, "Something's Missing: A Discussion between Ernst Bloch and Theodor W. Adorno on the Contradictions of Utopian Longing," in *The Utopian Function of Art and Literature: Selected Essays*, trans. Jack Zupes and Frank Mecklenburg (Cambridge, MA: The MIT Press, 1988), 3–4.
37 Adorno, *Minima Moralia*, 247.

Chapter 6

1 The millions murdered or immiserated to make possible the expansion of the liberal capitalist world system have been "cheated out of the single remaining thing that our powerlessness can offer them: remembrance." Although a tawdry imitation of remembrance springs from the bad conscience of the comfortable, who remind their children of those starving in Africa: "Precisely because famine continues to reign across entire continents when technically it could be eliminated, no one can really be so delighted at his prosperity." Theodor Adorno, "The Meaning of Working Through the Past," in *Critical Models: Interventions and Catchwords*, trans. Henry W. Pickford (New York: Columbia University Press, 2005), 91, 96.
2 Theodor Adorno, *Minima Moralia*, trans. E. F. N. Jephcott (London: Verso, 2005), 56, 59 [aphorism 33, 36].
3 Ibid., 73 [aphorism 45].
4 Ibid., 50 [aphorism 29].

5 Totality in Adorno's writing seems implicitly to be capitalist totality, although he does not always explicate it with Marxian categories. His students and immediate inheritors who formed the Neue-Marx-Lektüre undertook the project of grounding Adorno's dialectical method and conclusions about conceptual reality in Marx's critique of political economy. Cf. Hans-Georg Backhaus, "Between Philosophy and Science: Marxian Social Economy as Critical Theory," in *Open Marxism*, edited by Werner Bonefeld et al. (London: Pluto Press, 1992), 54–92.
6 Adorno, *Minima*, 17 ["Dedication"].
7 Ibid., 113 [aphorism 72].
8 Theodor Adorno et al., *The Positivist Dispute in German Sociology*, trans. Glyn Adey and David Frisby (London: Heinemann, 1977), 62.
9 Adorno, "Meaning," 98.
10 "The universality that reproduces the preservation of life simultaneously imperils it in more and more menacing stages. The power of the self-realizing universal is not, as Hegel thought, identical with the nature of the individuals in themselves; it is always also contrary to that nature. The individuals are not only character masks, agents of value in a supposedly separate economic sphere. Even where they think they have escaped the primacy of economics . . . they react under the compulsion of the universal. . . . There are innumerable times when unavoidable motives of self-preservation force people, even conscious people capable of criticizing the whole, to do things and to take attitudes which blindly help maintain the universal even though their consciousness is opposed to it." Theodor Adorno, *Negative Dialectics*, trans. E. B. Ashton (New York: Continuum, 1983), 311.
11 Adorno, "Meaning," 99.
12 Adorno, *Positivist*, 37.
13 Ibid., 247.
14 Theodor Adorno and Max Horkheimer, *Towards a New Manifesto*, trans. Rodney Livingstone (London: Verso, 2019), 31.
15 Walter Benjamin, *The Writer of Modern Life: Essays on Charles Baudelaire*, ed. Michael Jennings, trans. Howard Eiland et al. (Cambridge, MA: Harvard University Press, 2006), 29.
16 "Je contemple d'en Haut le globe en sa rondeur, / Et je n'y cherche plus l'abri d'une cahute." Charles Baudelaire, *Les Fleurs du Mal*, ed. Marthiel and Jackson Mathews (New York: New Directions, 1989), 315.
17 Benjamin, *Writer*, 201.
18 Theodor Adorno and Walter Benjamin, *The Complete Correspondence 1928-1940*, ed. Henri Lonitz, trans. Nicholas Walker (Cambridge, MA: Harvard University Press, 1999), 319.
19 Ibid., 272, 219.
20 Ibid., 301, 304.

21 Ibid., 283. I leave aside here, for reasons of space, the question of Adorno's fairness to Benjamin in his reading. Robert Kaufman, for example, argues that Adorno "bullheadedly fails to grasp . . . the necessity in poetry, literary-historical study, and critical theory of immanently dwelling in the experience of alienated social and existential life." Robert Kaufman, "Lyric Commodity Critique, Benjamin Adorno Marx, Baudelaire Baudelaire Baudelaire," *PMLA* 123, no. 1 (January 2008): 212.
22 Ibid. Original emphasis.
23 Karl Marx, *Capital: A Critique of Political Economy Volume 1*, trans. Ben Fowkes (London: Penguin, 1990), 142.
24 Adorno and Benjamin, *The Complete Correspondence 1928-1940*, 281, 107.
25 Benjamin, "Concept," 392.
26 Ibid., 394.
27 Walter Benjamin, "On the Concept of History," trans. Harry Zohn, in *Selected Writings: Volume 4*, ed. Howard Eiland et al. (Cambridge, MA: Harvard University Press, 2006), 393.
28 Adorno, *Minima*, 151 [aphorism 98].
29 The German word translated as calamity is *Unheil*. Adorno writes of "the harm [*Unheil*]" done by the thinker who misuses the dialectic by adopting "the standpoint of totality." The concept describes several related phenomena in the book: "the objective calamity [Unheil] visited on the world" by Hitler; the loss of individuality as "the subject performs, voluntarily and calamitously [*unheilvoll*], the annulment of the self"; and how "the abundance of commodities indiscriminately consumed is becoming calamitous [*unheilvoll*]." Ibid., 247, 57, 61, 119.

Jennifer Kapczynski writes of the use of the term "*Unheil*" as part of the presentation of Nazism as a disease that befell Germany: "While an altogether common phrase in postwar literature on the German condition, the term resonates particularly strongly with the prevailing discourses on national health. Although accurate, the translation of *Unheil* as 'calamity' or 'disaster' unfortunately loses the associative force of the original. Un negates the word Heil, which means 'whole' or 'healthy,' as in the English word hale. But the prefix also has the peculiar effect of inverting the infamous Hitler greeting—which, while generally understood to mean 'hail,' also carries with it the injunction to 'heal.' The deployment of the word *Unheil* thus, consciously or no, aligns conveniently with efforts by postwar thinkers to refute Nazi claims to heal the nation." Jennifer Kapczynski, *The German Patient: Crisis and Recovery in Postwar Culture* (Ann Arbor: University of Michigan Press, 2008), 64.
30 "Et le Temps m'engloutit minute par minute, / Comme la neige immense un corps pris de roideur." Baudelaire, *Les Fleurs du Mal*, 315.
31 Theodor Adorno and Max Horkheimer, *Dialectic of Enlightenment*, trans. Edmund Jephcott (Stanford, CA: Stanford University Press, 2002), 182–3.

32 Ibid., 166. What Adorno and Horkheimer call "ticket thinking" is further developed in a passage from "Elements of Anti-Semitism": "Anti-Semitic views always reflected stereotyped thinking. Today only that thinking is left. People still vote, but only between totalities. The anti-Semitic psychology has largely been replaced by mere acceptance of the whole fascist ticket, which is an inventory of the slogans of the belligerent big business. Just as, on the ballot paper of the mass party, voters are presented with the names of people remote from their experience for whom they can only vote en bloc, the central ideological concepts have been codified into a small number of lists. . . . When the masses accept the reactionary ticket containing the clause against the Jews, they are obeying social mechanisms in which individual people's experiences of Jews play no part."

33 Adorno, "Meaning," 90, 98.

34 Adorno, *Minima*, 104 [aphorism 67]. "The German ruling clique drove towards war because they were excluded from a position of imperial power. . . . They saw nothing before them except cheering assemblies and frightened negotiators: this blocked their view of the objective power of a greater mass of capital." Ibid., 106 [aphorism 69].

35 Adorno is careful never to ground an analysis of fascism's mass appeal in individual psychology. He criticizes Freud precisely for being "hardly interested in the political phase of the problem," so foreseeing "the rise and nature of fascist mass movements in purely psychological categories." Freud "did not concern himself with the social changes" that produced the conditions in which the mass psychological features of authoritarianism could take hold. Instead, Adorno argues, "only an explicit theory of society, by far transcending the range of psychology, can fully answer the question raised here": that is, what are the causes of authoritarian mass movements. Theodor Adorno, "Freudian Theory and the Pattern of Fascist Propaganda," in *Essential Frankfurt School Reader*, ed. Andrew Arato & Eike Gebhardt (New York: Continuum, 1985), 120, 134.

The collaborative study of *The Authoritarian Personality*, too, takes care to note that "personality is not, however, to be hypostatized as an ultimate determinant," as "personality evolves under the impact of the social environment and can never be isolated from the social totality within which it occurs." Further, the major influences on the development of personality are "profoundly influenced by economic and social factors," so the general approach that the authors of the study take is to "consider personality as an agency through which sociological influences upon ideology are mediated." T. W. Adorno, Else Frenkel-Brunswik et al., *The Authoritarian Personality* (London: Verso, 2019), 5–6. The beguiling ploys of the authoritarian demagogue are also everywhere tied to a determining and constitutive foundation in objective social forces, in Adorno's study of Martin Luther Thomas. The insinuating, personalistic appeal of Thomas

can be understood "as a sort of emotional compensation for the cold, self-alienated life of most people and particularly of innumerable isolated individuals of the lower middle classes." Theodor Adorno, *The Psychological Technique of Martin Luther Thomas' Radio Addresses* (Stanford, CA: Stanford University Press, 2000), 27.
36 Adorno, *Minima*, 132 [aphorism 85].
37 Adorno and Horkheimer, *Dialectic*, 165.
38 Ibid., 142–3.
39 Adorno, *Minima*, 34 [aphorism 14].
40 Ibid., 104 [aphorism 67].
41 Marx, *Capital*, 375.
42 Ibid., 381.
43 Ibid.
44 Adorno and Horkheimer, *Dialectic*, 175.
45 Adorno, *Minima*, 193–4 [aphorism 124].
46 Karl Marx, "Critique of Hegel's Philosophy of Right," in *Early Writings*, trans. Rodney Livingstone and Gregor Benton (London: Penguin, 1992), 256.
47 Karl Marx and Friedrich Engels, *The German Ideology*, in Collected Works Vol. 5 (New York: International Publishers, 1976), 77.
48 Adorno, *Minima*, 204–5 [aphorism 131].
49 Ibid., 202, 37 [aphorism 130, 17].
50 Ibid., 229 [aphorism 147].
51 Compare to Marx's description: "When we consider bourgeois society in the long view and as a whole, then the final result of the process of social production always appears as the society itself, i.e. the human being itself in its social relations. Everything that has a fixed form, such as the product etc., appears as merely a moment, a vanishing moment, in this movement. The direct production process itself here appears only as a moment. The conditions and objectifications of the process are themselves equally moments of it, and its only subjects are the individuals, but individuals in mutual relationships, which they equally reproduce and produce anew ... in which they renew themselves even as they renew the world of wealth they create." Karl Marx, *Grundrisse: Foundations of the Critique of Political Economy*, trans. Martin Nicolaus (London: Penguin, 1993), 712.
52 Adorno, *Minima*, 194 [aphorism 124].
53 Marx, *Grundrisse*, 709.
54 Ibid., 703, 706.
55 Alfred Sohn-Rethel, *Economy and Class Structure of German Fascism*, translated by Martin Sohn-Rethel (London: Free Association Books, 1987), 22–30. Sohn-Rethel writes from the bowels of the beast, having been a research assistant during the years of fascist consolidation inside the "Mitteleuropäischer Wirtschaftstag"

(MWT), which as "a unique vehicle for the re-unification of German big business on the basis of a new imperialistic policy" he called the active center of monopoly capitalism. Ibid., 19.

56 Adorno, *Minima*, 34 [aphorism 14].
57 Ibid., 195 [aphorism 125].
58 Ibid., 187 [aphorism 120].
59 Ibid., 114 [aphorism 73].
60 Marx, "Critique of Hegel's Philosophy of Right," 257.
61 Adorno, *Negative Dialectics*, 3.
62 Adorno, *Minima*, 123 [aphorism 79].
63 Adorno, "Education After Auschwitz," in *Critical Models*, 193.
64 Marx, *Capital*, 201. Although both the phrases "behind the back" and "second nature" were borrowed from Hegel.
65 Adorno, *Negative Dialectics*, 67.
66 Marx, *Capital*, 284.
67 Ibid., 174–5.
68 Adorno, *Minima*, 227–8 [aphorism 146].
69 Ibid., 148 [aphorism 97].
70 This observation follows Marx's insight that only with the high level of social organization developed under capitalism is the modern individual possible, despite the Robinson Crusoe fantasy of the natural individual that subtends so much back-projection in political economy and philosophy. In previous history, the natural subject was the family or clan; "only in the eighteenth century, in 'civil society', do the various forms of social connectedness confront the individual as a mere means towards his private purposes, as external necessity. But the epoch which produces this standpoint, that of the isolated individual, is also precisely that of the hitherto most developed social (from this standpoint, general) relations. . . . Production by an isolated individual outside society . . . is as much of an absurdity as is the development of language without individuals living together and talking to each other." Marx, Grundrisse, 84.
71 Adorno, *Minima*, 155 [aphorism].
72 Ibid., 232 [aphorism 148].
73 Ibid., 228 [aphorism 146].
74 Theodor Adorno, *Lectures on Negative Dialectics: Fragments of a Lecture Course 1965/1966*, edited by Rolf Tiedemann, translated by Rodney Livingstone (Cambridge: Polity, 2008), 58. Adorno mentions that he borrows this last phrase from Horkheimer.
75 Ibid., 59.
76 Adorno, *Minima*, 115 [aphorism 74]. In an exuberant passage, Marx describes the organized system of machines that comprise the productive infrastructure as a

monster, too: "a mechanical monster whose body fills whole factories, and whose demonic power, at first hidden by the slow and measured motions of its gigantic members, finally bursts forth in the fast and feverish whirl of its countless working organs." Marx, *Capital*, 503.

77 Adorno and Horkheimer, *Dialectic*, 149.
78 Adorno, *Minima*, 147 [aphorism 96].
79 Ibid., 190 [aphorism 121].
80 The superlative form of the title implies laws of second nature replace the laws of nature Francis Bacon studied in *Novum Organum*.
81 The insistence from Adorno in this aphorism that the inner constitution of individuals is determined by society and severed "from their instinctual basis and from the self," definitively not the "'hereditary taint' that biologism projects on to nature" stands in contrast to Deborah Cook's interpretation of his concept of self-preservation. Adorno, *Minima*, 229–30 [aphorism 147]. Cook recognizes the relevance of the concept to explain the horrors of the contemporary world in which "famine, disease, poverty, and malnutrition" persist while the environment is disastrously degraded, but writes that "self-preservation is now the exclusive prerogative of the owners of the means of production in Western countries" and war-mongering politicians. In other words, "having surrendered the task of self-preservation to the economic and political systems, we remain in thrall to untamed survival instincts that could well end up destroying not just the entire species, but all life on the planet." Cook undersells the radicality of Adorno's idea that "instinctual" self-preservation is not handed over to a power elite but entirely replaced by a self-preservation immanent to the capitalist system—so the system of domination perpetuates itself through and above the people dominated. Deborah Cook, "Staying Alive: Adorno and Habermas on Self-Preservation under Late Capitalism," *Rethinking Marxism* 18, no. 3 (2006): 445, 439.
82 Adorno, *Minima*, 228–30 [aphorism 147].
83 Quoted in Adorno, *Minima*, 230 [aphorism 147]. Lukács goes on to argue that the reification or commodification of the proletarian worker "dehumanises him and cripples and atrophies his 'soul,'" yet still "his humanity and his soul are not changed into commodities." Unlike the journalist or the intellectual or the bureaucrat for whom commodification precisely means the reification of those faculties that would allow rebellion, for Lukács the proletariat is potentially made revolutionary by reification. Adorno of course had a serious disagreement here. György Lukács, *History and Class Consciousness: Studies in Marxist Dialectics* (Cambridge, MA: MIT Press, 1971), 172.
84 Adorno, *Minima*, 185–6, 216 [aphorism 119, 138].
85 Ibid., 229–30 [aphorism 147].
86 Ibid., 231 [aphorism 147].

87 Ibid., 233 [aphorism 148].
88 Theodor Adorno, *Problems of Moral Philosophy*, ed. Thomas Schröder, trans. Rodney Livingstone (Cambridge: Polity, 2000), 2.
89 Adorno, *Negative*, 72.
90 "I am reluctant to use the term 'humanity' at this juncture since it is one of the expressions that reify and hence falsify crucial issues merely by speaking of them. When the founders of the Humanist Union invited me to become a member, I replied that 'I might possibly be willing to join if your club had been called an inhuman union, but I could not join one that calls itself "humanist".'" Adorno, *Problems*, 169.
91 Adorno, *Negative*, 322–3.
92 Adorno, *Minima*, 18 ["Dedication"].
93 However, Adorno's conversations with Horkheimer about writing a new manifesto for communism offer an interesting and rare look at his attempt to direct his thought toward political action. They find Adorno insisting, "we must not abandon Marxist terminology" though it had been corrupted into ideology by the Soviet Union. He wanted to rectify its failures, including the disregard for administered censorship of art, "and develop a theory that remains faithful to Marx, Engels and Lenin, while keeping up with culture at its most advanced." Adorno and Horkheimer, *Manifesto*, 25, 69.
94 Theodor Adorno, *Aesthetic Theory*, ed. Gretel Adorno and Rolf Tiedemann, trans. Robert Hullot-Kentor (New York: Continuum, 2002), 227.
95 Theodor Adorno, "Theses on Need," trans. Devi Dumbadze, in *Constelaciones* 6 (December 2014): 464.
96 Adorno, *Minima*, 62 [aphorism 38].
97 Ibid., 139 [aphorism 91].
98 Ibid., 51 [aphorism 31].
99 I borrow this use of "non-identity" and "class-transcending consciousness" from Moishe Postone, who is himself adapting Adorno's influence. Moishe Postone, "Necessity, Labor, and Time: A Reinterpretation of the Marxian Critique of Capitalism," *Social Research* 45, no. 4 (1978): 739–88. And I borrow the phrase "self-production of the living" from Guy Debord, who continues: "the living becoming master and possessor of its world—that is, of history—and coming to exist as consciousness of its own activity." Guy Debord, *The Society of the Spectacle*, trans. Donald Nicholson-Smith (New York: Zone Books, 1995), 48.
100 Adorno, *Minima*, 156 [aphorism 100].
101 Adorno, "Progress," in *Critical Models*, 144. Further development of the idea of overcoming blind domination of nature may be found in the work, supervised by Adorno as a doctoral dissertation, of Alfred Schmidt, who writes that "the just society would neither simply coincide with nature nor be radically distinct from it." Alfred Schmidt, *The Concept of Nature in Marx* (London: Verso, 2014), 83.
102 Adorno, *Minima*, 238 [aphorism 150].

Chapter 7

1. Andrew Hui, *A Theory of Aphorism: From Confucius to Twitter* (Princeton, NJ: Princeton University Press, 2019), 12. See Simone Weil, *Gravity and Grace*, trans. Arthur Wills (New York: Octagon Books, 1979).
2. Gillian Rose, *The Melancholy Science: An Introduction to the Thought of Theodor W. Adorno* (London: The Macmillan Press, 1978), ix–x. According to Rose, "fragments and aphorisms are easily detachable and equally easily misunderstood, since their significance can only be appreciated on the basis of an understanding of the whole of which they are the fragments—hence the paradoxes that such idiosyncratic and radical thinkers" like Adorno "can be so widely and quickly assimilated but so often misunderstood" (19).
3. Jakob Norberg, "Adorno's Advice: Minima Moralia and the Critique of Liberalism." *PMLA* 126, no. 2 (March 2011): 400–1.
4. Rose, *The Melancholy Science*, 17.
5. As Norberg puts it, the text's "relentlessly accumulating statements make clear that the room for meaningful individual action has dwindled to nothing" (Norberg, "Adorno's Advice," 404–5); "The text does not abstain from the modality of advice so much as it seeks to show how any advice has become impossible . . . when two (and only two) possible alternatives are equally bad, there can be no space for advice" (406).
6. Christina Gerhardt, "The Ethics of Animals in Adorno and Kafka," *New German Critique*, no. 97 (Winter, 2006), 169. As Gerhardt explains, "Allowing a recognition rather than a suppression of the animality within allows a recognition of the humanity, too" (178).
7. Gerhardt, "The Ethics of Animals in Adorno and Kafka," 161. See Adorno, *Negative Dialectics*, trans. E. B. Ashton (New York: Seabury, 1973), 299.
8. Max Horkheimer and Theodor W. Adorno, *Dialectic of Enlightenment*, ed. Gunzelin Schmid Noerr, trans. Edmund Jephcott (Redwood City, CA: Stanford University Press, 2002), 203.
9. See Gerhardt, "The Ethics of Animals in Adorno and Kafka," 176–7; and Andrew Bowie, *Adorno and the Ends of Philosophy* (Cambridge: Polity, 2013), 66: Adorno is "deeply convinced that the difference between human beings and animals is not to be taken as emphatically as idealist philosophy wishes to persuade us it should be."
10. As Eric S. Nelson puts it, "By not recognizing the animal in the human and the ethical in the animal . . . numerous human forms of life and suffering are silenced" ("Revisiting the Dialectic of Environment: Nature as Ideology and Ethics in Adorno and the Frankfurt School," *Telos* 155 [Summer 2011], 113).
11. Theodor W. Adorno, *Minima Moralia: Reflections from Damaged Life*, trans. E. F. N. Jephcott (London: Verso, 2005), 239.

12 Robert Savage, "Adorno's Family and Other Animals," *Thesis Eleven* 78 (August 2004): 110.
13 Jay Geller, *Bestiarium Judaicum: Unnatural Histories of the Jews* (New York: Fordham University Press, 2018), 7.
14 Geller investigates how Jewish-identified, predominately German-speaking writers deployed animal figures, inquiring, given this history of dehumanization, "what may be going on when they are telling animal tales and composing animal poems" (*Bestiarium Judaicum*, 5). These writers respond to the othering of society by undermining the identification of the Jew-Animal through uncanny renderings of Jewish *animot* (to borrow Derrida's terminology) in their irreducible singularity.
15 Aaron Gross, "Animal Others and Animal Studies," in *Animals and the Human Imagination: A Companion to Animal Studies*, ed. Aaron Gross and Anne Vallely (New York: Columbia University Press, 2012), 4.
16 See, for example, the intentional locution in the title of Paul Waldau and Kimberly Patton, *A Communion of Subjects: Animals in Religion, Science, and Ethics* (New York: Columbia University Press, 2006), indicating the agency and subjectivity of animals, rather than casting them as objects of human perception, consumption or use.
17 Helen Andersson points out that Hélène Cixous first used this term: "Cixous playfully invokes animots in plural, in which it is possible to read 'animated words' or 'animals', as early as 1976 in *Là* (more than twenty years before Derrida chose to adopt it), and mentions it explicitly once more in 'Writing blind: conversation with the donkey' from 1996," referring to "my magic animots, my animal-words" (Helen Andersson, "Traces of a Half-Forgotten Dog: Suffering and Animal Humanity in Hélène Cixous' Algerian Scenes," *Literature & Theology* 31, no. 4 [December 2017]: 422; citing Hélène Cixous, *Là* [Paris: Gallimard, 1976], 93; and Hélène Cixous, *Stigmata: Escaping Texts*, trans. E. Prenowitz [London: Routledge Classics, 2005], 186).
18 Jacques Derrida, *The Animal that Therefore I Am*, ed. Marie-Louise Mallet, trans. David Wills (New York: Fordham University Press, 2008), 41.
19 Derrida, *The Animal that Therefore I Am*, 47–51.
20 As popularized by Peter Singer, the term "speciesism" refers to the privileging of one's own species over other species, which usually means the privileging of humans over other animals; see Singer, *Animal Liberation: A New Ethics for our Treatment of Animals* (New York: Random House, 1975).
21 Beth A. Berkowitz, *Animals and Animality in the Babylonian Talmud* (Cambridge, UK: Cambridge University Press, 2018), 14. See also Mira Beth Wasserman, *Jews, Gentiles, and Other Animals: The Talmud after the Humanities* (Philadelphia: University of Pennsylvania Press, 2017), 73: "It is easy to see how the denial of our kinship with animals hurts animals . . . . [O]ur thinking about animals and the

animal also has repercussions for human welfare and sociality, conditioning the way we understand ourselves as human, and shaping the ways in which we relate to others."

22 Berkowitz, *Animals and Animality in the Babylonian Talmud*, 14.
23 Andrew Benjamin, *Of Jews and Animals* (Edinburgh: Edinburgh University Press, 2011), 4.
24 Benjamin, *Of Jews and Animals*, 4.
25 Che Gossett, "Blackness, Animality, and the Unsovereign," September 8, 2015, http://www.versobooks.com/blogs/2228-che-gossett-blackness-animality-and-the-unsovereign. On the "absent presence" at the heart of the sexuality-animality nexus, in which women, alongside animals, are made to be absent referents in patriarchal culture, see Carol J. Adams, *The Sexual Politics of Meat: A Feminist-Vegetarian Critical Theory* (New York: Bloomsbury, 1990).
26 Zakiyyah Iman Jackson, *Becoming Human: Matter and Meaning in an Antiblack World* (New York: New York University Press, 2020), 16.
27 Bénédicte Boisseron, *Afro-Dog: Blackness and the Animal Question* (New York: Columbia University Press, 2018), 2. In the humanities and social sciences, the "animal turn" results from a counterlinguistic turn which pays attention to bodies, emotions, and other affective experiences, along with the ethical impulse to interrogate our human responsibility to animal others (Kari Weil, *Thinking Animals: Why Animal Studies Now?* [New York: Columbia University Press, 2012], 6–7.)
28 Jackson, *Becoming Human*, 82.
29 Ibid., 23.
30 Ibid., 60.
31 Adorno, *Minima Moralia*, 102.
32 Ibid.
33 Ibid., 103.
34 "The spokesmen of unitary tolerance are, accordingly, always ready to turn intolerantly on any group that remains refractory: intransigent enthusiasm for blacks does not exclude outrage at Jewish un-couthness" (Adorno, *Minima Moralia*, 103).
35 Jackson suggests an alternative to the discourse of exclusion: "I replace the notion of 'denied humanity' and 'exclusion' with bestialized humanization, because the African's humanity is not denied but appropriated, inverted, and ultimately plasticized in the methodology of abjecting animality" (Jackson, *Becoming Human*, 23); "Too often, our conception of antiblackness is defined by the specter of 'denied humanity,' 'dehumanization,' or 'exclusion,' yet, as Saidiya Hartman has identified in her path-breaking study *Scenes of Subjection: Terror, Slavery, and Self-Making in Nineteenth-Century America*, the process of making the slave relied on the

abjection and criminalization of the enslaved's humanity rather than merely on the denial of it. Thus, humanization is not an antidote to slavery's violence; rather, slavery is a technology for producing a kind of human" (46).

36 Jackson, *Becoming Human*, 38.
37 Joseph R. Winters, *Hope Draped in Black: Race, Melancholy, and the Agony of Progress* (Durham, NC: Duke University Press, 2016), 21.
38 Jackson, *Becoming Human*, 23, 46; see Saidiya Hartman, *Scenes of Subjection: Terror, Slavery, and Self-Making in Nineteenth-Century America* (New York: Oxford University Press, 1997).
39 Geller, *Bestiarium Judaicum*, 4.
40 Adorno, *Minima Moralia*, 228.
41 This link is later evoked by Adorno and Horkheimer in *Towards a New Manifesto*, a collection of discussions from 1956 taken down by Gretel Adorno. Horkheimer observes of the connection between animals, childhood, and labor, "Originally, the position of man is like that of a dog you want to train. He would like to return to an earlier state of being. He works in order not to have to work. The reification of labour is a stage in the process that enables us to return to childhood, but at a higher level.... Both Marxism and the bourgeois world take good care to make sure that people cannot revert to the pre-civilized phase, the phase in which man has sought refuge from work by reverting to childhood" (Theodor Adorno and Max Horkheimer, *Towards a New Manifesto*, trans. Rodney Livingstone [London: Verso, 2011], 14; 23).
42 Leigh Claire La Berge, *Wages Against Artwork: Decommodified Labor and the Claims of Socially Engaged Art* (Durham, NC: Duke University Press, 2019), 162. As La Berge succinctly puts it, "whether in art or critical theory, often where we find animals, we find children" (160). See also Kimberly Patton: "The genre of children's literature around the world seems to reflect a kind of yearning for a lost age when animals and human beings could indeed speak the same language, and co-existed without the antagonism and complicated tensions of the predator-prey relationship that are now expected between them, both for biological and cultural reasons. The child, whether as the story's protagonist or as its reader, is somehow seen as the symbolic catalyst and center of this picture of peace" ("'Caught with Ourselves in the Net of Life and Time:' Traditional Views of Animals in Religion," *A Communion of Subjects: Animals in Religion, Science, and Ethics*, 31–2).
43 Theodor Adorno, *Aesthetic Theory*, trans. Robert Hullot-Kentor (London: Continuum, 2002), 119.
44 Adorno, *Aesthetic Theory*, 119.
45 Kimberly Patton, "Caught with Ourselves in the Net of Life and Time," 32.
46 Adorno, *Minima Moralia*, 16.

47 Ulrich Plass, "Expropriated Death: Alienation and Nullification in Adorno's *Minima Moralia*," in *Adorno and the Concept of Genocide*, ed. Ryan Crawford and Erik M. Vogt (Leiden: Brill, 2016), 89.
48 Adorno, *Negative Dialectics*, 362.
49 Plass, "Expropriated Death," 92.
50 See Adorno, *Minima Moralia*, aphorism 17: "The objective end of humanism is only another expression for the same thing. It signifies that the individual as individual, in representing the species of man, has lost the autonomy through which he might realize the species" (38).
51 Adorno, *Minima Moralia*, 105.
52 Ibid.
53 Jackson, *Becoming Human*, 23.
54 Adorno, *Minima Moralia*, 105.
55 I thank Eugene Sheppard for this observation, and for his translation of aphorism 68, which highlights these valences.
56 Adorno, *Minima Moralia*, 105.
57 Arendt, *The Origins of Totalitarianism*, 438.
58 As David Engel explains, the literal Nazi conception of the Jew as noxious parasite meant that "Jews were mortal enemies not of Germany alone but of all of humanity." Jews were cast as "non-human pathogens who threatened human survival" (David Engel, *The Holocaust: the Third Reich and the Jews* (Harlow: Longman, 2000), 14–15.
59 See Geller, *Bestiarium Judaicum*: "Here the objectifying telos of dehumanizing animalization is fully realized" (230).
60 Donna Haraway, *When Species Meet* (Minneapolis, MN: University of Minnesota Press, 2007), 20. Haraway finds Derrida's encounter with his cat promising, but ultimately limiting. She contrasts what she views as his insufficient animal curiosity with bioanthropologist Barbara Smuts's innovative research method of socializing with baboons on their own terms, and learning how to "become with" other animals (23).
61 "Mister's gaze is a provocation inviting us to reconsider how we define ourselves especially with regard to the racialized, gendered, and sexual dimensions of our fleshly being" (Jackson, *Becoming Human*, 78).
62 Although Jackson suggests that Mister's gaze may lead beyond the ocularcentric, her reading does not explore this mode further: "Surely a different mode of relating and a different grammar of value is behind (and reflected in) Mister's eyes—one that might even disorder the ocularcentrism that underwrites the hierarchical arrangements of taxonomy and typology" (Jackson, *Becoming Human*, 80).
63 Horkheimer and Adorno, *Dialectic of Enlightenment*, 213.
64 Ibid.

65 Adorno and Horkheimer, *Towards a New Manifesto*, 71.
66 For a theoretical examination of cultural approaches to visuality alongside disability studies, see Rosemarie Garland-Thomson, *Staring: How We Look* (Oxford: Oxford University Press, 2009).
67 On the links between disability and animality, see Sunaura Taylor, *Beasts of Burden: Animal and Disability Liberation* (New York: The New Press, 2016).
68 Hannah Arendt, *The Origins of Totalitarianism* (Orlando: Harcourt, Inc., 1973), 438.
69 Hannah Arendt, "The Concentration Camps," in *A Holocaust Reader: Responses to the Nazi Extermination*, ed. Michael L. Morgan (New York: Oxford University Press, 2001), 57.
70 Arendt, *The Origins of Totalitarianism*, 449. Plass notes that Arendt "anticipates Adorno's interest in the constitutive nexus of production and elimination when she describes the rationality of the camps as the 'mass production of corpses.' Even though Arendt's perspective is legal and political whereas Adorno's is social and economic, their accounts of the nullification of subjectivity in the camps are structurally similar. . . . By contrast, Adorno attempts to understand the fabrication of corpses as part of a rationalistic continuum with capitalistic socio-economic conditions in which the needs of production for production's sake have forced human needs to regress to mythical forms of mere self-preservation. These conditions prevail not only in totalitarian societies [as Arendt argues], but also in liberal free-market states" (Plass, "Expropriated Death," 90–1).
71 Arendt, *The Origins of Totalitarianism*, 455.
72 Ibid., 456–7.
73 Ibid., 458–9.
74 Primo Levi, *Survival in Auschwitz: the Nazi Assault on Humanity*, trans. Stuart Woolf (New York: Collier Books, 1961), 79.
75 Levi, *Survival in Auschwitz*, 82.
76 Ibid.
77 Ibid., 80.
78 Sarah Kofman, *Smothered Words*, trans. Madeleine Dobie (Evanston, IL: Northwestern University Press, 1998), 82n44.
79 Ibid., 42–3.
80 Ibid., 57.
81 Giorgio Agamben, *The Open: Man and Animal*, trans. Kevin Attell (Redwood City, CA: Stanford University Press, 2004), 37.
82 See Giorgio Agamben, *Homo Sacer: Sovereign Power and Bare Life*, Trans. Daniel Heller-Roazen (Redwood City, CA: Stanford University Press, 1998).
83 Alexander Weheliye, *Habeas Viscus: Racializing Assemblages, Biopolitics, and Black Feminist Theories of the Human* (Durham, NC: Duke University Press, 2014), 36;

"Instead of advancing an ethos of historical determinism . . . I am interested in the crosscurrents and discontinuities of the irreducible relation at the heart of modern terror and encampment that gets lost in the shuffle between the state of exception and the zone of indistinction" (36).

84 Weheliye, *Habeas Viscus*, 36. On placing Holocaust memory within the context of slavery, colonialism, and historical genocide, see Michael Rothberg, *Multidirectional Memory: Remembering the Holocaust in the Age of Decolonization* (Redwood City, CA: Stanford University Press, 2009); "Against the framework that understands collective memory as competitive memory—as a zero-sum struggle over scarce resources—I suggest that we consider memory as multidirectional: as subject to ongoing negotiation, cross-referencing, and borrowing; as productive and not privative" (3).
85 Weheliye, *Habeas Viscus*, 37.
86 Weheliye, *Habeas Viscus*, 38; see Hortense J. Spillers, *Black, White, and in Color: Essays on American Literature and Culture* (Chicago: University of Chicago Press, 2003).
87 Primo Levi, *The Drowned and the Saved*, trans. Raymond Rosenthal (New York: Summit Books, 1988), 75.
88 Levi, *Survival in Auschwitz*, 84.
89 See Gerhardt, "The Ethics of Animals in Adorno and Kafka," 169.
90 Adorno, *Towards a New Manifesto*, 16.
91 Ibid., 45.
92 Cixous, *Stigmata: Escaping Texts*, 156.
93 Scholars working in religious studies and animal studies have inquired about the possibility of animals themselves being considered religious subjects. For example, drawing on observations of animal spirituality by primatologist Jane Goodall, Donavan Schaefer argues that religion need not be predicated on language, as it is neither exclusively cognitive nor exclusively human. In emphasizing links between human and nonhuman animal bodies, he writes, we can have access to "better understandings of the shared worlds spiraling around, through, and between us, as well as new modes of interspecies community" (Donovan Schaefer, *Religious Affects: Animality, Evolution, and Power* [Durham, NC: Duke University Press], 2015, 18). See also Aaron Gross, *The Question of the Animal and Religion: Theoretical Stakes, Practical Implications* (New York: Columbia University Press, 2015).
94 Adorno, *Minima Moralia*, 115.
95 Ibid.
96 Rose, *The Melancholy Science*, 25.
97 Ibid., 25–6.
98 Adorno, *Minima Moralia*, 57.

99 Ibid., 18.
100 Ibid.: "In each of the three parts the starting-point is the narrowest private sphere, that of the intellectual in emigration. From this follow considerations of broader social and anthropological scope; they concern psychology, aesthetics, science in its relation to the subject. The concluding aphorisms of each part lead on thematically also to philosophy, without ever pretending to be complete or definitive: they are all intended to mark out points of attack or to furnish models for a future exertion of thought."
101 On the assumption of individual "authenticity," see Plass, "Expropriated Death," 88–9.
102 Adorno, *Minima Moralia*, 27, 79.
103 See aphorism 6, "Antithesis": "He who stands aloof runs the risk of believing himself better than others and misusing his critique of society as an ideology for his private interest. While he gropingly forms his own life in the frail image of a true existence, he should never forget its frailty, nor how little the image is a substitute for true life. Against such awareness, however, pulls the momentum of the bourgeois within him. The detached observer is as much entangled as the active participant; the only advantage of the former is insight into his entanglement, and the infinitesimal freedom that lies in knowledge as such" (Adorno, *Minima Moralia*, 26). Accordingly, Rose calls *Minima Moralia* the "prose poem of [Adorno's] own existential pathos" (Gillian Rose, *The Broken Middle: Out of our Ancient Society* [Oxford, UK: Blackwell, 1992], 9).
104 Adorno, *Minima Moralia*, 234.
105 Ibid., 83; or, in the twenty-first-century idiom of the prophetic television show *Buffy the Vampire Slayer*, "I suddenly find myself needing to know the plural of apocalypse" (*Buffy the Vampire Slayer*, "A New Man," season 4 episode 12, written by Jane Espenson, directed by Michael Gershman, aired January 25, 2000, on the WB Television Network).
106 Adorno, *Minima Moralia*, 234.
107 See Donna Haraway, *Staying with the Trouble: Making Kin in the Chthulucene* (Durham, NC: Duke University Press, 2016).
108 Adorno, *Minima Moralia*, 247.

Chapter 8

1 Theodor W. Adorno, "The Idea of Natural-History" (1932) reprinted in Robert Hullot-Kentor and Lydia Goehr, *Things Beyond Resemblance: Collected Essays on Theodor W. Adorno* (New York: Columbia, 2006), 252. Subsequent citations in text.
2 In *A History of the World in Seven Cheap Things: A Guide to Capitalism, Nature, and the Future of the Planet* (Berkeley: University of California Press, 2017), Raj

Patel and Jason Moore define cheapening as "a strategy, a practice, a violence that mobilizes all kinds of work—human and animal, botanical and geological—with as little compensation as possible" (11).

3. Deborah Cook, *Adorno on Nature* (New York: Routledge, 2014): 1.
4. Detlav Klaussen, *Theodor W. Adorno: One Last Genius*, trans. Rodney Livingstone (Cambridge, MA: Harvard University Press, 2010), 142.
5. Theodor W. Adorno, *Minima Moralia: Reflections from Damaged Life*, trans. E. F. N. Jephcott. (London, 1951; Verso, 1978), 47. Subsequent citations appear in the body of the text.
6. Ross Wilson, *Theodor Adorno* (London: Taylor & Francis, 2007), np.
7. Nico Israel, "Damage Control: Adorno, Los Angeles, and the Dislocation of Culture" in James Schmidt, ed. *Theodor Adorno* (Burlington, VT: Ashgate, 2007), 222.
8. Paul A. Cantor, "Film Noir and the Frankfurt School: America as Wasteland in Edgar Ulmer's *Detour*," in *The Philosophy of Film Noir*, ed. Mark T. Conard (Kentucky, 2005), 153.
9. Quoted in Detlav Klaussen, *Theodor W. Adorno*, 135.
10. Lorenz Jaeger, *Adorno: A Political Biography* (New Haven: Yale University Press, 2004), 105.
11. In "Film Noir and the Frankfurt School" Cantor reports that "it is documented that at least Adorno never learned to drive" (153).
12. Quoted in Klaussen, *Theodor W. Adorno*, 135.
13. Quoted in *Aesthetic Technologies of Modernity, Subjectivity, and Nature: Opera, Orchestra, Photograph, Film*. Richard Leppert (California, 2015), 192.
14. Matthew Battles, *tree* (New York: Bloomsbury, 2017), 82.
15. Matthias Benzer develops the motif of microsociology in *The Sociology of Theodor Adorno* (Cambridge, 2011), 81.
16. See Raymond Williams's discussion of the limits of place-based writing of the countryside, a tradition he sets in opposition to accounts of the ongoing struggle between visions of country and city; this vision of a common system governing the division of labor in country and city states in positive terms something that Adorno discovers in its negation. *Country and the City* (New York: Oxford University Press, 1975), 305–7.
17. Here, I draw on Deborah Cook's deep insight into the role of determinate negation in Adorno's treatment of nature in *Adorno and Nature* (New York: Routledge, 2014).
18. Karl Marx, "Excerpt from *The Grundrisse*," in *The Marx-Engels Reader*, ed. Robert C. Tucker (New York: Norton, 1978), 245.

Index

Abensour, Miguel 51
abstractionist aesthetics 154 n.21
abstractionist artwork 154 n.21
Accra 69, 70
Actor-Network-Theory (ANT) 153 n.5
acts *vs.* gestures 45
Adagia (Erasmus) 49
Adorno, Gretel 169 n.41
Adorno and Existence (Gordon) 4
adult education 18, 23
advanced capitalism 20, 23, 24, 37
aesthetics 7–9
Aesthetic Theory (Adorno) 36, 119, 132, 137
African diaspora 71
African literature 68
African Renaissance 66
Afro-Americans 63, 117
Afro-Brazilians 69
Afrocentricism 66
Afro-Cuban people 65
Afromodernity 70
Agamben, Giorgio 46, 51, 124, 125
Aktualität xv
alienation 8, 21, 94, 114, 120, 136
Amazon 39
America. *See* United States
American tradition 25
Andersson, Helen 167 n.17
animality 9, 10, 56, 113, 114–26
animalization 116–18, 121, 123, 125
animalized humans 117
"animal question" 114–18
animals xiv, 10, 55, 56, 103, 104, 113–19, 121–6, 139, 172 n.93
Animal that Therefore I am, The (Derrida) 122
"animot" 115
Anschluss 91
anschmiegen (nestle close to it) 33
Antelme, Robert 124
anthropocene 10, 129–41

anthropocentric framework 122
anti-Black racism 10
anti-fascism 8, 13, 23
anti-Semitism 10, 15, 23, 95, 96, 161 n.32
aphorisms (*aphorizein*) x, viii, 2–4, 7–10, 13, 14, 25, 28, 29, 31, 33, 35, 36, 38, 39, 47–50, 61–3, 65–8, 72, 73, 102, 105, 113, 118, 120, 124, 126, 128, 132, 133, 135, 138, 153 n.5
aphoristic anthropologies 65–70
aphoristic assemblages 63–5
aphoristic rhythms 70–3
Apple 39
Arendt, Hannah 5, 121, 123, 124, 171 n.70
Aristotle xii, 115
"Art and Mass Culture" (Horkheimer) 49
"Asylum for the Homeless" (Adorno) x
attentive activity 45, 46
Aufhebung (transcendence/self-abolition) 101
Auschwitz 29, 32, 38, 39, 42, 53, 92, 113, 114, 118–25
authoritarianism 15, 21, 23, 26, 96, 135, 161 n.35
Authoritarian Personality, The (Adorno, Frenkel-Brunswik er al.) 161 n.35
autonomy 4, 5, 8, 13, 14, 18–20, 24, 26, 70, 120

Ballaga, Emilio 65
barbarism x, 2, 31, 91, 122, 138
Battles, Matthew 139
Baudelaire, Charles 93, 94
Becker, Hellmut 18, 19
Becoming Human: Matter and Meaning in an Antiblack World (Jackson) 116
Beloved (Morrison) 122
Benjamin, Andrew 116
Benjamin, Walter xiv, 5, 32, 33, 59, 93–5, 130, 138, 160 n.21
Benzer, Matthias xiii

Berkowitz, Beth 115
Berlin Childhood around Nineteen Hundred (Benjamin) xiv
Bernes, Jasper 83
Bernhard, Andreas 31
beschädigte (mutilated) 30, 51
Best, Stephen 62
beurteilende Menschenkenntnis (appraising assessment of people) 37
Black art 63
Black artists 67
Black avant-garde 65
Black identity 63, 69
Blackness 69, 71, 116
"Black Orpheus" (Sartre) 71
Bloch, Ernst 78, 79, 88, 153 n.6
Boisseron, Bénédicte 116–17
Bolsheviks 104
bourgeois society 4, 7, 16, 17, 20, 24, 26, 38, 98, 100, 127, 135, 169 n.41
Bradley, F. H. 128
Brahms, Johannes x
Brittain, Christopher Craig 4

Calvelli-Adorno, Maria ix
capital xiii, 80–2, 85, 86, 96–100, 104–6
Capital (Marx) xiv, 80, 90
capitalism 7, 8, 14, 17, 20, 23, 24, 31, 36, 38–42, 72, 79, 80, 82–5, 90–8, 100, 101, 114, 134, 138, 141, 163 n.70. *See also* advanced capitalism
capitalist production 80–3, 98, 101, 102
capitalist society xiii, 19, 24, 26, 31, 35, 36, 39, 91, 102
capitalist system 86, 98, 104, 109, 124, 158 n.1
Capitalocene 9, 77–9, 81, 82, 85, 88, 156 n.1
carboniferous capitalism 81, 82
Caribbean futurism 68
Carnegie, Dale 25
Carpentier, Alejo 65
Carter, Jimmy 40
chiasmus 8, 105, 132, 133
child-animal link 103, 119
children xiv, 19, 56
Chinweizu, Ibekwe 69
Chrostowska, S. D. 8, 9
Cixous, Hélène 115, 126, 167 n.17
class formation 98, 108

classless society 100, 104
climate change 108, 129, 138
coldness 39–42
colonialism 64, 67, 70, 72, 121, 125
Comaroff, Jean 65, 66, 70
Comaroff, John L. 65, 66, 70
commercial gesture 46
commissive speech act 45
commodification xiv, 16, 17, 35, 38, 105
commodity fetishism 94, 102
communal mourning 72
communism 80, 83, 85, 91, 93
Communist Manifesto, The (Engels and Marx) 86
concentration camp 2, 96, 117, 120, 121, 123–5
connoisseurship 16
consumerism 6
contestatory dialogue 4
Cook, Deborah 4, 132, 164 n.81
corporatization 39
Covid-19 pandemic 61
"Cradle Song" (Brahms) x
Crary, Jonathan 77
crisis 91, 101, 113, 126. *See also* economic crises
critical theory 8, 16, 49, 54, 55, 57, 59, 63, 118
Cruising Utopia (Muñoz) 153 n.6
Cuba 64, 65
Cuban Counterpoint (Orti) 65, 68
Cuban culture 68
cubism 64
cultural criticism ix
culture
    memory 131
    production 65–70, 73
    tradition 16
Cumming, John 5

damage 2, 3, 10, 33, 52, 130–2, 136, 138, 139
damaged life 2, 7–10, 36, 39, 41, 51, 57, 86, 89, 113, 132, 133, 137, 140
Danish Euro-Africans 69
death 90, 91, 104–6, 120, 123–5
"Dedication" (Adorno) 5, 120, 127
dehumanization 115, 118, 125, 167 n.14
déjà vu 131, 134, 138
democracy 18, 23, 24, 26, 95, 96, 100

Denkanstoß 31
Derrida, Jacques 72, 77, 115, 119, 122, 170 n.60
detail xiii, 9, 125, 132
dialectical theory 50
Dialectic of Enlightenment (Adorno and Horkheimer) xv, 5, 38, 49, 51, 57, 58, 95, 122, 132, 138
dialectic of nostalgia 58
Differenzen ums Ganze (crucial differences) 34
Differenzen ums Kleinste (minimal differences) 34
Disidentifications (Muñoz) 72
Dissonanzen (Adorn) 16
domination 3, 10, 36, 57, 90–2, 95, 97, 102–4, 107, 114, 129, 130, 132, 140, 141
du Bois, W. E. B. 67

ecology 3, 9, 57, 63, 69, 72, 113, 128, 132, 139–41
economic crises 21, 96
economic growth 91, 95
education 17, 19, 23
"Education After Auschwitz" (Adorno) 23
educational reform 23–4
Eipper, Paul 118, 119
Elias, Norbert 5
Engel, David 170 n.58
Enlightenment 13, 18–20, 24, 26, 114, 115
entanglements 10, 16, 25, 125–8, 132
epithymia 68
Erasmus, Desiderius 49
Erziehung zur Mündigkeit (*Education for Autonomy*, Adorno) 23
Essais (Montaigne) viii
"The Essay as Form" (Adorno) 48
ethical relationships 122
ethics 2, 9, 29, 34, 41, 42, 46, 54, 113, 117, 122, 126
Ethiopianism 66
ewiger Friede (perpetual peace) 56
exaggeration 9, 31, 32, 59
exile 2, 7, 9, 28–30, 51, 71, 113, 139
existentialism 4, 71, 72

Facebook 39
Fanon, Franz 71

fascism ix, 2, 3, 8, 9, 16, 23, 24, 26, 30, 36, 38–41, 93–100, 104, 109, 161 n.35
fascist recidivism 15, 23
Faulkner, William 156 n.41
Faust (Goethe) xi
film 3
First World War 51
Flaschenpost ix
form xii, xiv, 2–5, 7–10, 13, 14, 17, 19–22, 24, 28, 30, 31, 36–8, 40, 47–9, 58, 59, 61, 63, 64, 66–71, 82, 86, 91, 94, 97, 98, 100, 102–4, 106–8, 113, 119–22, 125, 128, 131, 132, 134, 137–9
Foster, Roger 7
Foucault, Michel 124
fragments 7, 9, 48–50, 52, 58, 59, 72, 86, 93, 131, 132, 135, 137
Franco, Francisco 94
Frankenstein 131
Frankfurt Institute of Social Research 15
Frankfurt School 15, 118
Franklin, Benjamin 25
freedom 8, 18, 34, 35, 88, 100
Freyenhagen, Fabian 4
Führer 21, 22

gay marriage 2
gaze xiv, 1, 30, 31, 47, 55, 56, 121–3, 139
Geller, Jay 118, 119, 167 n.14
generic nonidentity 50
genocide 22, 38, 40, 71, 120, 123, 125
genre xii, 9, 14, 25, 47–50, 61, 70, 113
Gerhardt, Christina 114
German Association of Sociologists 15
German Ideology, The (Marx) 85
German nationalism 21
German philosophical tradition 15
Germans 21, 22
Germany 13, 15, 17, 22, 24, 25, 38, 96, 98
geschliffen (polished) 38
gesticulations 58–60
gesture of friendship 46
gestures 45–52, 55, 57–9, 63
Geuss, Raymond 54, 55
gleichgemacht (same) 38
global capitalism 70
Goethe, Johann Wolfgang von xi
Goodall, Jane 172 n.93

Google 39
Gordon, Peter 4
Gossett, Che 116
Gravity and Grace (Weil) 113
Grundrisse (Marx) 141
Guillén, Nicolás 65

Hall, Stuart 155 n.36
happiness 55–7, 91
Haraway, Donna 122, 128, 170 n.60
Harlem Renaissance 63
Harper, Phil 154 n.21
Hartman, Saidiya 118
Harvey, David 65
Havana 64, 68
Hebbel, Friedrich 33, 102, 103
Hegel, G. W. F. xi, xii, 30, 49, 50, 58, 133, 159 n.10
Hegelianism 50
Heidegger, Martin 4, 115, 130
high arts 15
high-culture 71
Hippocrates 50
historical materialism 130, 131
historicization of nature 130–1
History and Class Consciousness (Lukacs) 149 n.24
Hitler, Adolf 21, 94, 95, 160 n.29
Hohendahl, Peter 7
Holocaust 9
Holocaust survivors 53
horizontal archaeologies 69
Horkheimer, Max viii, xiii, xv, 15, 38, 40, 49–51, 86–8, 93, 97, 114, 132, 138, 165 n.93, 169 n.41
How to Make Friends and Influence People (Carnegie) 25
human beings 4, 10, 19, 21, 26, 35, 38, 41, 46, 55, 58, 87, 94, 97, 99, 102, 104–6, 108, 113–17, 119–22, 123–6
human injustice 114, 118
humanist tradition 115
humanity viii, 66, 94, 101, 102, 107, 108, 114–18, 124, 126, 130, 168 n.35
human life 9, 77, 105, 149 n.24
Humboldt, Wilhelm von 18, 19
Hume, David 36
Husserl, Edmund 4
Huxley, Aldous x
Huyssen, Andreas 7

idealism 94, 130
"The Idea of Natural History" (Adorno) 132
identity xii, 36, 37, 48, 52, 67, 116, 123, 126
IMF programs 70
immigrant children 40
imperialism 97
individuality 21, 38, 39, 41, 103, 120, 123
"In Fascism" (Adorno) x
inhumanity 10, 40, 81, 114
inhuman union 106–9
"In psycho-analysis" (Adorno) xii
"intellectus sacrificium intellectus" (the intellect is sacrificed to the intellect) 33
interhuman relationships 10, 39
Irr, Caren 10

Jackson, Zakiyyah Iman 116–18, 121, 168 n.35
Jaeger, Lorenz 135
Jaeggi, Rahel xiv, 28, 30
Jameson, Frederic 68
Jephcott, Edmund 5, 6, 30, 118
Jews 95–7, 116–21, 124, 136, 170 n.58
Juden sehen Dich an ("Jews are looking at you," Leers) 118–19
Jungle, The (Lam) 64–7

Kant, Immanuel 4, 13, 18–20
Kant Society 130
Kapczynski, Jennifer 160 n.29
Kaufman, Robert 160 n.21
Kierkegaard, Søren 4
Kofman, Rabbi Bereck 124
Kofman, Sarah 124
kosmios 67
Kraus, Karl xii
krinein 47
Kulturträger viii
Kürnberger, Ferdinand xiii, 38

La Berge, Leigh Claire 119, 169 n.42
labor 3, 9, 56, 78–87, 91, 97–9, 101, 102, 105, 106, 119, 124
labor time 78, 80, 97–9, 103
Lam, Wifredo 64, 66–8, 154 n.21
language 46, 133

Latour, Bruno   153 n.5
Lectures on Negative Dialectics
    (Adorno)   32–4, 36, 52, 53, 120
Leers, Johann von   118–19
Lefebvre, Henri   65
"Le Goût du Néant" (Baudelaire)   93
Les Fleurs du Mal (Baudelaire)   93
L'Espèce humaine (*The Human Race/The Human Species,* Antelme)   124
Levi, Primo   124, 125
liberal humanism   116, 117
liberation   65, 84, 91, 95, 96, 99, 107
"live contact with the warmth of things" (Adorno)   xiii, xv, 33
Los Angeles   viii, 2
Lukacs, György   105, 131, 149 n.24, 164 n.83

Machado, Geraldo   65
machinery   25, 38, 98, 99, 104
Magna Moraliar ("Great Ethics," Aristotle)   xii
Mahler, Gustav   5
Malm, Andreas   156 n.1
"Mammoth" (Adorno)   126
"Man and Beast" (Adorno and Horkheimer)   114
Mariotti, Shannon   4
market economy   20
marriage   2
Marx, Karl   xiii, xiv, 53, 80, 82, 85, 90, 94, 97–9, 101–4, 119, 141, 159 n.5, 162 n.51, 163 n.70
Marxism   8, 71, 86, 87, 92, 94, 120, 169 n.41
Marxist humanism   65
Massey, Doreen   65
mass media   3
mass murder   95
Max-Planck Institute for Educational Research   18
Mbembe, Achille   72
melancholy   53, 54, 62, 73
melancholy historicism   62, 63
"Mélange" (Adorno)   117
metabolic interaction   102
metaphysics   52, 57, 70, 71
micrological approach   33
"micrological" glance   31, 52
microsociology   xiii

migrant identity   69
mikrologisch verblendete Moral ("micrologically deluded ethics")   29, 34, 41, 42
mining   81
modernity   21, 63, 64, 66, 67, 72, 125, 137
modernization   21, 66, 67, 72
Mok, Maurits   5
Molecular Red: Theory for the Anthropocene (Wark)   129
monopoly capitalism   31, 38, 40, 41
Montaigne, Michel de   viii
Moore, Jason   130
Morrison, Toni   122
Moses, Stefan   1
Mumford, Lewis   81, 82, 84
Mündigkeit ("maturity")   18
Muñoz, José Esteban   61, 66, 72, 153 n.6
Museum of Modern Art (MoMA)   64
music   3, 15, 68, 70–3

national literary traditions   9
National Socialism   16, 21, 95, 96, 106
national unity   96
natural-history   130–3, 136–9, 141
naturalization of history   130–1, 133
Nazi Germany   15, 21
Nazi regime   21, 22, 97
Nazis   16, 22, 31, 118, 121, 123, 125, 160 n.29
Nazism   40, 96, 160 n.29
negation   xii, 4, 38, 46–8, 50, 63, 70
negative dialectics   4, 5, 8, 10, 52, 53, 65, 67, 132
negrismo   63, 65
Negritude   66
négritude   63, 71, 72
neoliberal capitalism   68, 70
neoliberal hegemony   42
neoliberalism   6, 40
Nietzsche, Friedrich   xii
"'No Individual Can Resist': *Minima Moralia* as Critique of Forms of Life" (Jaeggi)   28
Nollywood movies   66
nonhuman animals   113, 117
non-identity   xii, 36, 50, 108, 165 n.99
Norberg, Jakob   113
Novalis   49
"Novissimum organum" (Adorno)   105

Obama, Barack 40
objects and beings 36
ocularcentrism 122, 123
Offe, Claus 31
Of Jews and Animals (Benjamin) 116
One-Way Street (Benjamin) xiv
online platforms 59
"On parle français" (Adorno) 133
ontology 48, 52, 62, 71, 83, 125, 131, 133, 138, 139
organized heteronomy 14, 20-4, 26
organized massacre 117, 121
Ortiz, Fernando 65, 68, 70, 72
Oxford Street, Accra (Quayson) 69, 70

Palster, Jann 67
Pan-Africanism 63, 65-7
Patel, Raj 130
patriarchal structure 21
Patton, Kimberly 119
"Paysage" (Adorno) 133-7
Paz, Norberto Silvetti 5
pedagogy 13, 14, 18, 23, 25
"People are looking at you" (Adorno) 118
petrified fragments 131, 132
Phenomenology of Spirit (Hegel) xii
philia (concordance) 67, 68
philosophical knowledge 32
philosophical system 50
philosophical tradition 15, 25
Pierre Matisse Gallery 64
planetary stupidity 137-9, 140
Plass, Ulrich 120, 171 n.70
plurality 5, 115
poiēsis (making) 46
political economy xiii, 96, 100, 103, 108, 159 n.5
political resistance 90, 93
Pollen (Novalis) 49
popular culture 3, 15
positive dialectic 4
postcolonial literary ethnography 70
post-Hegelian philosophy 54
postwar and prewar society 23
postwar Germany 13, 14, 17, 22, 59
postwar pedagogy 14, 24-7
praxis (deliberate acting) 46
pre-philosophical experience 32
primitivism 64, 73

Prismen (Adorn) 16
Produktionsorganismus (organization of production) 102
professorships 15
proletariat and proletarians 97-101, 108
Proust, Marcel viii, ix, 5
pseudo-activity 85, 108
public roles of Adorno 14-17
public zoos 126, 127
Puchner, Martin 71

quaelbare Leib (torturable body) 32
Quayson, Ato 69-70, 72

races 2, 117, 118
racialization 117, 118, 123, 125
racism 2, 40
redemption 34, 55, 57, 58, 89, 93, 125
Redmond, Dennis 5, 6, 145 n.22
reflexionen (reflection) 2, 8
"Regressions" (Adorno) x
relations without purpose 36
religious traditions 119
Revolt of the Sergeants (1933) 65
Revolución cubana (1959) 65
Richter, Gerhard 1
Rilke, Rainer Maria 5
Rose, Gillian 113, 127
Rumsfeld, Donald 134

Santí, Erico Mario 65
Sartre, Jean-Paul 71, 72, 156 n.41
Schaefer, Donavan 172 n.93
Schlegel, Friedrich 49
Schönberg, Arnold 91
Schweppenhäuser, Gerhard 4
Sedgwick, Eve 61
self-incurred immaturity 18, 19
self-preservation 92, 104-8, 164 n.81
semi-*Bildung* 23
Sengho, Léopold Sédar 70-1
settler colonialism 10
sexual revolution 2
slavery 63, 64, 71, 118, 121, 125
Smothered Words (Kofman) 124
social critique 53
socialism 82, 95
socialization 14, 19, 23, 103
social media 3, 59

social relations   90, 91, 93, 96, 98, 101, 103, 105–7, 120
sociology   15, 16, 20, 21, 25, 141
Sohn-Rethel, Alfred   99
Solmi, Renato   5
Sound and the Fury, The (Faulkner)   156 n.41
Soviet Union   104
speciesism   117
Spillers, Hortense   125
spleen   54
state bureaucracies   14, 20, 21
Strauss, Richard   5
subject-object interaction   35, 37
suffering   xi, 51–6, 58, 59, 114, 121
Suhrkamp   15
"Sur l'eau" (Adorno)   56
surplus value   80, 97, 103, 104
surrealist art   66
Survival in Auschwitz (Levi)   124

tabula rasa   84
Technics and Civilization (Mumford)   81
Teilmomente ("partial moments")   99
Theory from the South (Comaroff and Comaroff)   65, 70
thinking   2–4, 7, 10, 34, 36, 37, 48, 57–9, 114, 117, 122, 137
Third Reich   viii, 22
"This Side of the Pleasure Principle" (Adorno)   56
Tiere sehen dich an ("Animals are looking at you," Eipper)   118
totalitarianism   92, 121, 124
totality   50, 52, 57, 88, 91, 104, 107, 159 n.5
Towards a New Manifesto (Adorno and Horkheimer)   122, 126, 169 n.41
"Toy Shop" (Adorno)   xiv, 102, 119, 120
transculturation   65, 68–9
transnational approach   9
transnationalism   64, 68–70, 73
transnational migration   63
Trauer (sadness)   54
traumatic history   67, 73

traurige Wissenschaft (melancholy science)   53, 90–109, 145 n.22
tree (Battles)   139

unemployment   20–2
Unheil ("the harm")   160 n.29
United States   38, 81, 113, 121, 134, 136
universal ethics   9
University of Cambridge   5
US-Mexican border   40
US-Spanish imperialism   65
utopia   xiv, xv, 55–60, 78, 84–9, 103, 108, 117, 138–40

Veblen, Thorstein   54, 78
Verblendungszusammenhang (context of delusion)   31
Vergesellschaftung (socialization)   102
Verwirklichung (realization)   101
violence   19, 35–7, 40–1, 106, 116, 121, 122, 127, 134
Volksgemeinschaft   21, 22
vulgar materialism   94

Wark, McKenzie   129
wa Thiong'o, Ngũgĩ   69
Weheliye, Alexander   125
Weil, Simone   113
Weimar Republic   38
Weltanschauung   67
West Germany   13–16, 18, 23, 26, 59
"What Is Enlightenment?" (Kant)   18
white culture   71, 72
Wiesengrund, Oscar   ix
Winters, Joseph R.   118
working class   20, 91, 94, 100, 101
"The Working Day" (Marx)   82
"work of leisure"   78, 79, 88
work   78, 79, 82, 84, 87
wound of history   63–5
Wunderkammer   ix

xenophobia   71

zartes Gefühl (delicate sentiment)   36
Zartheit   36, 37, 39, 41
"zealous excessiveness"   31
Zeitschrift für Sozialforschung   93

www.ingramcontent.com/pod-product-compliance
Lightning Source LLC
Chambersburg PA
CBHW061833300426
44115CB00013B/2363